Keto Vegetarian Cookbook 2 in 1

30 days meal Plan
Breakfast-Lunch-Dinner

90 desserts recipes

FOREWORD

Congratulations on taking the first step towards a healthy lifestyle!

This book presents a combination of 2 books: keto vegetarian cookbook 30-days meal plan and 90 keto vegetarian desserts recipes. I have made all efforts to make the recipes in this book "beginner friendly", with ingredients that are quite accessible and with as little preparation time as possible. I realize how difficult and overwhelming it can be to change your eating habits, and I wanted to make this journey as easy for you as possible.

Take note to always refer the keto vegetarian diet as more than just a diet, but a lifestyle. Embracing a healthy lifestyle means letting it influence all areas of your life – from having a healthy diet, to getting regular exercise, and getting enough sleep every day. It takes a conscious decision and constant effort to change how you do things, and to achieve physical, mental, and spiritual health.

I encourage that you don't think of a healthy "diet" as something you will only do for 30 days. What I provide in this book is an opportunity for you to take the first steps towards transforming your lifestyle and becoming a healthier version of you.

For those who are not new to the keto vegetarian lifestyle, we hope that this book opens up and expands your dining choices. We have made an effort to come up with recipes that are not only healthy, but also taste great. The point that we are trying to make is that you don't have to feel deprived when you're on a keto vegetarian diet. After all, life is too short to not enjoy.

"I really recommend that before trying a ketogenic diet or any kind of diet please see a physician first to check if it will be safe for you. I will not be held responsible for any health problems you may encounter due to improper usage of the diet"

Again, thank you for buying our book. Best of luck!

Erin Mira

Table of Contents

FREE E-book Version at the End page

INTRODUCTION

What is a ketogenic diet

The ketogenic diet is a high fat, low carbohydrates, and adequate protein diet. It was originally used to treat epilepsy in children. What this diet does is instead of burning carbohydrates (which is converted into glucose which fuels the body especially the brain activity) the body uses FATS!

If little carbohydrate is consumed by our body, the liver is forced to convert the fats into fatty acid and ketone bodies. The ketone bodies pass in the brain and replace the glucose as a source of energy. The high level of ketone bodies present in our system can cause to be in a state called "KETOSIS", in which can result to weight loss.

What are the signs you are under the state of ketosis?

1. BAD BREATH

This might be a not so sexy symptom especially when you are a social person, but it is indeed a sign that you are under the state of ketosis.
It is caused by the high amount of ketone in your system. The specific culprit is acetone, a ketone that exits the body in your urine and breath.
People who experience this symptom tend to brush their teeth often or take a sugar-free/ carb free gum.

2. INCREASED KETONES IN THE BLOOD

Some ketogenic diet experts say nutritional ketosis is defined as blood ketones ranging from 0.5–3.0 mmol/L. Measuring ketones in your blood is the most accurate way of testing and is used in most research studies. It requires a small pinprick to draw blood from your finger and measure it using the test kit designated to track ketones. Ask the pharmacy for this.

3. WEIGHT LOSS

Studies have found out that one of the first and obvious symptoms of ketosis is weight loss, but the loss in weight may vary to people. The drop in weight may be caused by the switching to a low carb diet, the glucose level becomes low and your muscle cells begin to lose water.

Given that carbohydrates bind water molecules to muscles, a decline in the intake of carbohydrates results in the dumping of water from your body cells resulting in weight loss. As your body water weight starts to decline, the body fat level also falls if you maintain your diet and remain in a calorie deficit.

4. INCREASE IN FOCUS AND ENERGY

People often report brain fog, tiredness and feeling sick when first starting a very low-carb diet. This is termed the "low carb flu" or "keto flu." However, long-term ketogenic dieters often report increased focus and energy. Once the body is adapted on the shift on carbs to fats as fuel and energy source the good benefits take place. Ketones are an extremely potent fuel source for your brain. They have even been tested in a medical setting to treat brain diseases and conditions such as concussion and memory loss

5. SHOR TERM TIREDNESS

Like all kinds of diets, it takes some time till your body gets used to the change. One of the short term side effects of the ketogenic diet is fatigue. This is due to the loss in water during the ketosis. It is suggested that the person take some electrolyte supplements. When adding these supplements, try to get 2,000–4,000 mg of sodium, 1,000 mg of potassium and 300 mg of magnesium per day. This tiredness may pass when your body gets used to the new diet.

6. DIGESTIVE ISSUES

Some people experience constipation, one of the symptoms of ketosis. Well it's pretty normal that a sudden change in your bowel movements may be noticed because you are changing the food intake and the eating habits. On the other hand, some people experience diarrhea. With the addition of more fat and protein to your diet, you might have to run to the bathroom more frequently. Make sure you are drinking enough water and taking fiber-rich diet or a supplement.

7.DRY MOUTH

Dry mouth is one of the symptoms of ketosis. Due to loss of water in the body, it is normal to feel dry mouth during the process. It is suggested to have more water intake and brushing your teeth more frequent also for the bad breath we mentioned before.

8.HEART PALPITATION

Some dieters report health palpitations during the early phases of ketosis. The change in dietary intake causes mineral imbalance, glucose level adjustment, and loss of water. Because of hypoglycemia, our brain goes into an emergency state of starvation causing sugar cravings which lead to burning of stored glycogen and cause HPA axis dysregulation.
Also, the reduction of minerals, especially potassium is responsible for a decrease in blood volume and pressure causing blood vessels to pump faster. When potassium level in our body is low, blood cells cannot repolarize as easily, and the cardiac muscles and nerves may not function normally causing a change in heartbeat rate.

9.INSOMNIA

As all takes effect when something is changed within our system, Insomnia is also one of the effect of ketosis. It is reported at the early phase of the ketogenic diet. But some people reported that once your body adapts to the new diet, your sleep becomes better.

10. INCREASED IN FOCUS AND ENERGY

Yup. ironically to the tiredness we mentioned above. The reason behind this is, when the body gets used to the ketogenic diet, you will experience an increase in focus and energy!

What is the breakdown of macronutrients to experience the state of ketosis?

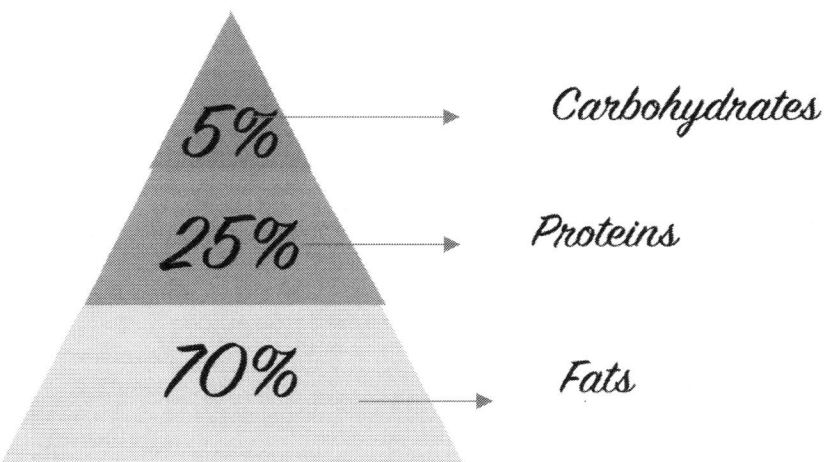

The suggested calories count for a normal person in general is 2000 calories per day, but that may vary depending on your height, weight, measurements, age, gender and level of activity.

What are the benefits of

KETOGENIC DIET?

1.Weight loss

As you cut your CARBOHYDRATE intake, you deprive your body of glucose, which is the main source of energy for all cells in the body. At this state, the tendency of your body is to find another source of fuel to sustain activity. This is where ketones come to the rescue!

During diet where very little carbohydrate is eaten, the body first pulls stored glucose from the liver and temporarily breaks down muscle to release glucose. If this continues for 3-4 days and stored glucose is fully depleted, blood levels of a hormone called insulin decrease, and the body begins to use fat as its primary fuel. The liver produces ketone bodies from fat, which can be used in the absence of glucose.

ATTENTION!

Excessive ketone bodies can produce a dangerously toxic level of acid in the blood, called ketoacidosis. During ketoacidosis, the kidneys begin to excrete ketone bodies along with body water in the urine, causing some fluid-related weight loss. Ketoacidosis most often occurs in individuals with type 1 diabetes because they do not produce insulin, a hormone that prevents the overproduction of ketones. However, in few rare cases, ketoacidosis has been reported to occur in non-diabetic individuals following a prolonged very low carbohydrate diet. This means that it is important that you ask your doctor for advice before you start this kind of diet.

As the old saying goes, "EVERYTHING IN MODERATION."

2. Reduced risk for Type 2 Diabetes

The process of burning fat provides more benefits than simply helping us to shed extra weight — it also helps control the release of hormones like insulin, which plays a role in the development of diabetes and other health problems. When we eat carbohydrates, insulin is released as a reaction to elevated blood glucose (an increase in sugar circulating in our blood) and insulin levels rise. Insulin is a "storage hormone" that signals cells to store as much available energy as possible, initially as glycogen (aka stored carbohydrates in our muscles) and then as body fat.

The ketogenic diet works by eliminating carbohydrates from the diet and keeping the body's carbohydrate stores almost empty, therefore preventing too much insulin from being released following food consumption and creating normal blood sugar levels. This can help reverse "insulin resistance," which is the underlying problem contributing to diabetes symptoms. In studies, low-carb diets have shown benefits for improving blood pressure, postprandial glycemia and insulin secretion. (7) Therefore, diabetics on insulin should contact their medical provider prior to starting a ketogenic diet; however, as insulin dosages may need to be adjusted.

3. Reduced risk of heart disease

The keto diet can reduce the risk of heart disease markers, including high cholesterol and triglycerides. In fact, the keto diet is unlikely to negatively impact your cholesterol levels despite being so high in fat. Moreover, it's capable of lowering cardiovascular disease risk factors, especially in those who are obese.

For instance, one study found that adhering to the ketogenic diet for 24 weeks resulted in decreased levels of triglycerides, LDL cholesterol and blood glucose in a significant percentage of patients, while at the same time increasing the level of HDL cholesterol.

4. Help protect against Cancer

Certain studies suggest that ketogenic diets may "starve" cancer cells. A highly processed, pro-inflammatory, low-nutrient diet can feed cancer cells causing them to proliferate. What's the connection between a high-sugar diet and cancer? The regular cells found in our bodies are able to use fat for energy, but it's believed that cancer cells cannot metabolically shift to use fat rather than glucose.

There are several medical studies — such as two conducted by the Department of Radiation Oncology at the Holden Comprehensive Cancer Center for the University of Iowa, and the National Institutes of Health's National Institute of Neurological Disorders and Stroke — that show the ketogenic diet is an effective treatment for cancer and other serious health problems.

Therefore, a diet that eliminates excess refined sugar and other processed carbohydrates may be effective in reducing or fighting cancer. It's not a coincidence that some of the best cancer-fighting foods are on the ketogenic diet food list.

5. Fight brain disease and neurological disorders

Over the past century, ketogenic diets have also been used to treat and even help reverse neurological disorders and cognitive impairments, including epilepsy and Alzheimer's symptoms. Research shows that cutting off glucose levels with a very low-carb diet makes your body produce ketones for fuel. This change can help to reverse neurological disorders and cognitive impairment. The brain is able to use this alternative source of energy instead of the cellular energy pathways that aren't functioning normally in patients with brain disorders.

For example, clinical improvement was observed in Alzheimer's patients fed a ketogenic diet, and this was marked by improved mitochondrial function. In fact, a European Journal of Clinical Nutrition study pointed to emerging data that suggested the therapeutic use of ketogenic diets for multiple neurological disorders beyond epilepsy and Alzheimer's, including headaches, neurotrauma, Parkinson's disease, sleep disorders, brain cancer, autism, and multiple sclerosis.

The report goes on to say that while these various diseases are clearly different from each other, the ketogenic diet appears to be so effective for neurological problems because of its "neuroprotective effect" — as the keto appears to correct abnormalities in cellular energy usage, which is a common characteristic in many neurological disorders.

Researchers believe that the ketogenic diet can also help patients with schizophrenia to normalize the pathophysiological processes that are causing symptoms like delusions, hallucinations, lack of restraint and unpredictable behavior. One study found that the ketogenic diet leads to elevated concentrations of kynurenic acid (KYNA) in the hippocampus and striatum, which promotes neuroactive activity. Some studies even point to the elimination of gluten under the ketogenic diet as a possible reason for improved symptoms, as researchers observed that patients with schizophrenia tended to eat more carbohydrates immediately before a psychotic episode.

Although the exact role of the ketogenic diet in mental and brain disorders is unclear, there has been proof of its efficacy in patients with schizophrenia. And, to boot, the ketogenic diet works to reverse many conditions that develop as a side effect of conventional medications for brain disorders, like weight gain, type 2 diabetes, and cardiovascular risks. More research is needed to understand the role of the ketogenic diet in treating or improving schizophrenia, as the currently available studies are either animal studies or case studies, but the benefits of this high-fat, low-carbohydrate diet in neurology is promising.

6. Live longer

There's even evidence that a low-carb, high-fat diet helps you live longer, compared to a low-fat diet. In a study by the medical journal The Lancet that studied more than 135,000 adults from 18 countries, high carbohydrate intake was associated with higher risk of total mortality, whereas total fat and individual types of fat were related to lower total mortality. Total fat and types of fat were not associated with cardiovascular disease, myocardial infarction or cardiovascular disease mortality.

In fact, saturated fat intake had an inverse association with the risk for suffering from a stroke, meaning the more saturated fat included in someone's diet, the more protection against having a stroke they seemed to have.

"Now that we know the important things we need to know about ketogenic diet, we can now proceed to the Things we need to know about VEGETARIAN"

What is a Vegetarian?

A vegetarian is someone who doesn't eat meat, and mostly eats foods that come from plants, like grains, fruits, vegetables, and nuts. Some stricter vegetarians avoid more than just meat. They also avoid animal products, which are nonmeat foods that come from animals. Some examples would be milk (from cows) and eggs (from chickens).

Types of Vegetarians

Lacto-ovo vegetarian: eats no meat, but will eat dairy products (milk, butter, cheese) and eggs; this is the most common type of vegetarian diet

Lacto vegetarian: eats dairy products but does not eat eggs

Ovo-vegetarian: eats eggs, but not dairy products

Vegan: does not eat eggs, dairy products, or any other food derived from animals

What is a keto vegetarian diet?

Simply put, a keto vegetarian diet restricts all forms of animal meat while restricting carbohydrate intake. The goal of this diet is to speed up weight loss by stimulating fat burning. Aside from promoting a better overall health, having a keto vegetarian diet is also an exhibit of disapproval of animal cruelty and abuse that runs rampant in the production of food derived from animal meat.

A traditional keto diet focuses on a meal plan that is very high in fat, very low in carbohydrates, and a moderate level of protein. The keto vegetarian diet does not stray from this general template but eliminates animal meat from the equation. As a general rule of thumb a keto vegetarian diet should be broken down as less than 5 percent carbohydrates, 15 to 20 percent protein, and 75 to 80 percent fat.

What can I eat and cannot eat under a keto vegetarian diet?

In preparing a meal plan for a keto vegetarian diet, it is often easier to start by listing down the foods that you avoid to eat or be responsible on the amount when you eat This list includes:

1.   Grains – rice, corn, oats, cereal, wheat, bran
2.   Legumes – peas, lentils, beans, chickpeas
3.   Fruit – apples, bananas, mangoes, oranges
4.   Sugar – honey, maple syrup, agave
5.   Tubers – yams, sweet potatoes, potatoes
6.   Animal meat – poultry, fish, pork, beef, lamb, seafood

"The restriction against meat is particularly challenging, as it acts as the primary source of protein for the traditional keto diet. However, a keto vegetarian diet does not have to be so limited. "

Below is the list of foods recommended for a keto vegetarian diet:

1. Eggs
2. Avocado
3. High fat dairy – butter, high fat cream and milk, different types of cheeses
4. Nuts and seeds – almonds, walnuts, sunflower seeds, pumpkin seeds, flaxseed
5. Coconut products – coconut milk, coconut flour, desiccated coconut
6. Soy products – tofu, soy milk,
7. Leafy greens – spinach, collard greens, cabbage, lettuce
8. Sweeteners – Stevia, erythritol, monk fruit
9. Fats and oils – olive oil, sesame oil, coconut oil, butter, ghee
10. Above ground vegetables – zucchini, cauliflower, broccoli

NOTE: Please use the vegetarian version of all the ingredients in this book. They absolutely exist.

It's a sure thing that being a vegetarian might have some food restrictions, and what more if we mixed it to ketogenic, but with a little imagination and creativity, we can make delicious meals and won't feel that there are restrictions in the first place.

30 Days
Meal Plan

DAY 1

Meal	Recipe	Calories
Breakfast	Scrambled Eggs with Spinach and Feta + Spinach Cucumber Smoothie	369 + 244
Lunch	Low-Carb Fried Eggplant	822
Dinner	Zoodles with Italian style hard cheese and Walnuts	475

Scrambled Eggs with Spinach and Feta

INGREDIENTS	Fats	Proteins	Carbs
2 eggs	8.37 g	11.05 g	0.63 g
1 cup spinach	0.12 g	0.86 g	1.09 g
1/4 cup feta cheese	7.98 g	5.33 g	1.53 g
1/8 cup fat-free cream	0.42 g	0.79 g	2.72 g
1 tbsp. olive oil (for frying)	13.5 g	0 g	0 g

Nutrition Facts

Amount per 199 g
1 serving (7 oz)

Calories 369
From fat 270

Amount	% Daily Value*	Amount	% Daily Value*
Total Fat 30.4g	47%	Total Carbohydrates 6g	2%
Saturated 10.5g	52%	Dietary Fiber 1g	3%
Trans Fat 0g		Sugars 4g	
Cholesterol 362mg	121%	Protein 18g	36%
Sodium 523mg	22%		
Calcium 29% • Iron 15%		Vitamin A 69% • Vitamin C 14%	

* Percent Daily Values are based on 2000 calorie diet. Your Daily Values may be higher or lower depending on your calorie needs.

Directions

1.   Crack open 2 eggs and whisk in a small bowl until thoroughly combined.

2.   Mix the fat-free cream with the eggs. Whisk the mixture until slightly airy.

3.   Brush a frying pan lightly with olive oil. Start heating the pan over a stove at low heat. When the pan is hot enough, pour in the egg mixture.

4.   Cook on one side for 2 to 3 minutes, or until the bottom has started to set. At this point, mix in the spinach.

5.   Start stirring the egg mixture continuously to keep the scrambled eggs creamy.

6.   Allow the spinach to cook and wilt a little for about 1 minute.

7.   Break up the feta cheese into small chunks and distribute evenly over the scrambled eggs.

8.   Continue cooking until the eggs are done to your liking.

9.   Season with salt and pepper, if desired.

Did you know?

Spinach is in fact, one of the most nutritious vegetables. It's high in iron, which helps build red blood cells. Red blood cells carry oxygen through the body and provide energy. Spinach is also a good source of vitamin A, vitamin K, and vitamin

Spinach Cucumber Smoothie

INGREDIENTS	Fats	Proteins	Carbs
2 cups spinach	0.23 g	1.72 g	2.18 g
1/2 cup cucumber, cubed	0.10 g	0.35 g	1.29 g
1 cup coconut milk	24.1 g	2.28 g	3.18 g
12 drops Stevia	0 g	0 g	1 g
7 ice cubes	-	-	-

Nutrition Facts

Amount per 234 g
1 serving (8.2 oz)

Calories 244
From fat 205

Amount	% Daily Value*	Amount	% Daily Value*
Total Fat 24.4g	38%	**Total Carbohydrates** 8g	3%
Saturated 21.4g	107%	Dietary Fiber 2g	7%
Trans Fat 0g		Sugars 1g	
Cholesterol 0mg	0%	**Protein** 4g	9%
Sodium 63mg	3%		
Calcium 9% • **Iron** 31%		**Vitamin A** 113% • **Vitamin C** 33%	

* Percent Daily Values are based on 2000 calorie diet. Your Daily Values may be higher or lower depending on your calorie needs.

Directions

1.   In a blender, mix in the spinach, Stevia, coconut milk, and ice cubes. Blend until smooth.

2.   Top with cubed cucumber and serve.

Did you know?

Cucumbers contain insoluble and soluble fiber that helps you feel full and also lowers bad cholesterol in your body

Low-Carb Fried Eggplant

INGREDIENTS	Fats	Proteins	Carbs
1 small eggplant (approx. 0.1 kg)	0.10 g	0.54 g	3.22 g
1/8 cup almond flour	6.19 g	2.62 g	2.67 g
1/2 tbsp. grated Italian style hard cheese	0.13 g	1 g	1 g
2 eggs	8.37 g	11.05 g	0.63 g
1/2 tsp Italian seasoning	0 g	0.06 g	0.81 g
5 tbsp. olive oil	67.5 g	0 g	0 g

Nutrition Facts

Amount per 227 g
1 serving (8 oz)

Calories 822
From fat 726

	Amount	% Daily Value*	Amount	% Daily Value*
Total Fat	82.3g	127%	Total Carbohydrates 8g	3%
Saturated	12.6g	63%	Dietary Fiber 3g	14%
Trans Fat	0.1g		Sugars 3g	
Cholesterol	328mg	109%	Protein 15g	31%
Sodium	257mg	11%		
Calcium	11% • Iron 15%		Vitamin A 11% • Vitamin C	2%

* Percent Daily Values are based on 2000 calorie diet. Your Daily Values may be higher or lower depending on your calorie needs.

Directions

1.   Combine the almond flour, grated Italian style hard cheese, and Italian season in a large plate. Set aside.

2.   Break the eggs into a small bowl and whisk until thoroughly mixed. Set aside.

3.   Slice the eggplant lengthwise into 1/4-inch slices. You may leave the skin on. Pat the slices dry using a paper towel.

4.   Heat the olive oil in a frying pan over medium heat.

5.   Dip each piece of eggplant into the egg mixture and coat lightly with the breading mixture. Make sure that each eggplant slice has been completely covered.

6.   Fry the eggplant slices until the coating is golden brown. You may fry several pieces at the same time, but make sure that the pan does not get overcrowded.

7.   After frying, drain the excess oil over paper towels.

8.   Season with salt and pepper before serving, if desired.

Did you know?
Salting eggplant will reduce the amount of oil absorbed in cooking.

Zoodles with cheese And Walnuts

INGREDIENTS	Fats	Proteins	Carbs
1 large zucchini (approx. 0.3 kg)	0.06 g	0.43 g	0.50 g
1/4 cup ricotta cheese	4.18 g	3.63 g	0.98 g
1/4 cup chopped macadamia nuts	6.06 g	0.63 g	1.11 g
1 cup raw radicchio	0.1 g	0.57 g	1.79 g
1/8 cup olive oil	28.1 g	0 g	0 g
1 tbsp. lemon juice	0.02 g	0.03 g	0.52 g
1 tsp chopped garlic	0.01 g	0.18 g	0.93 g
1/4 cup Greek yogurt	0.23 g	6.11 g	2.16 g

1/8 cup shredded cheddar	4.97 g	3.53 g	0.2 g

Directions

1. Slice the zucchini into noodles using a spiralizer. If you don't have a spiralizer, a mandolin slicer will do to slice it into thin strips.

2. Shred or slice the radicchio into bite-sized strips.

3. Mix together the spiralized zucchini, radicchio, ricotta cheese, shredded cheddar cheese, Greek yogurt, and macadamia nuts.

4. For the dressing, mix together the olive oil, lemon juice, and chopped garlic. Add a pinch of salt and pepper.

5. Add the dressing and salad and toss thoroughly. Serve immediately. Enjoy!

Did you know?

Cheese can be produced using a variety of milk including cow, buffalo, goat, horse, and even camel.

DAY 2

Meal	Recipe	Calories
Breakfast	Keto Pumpkin Pancakes	551
Lunch	Cauliflower Spinach Bowl	499
Dinner	Broccoli and Cheese Fritters	932

Keto Pumpkin Pancakes

INGREDIENTS	Fats	Proteins	Carbs
1/4 cup pumpkin puree	0.17 g	0.67 g	4.96 g
2 eggs	0.11 g	7.19 g	0.48 g

2 tbsp. coconut flour	5.16 g	0.55 g	1.89 g
1/4 tsp cinnamon powder	0.01 g	0.03 g	0.56 g
1/4 tsp. vanilla extract	0 g	0 g	0.14 g
2 tbsp. coconut oil (for frying)	27.2 g	0 g	0 g
2 tbsp. butter	23.04 g	0.24 g	0.02 g

Nutrition Facts

Amount per 193 g
1 serving (6.8 oz)

Calories 551
From fat 483

Amount	% Daily Value*	Amount	% Daily Value*
Total Fat 55.7g	86%	Total Carbohydrates 8g	3%
Saturated 42.8g	214%	Dietary Fiber 4g	14%
Trans Fat 1g		Sugars 3g	
Cholesterol 61mg	20%	Protein 9g	17%
Sodium 298mg	12%		
Calcium 4% • Iron 7%		Vitamin A 205% • Vitamin C 5%	

* Percent Daily Values are based on 2000 calorie diet. Your Daily Values may be higher or lower depending on your calorie needs.

Directions

1.   Whisk together the pumpkin puree and eggs in a large bowl.

2.   Whisk in the cinnamon powder and vanilla extract.

3.   Gradually add in the coconut flour while continuing whisking. Mix until just after all the lumps are gone.

4.   Heat coconut oil on a frying pan at medium heat.

5.   When the frying pan is hot enough, add the pancake batter one tablespoon at a time.

6.   Cook one side until bubbles start appearing at the surface. Flip and cook the other side. Cook until both sides are a golden brown color.

7.   Serve pancakes with butter.

Did you know?
September 26th is National Pancake Day.

Cauliflower Spinach Bowl

INGREDIENTS	Fats	Proteins	Carbs
3/4 cups cauliflower, chopped	0.22 g	1.54 g	3.99 g
1 cup spinach	0.12 g	0.86 g	1.09 g
1/4 cup almonds, chopped	0.15 g	0.06 g	0.06 g
0.25 tbsp garlic, chopped	0.01 g	0.13 g	0.69 g
1/2 cup cilantro leaves	0.04 g	0.17 g	0.29 g
2 tbsp. olive oil	27 g	0 g	0 g

1/2 tbsp. sunflower seeds	1.13 g	0.46 g	0.44 g
1/2 cup ricotta cheese	15.97 g	13.85 g	3.74

Nutrition Facts

Amount per 273 g
1 serving (9.6 oz)

Calories 499
From fat 393

Amount	% Daily Value*	Amount	% Daily Value*
Total Fat 44.6g	69%	Total Carbohydrates 10g	3%
Saturated 14.2g	71%	Dietary Fiber 3g	11%
Trans Fat 0g		Sugars 2g	
Cholesterol 63mg	21%	Protein 17g	34%
Sodium 156mg	7%		
Calcium 31% • Iron 12%		Vitamin A 78% • Vitamin C 83%	

* Percent Daily Values are based on 2000 calorie diet. Your Daily Values may be higher or lower depending on your calorie needs.

Directions

1.   Pre-heat your oven to 375 F. Spread the almonds evenly over a small baking tray and bake until golden brown, about 7 to 10 minutes Set aside.

2.   Separate the cauliflower into florets and place into a food processor. Pulse repeatedly until you obtain a rice-like texture.

3.   In a separate pan, heat 1 tbsp. of olive oil over medium heat. Add in the cauliflower rice and chopped garlic. Cook while stirring occasionally. The cauliflower rice is done when it has turned golden brown. Season with salt and pepper.

4.   To the same pan as the cauliflower rice, add in the spinach and cilantro. Don't stir the leaves in, but just let them sit on top of the cauliflower rice. Cover the pan and let the leaves sit for about 2 to 3 minutes.

5.   Garnish the dish with sunflower seeds and ricotta cheese. Serve.

Did you know?

Cauliflowers can be eaten raw, cooked or pickled

Broccoli And Cheese Fritter

INGREDIENTS	Fats	Proteins	Carbs
1 cup broccoli, chopped	0.2 g	1.27 g	1.14 g
1/8 cup almond flour	6.19 g	2.62 g	2.67 g
1/2 cup mozzarella cheese	0 g	17.91 g	1.98 g
1 egg	9.64 g	8.97 g	1.02 g
0.5 tbsp. flaxseed meal	1.48 g	0.64 g	1.01 g
0.5 tsp. baking powder	0.01 g	0 g	1.17 g
3 tbsp. mayonnaise	14.31 g	2.68 g	1.38 g
1 tbsp. lemon juice	0.04 g	0.05 g	1.06 g
1 tbsp. fresh dill	0.09 g	0.28 g	0.56 g
4 tbsp coconut oil	54.4 g	0 g	0 g

Nutrition Facts	Amount	% Daily Value*	Amount	% Daily Value*
Amount per 212 g	**Total Fat** 38g	58%	**Total Carbohydrates** 13g	4%
1 serving (7.5 oz)	Saturated 16.6g	83%	Dietary Fiber 4g	14%
	Trans Fat		Sugars 7g	
Calories 431	**Cholesterol** 84mg	28%	**Protein** 13g	26%
From fat 329	**Sodium** 96mg	4%		
	Calcium 32% • **Iron** 12%		**Vitamin A** 27% • **Vitamin C** 17%	

* Percent Daily Values are based on 2000 calorie diet. Your Daily Values may be higher or lower depending on your calorie needs.

Directions

1.   Cut up the broccoli into florets and place inside a food processor. Pulse until the broccoli has been cut down to very small pieces.

2.   To the broccoli, add the almond flour, mozzarella cheese, 1 tbsp. flaxseed meal, and baking powder. You may also add salt and pepper at this point, if desired. Mix thoroughly.

3.   Add the egg to the mixture and mix thoroughly until everything is well-incorporated.

4.   Using your hands, form the mixture into balls of around 1 inch in diameter.

5.   Roll the balls around the remaining flaxseed meal, ensuring that they are completely covered. Continue doing this for all the balls and set them aside.

6.   Prepare the deep fryer. Add enough coconut oil to the deep fryer to fully submerge the balls you have made. Heat the deep fryer to about 375 F.

7.   Drop the balls one by one to the deep fryer, making sure that they don't stick to each other. Allow them to cook until golden brown, which should only take about 3 to 5 minutes.

8.	Once they are cooked, drain the excess oil by placing the fritters on dish lined with paper towels.

9.	To make a dip for the fritters, combine mayonnaise, dill, and lemon juice.

10.	Serve the fritters with a side of dip. Enjoy!

Did you know?

Broccoli contains the flavonoid kaempferol. Kaempferol is an anti-inflammatory, helps fight against cancer and heart disease, and has been shown to be preventative in adult diabetes onset.

DAY 3

Meal	Recipe	Calories
Breakfast	Keto Smoothie Bowl	431
Lunch	Zucchini Grilled Cheese Sandwich	936
Dinner	Tofu and Bok Choy Salad	426

Keto Smoothie Bowl

INGREDIENTS	Fats	Proteins	Carbs
1/2 cup whole milk	1.04 g	1 g	1.52 g
1/2 cup cream	23.17 g	3.24 g	4.39 g
1/4 cup avocado, chopped	5.5 g	0.75 g	3.2 g
1/2 scoop protein powder	1.5 g	6.25 g	2.75 g
2 ice cubes	-	-	-
1/8 cup walnuts, chopped	6.78 g	1.58 g	1.43 g

Nutrition Facts

	Amount	% Daily Value*	Amount	% Daily Value*
	Total Fat 38g	58%	**Total Carbohydrates** 13g	4%
	Saturated 16.6g	83%	Dietary Fiber 4g	14%
	Trans Fat		Sugars 7g	
	Cholesterol 84mg	28%	**Protein** 13g	26%
	Sodium 96mg	4%		
	Calcium 32% • **Iron** 12%		**Vitamin A** 27% • **Vitamin C** 17%	

Amount per 212 g
1 serving (7.5 oz)

Calories 431
From fat 329

* Percent Daily Values are based on 2000 calorie diet. Your Daily Values may be higher or lower depending on your calorie needs.

Directions

1.   Place all the ingredients into a blender.

2.   Blend until smooth.

3.   Pour into a bowl.

4.   Top with chopped walnuts and serve.

Did you know?

Walnuts are the oldest known tree food — they date back to 10,000 BC

Zucchini Grilled Cheese Sandwich

INGREDIENTS	Fats	Proteins	Carbs
2 cups zucchini, shredded	0.04 g	0.3 g	0.34 g
1 egg	9.64 g	8.97 g	1.02 g
1/8 cup Italian style hard cheese, shredded	3.62 g	3.69 g	1.81 g
1/2 cup cheddar, shredded	22.32 g	15.87 g	0.88 g
1/4tbsp. cornstarch	0 g	0.01 g	1.83 g

1/4 cup green onions, sliced	0.08 g	0.17 g	1.02 g
4 tbsp. coconut oil	54.4 g	0 g	0 g

Nutrition Facts

Amount per 234 g
1 serving (8.3 oz)

Calories 936
From fat 790

Amount	% Daily Value*	Amount	% Daily Value*
Total Fat 90.1g	139%	Total Carbohydrates 7g	2%
Saturated 64.4g	322%	Dietary Fiber 1g	2%
Trans Fat 1g		Sugars 2g	
Cholesterol 697mg	232%	Protein 29g	58%
Sodium 765mg	32%		
Calcium 61% • Iron 17%		Vitamin A 40% • Vitamin C 10%	

* Percent Daily Values are based on 2000 calorie diet. Your Daily Values may be higher or lower depending on your calorie needs.

Directions

1.   Wrap the shredded zucchini in several pieces of kitchen towels. Place a weight (such as a pot with water) on top of the zucchini and allow it to squeeze the excess moisture out of it for at least an hour.

2.   After enough water has been squeezed out of the zucchini shred, combine it with the egg, Italian style hard cheese, cornstarch, and green onions. Season with salt and pepper. Mix thoroughly.

3.   In a large pan, pour enough coconut oil to coat the bottom of the pan. Heat the pan over medium heat.

4.   When the pan is sufficiently hot, place about 1/4 cup of the zucchini mixture on the pan. Shape the zucchini mixture into a square.

5.   Cook until golden brown on both sides. At this point, the fried mixture should resemble patties and should hold their shape.

6.   Repeat until all of the zucchini mixture has been cooked. Drain excess oil from all cooked patties using paper towels.

7.   To the same pan, place two zucchini patties. Top each patty with shredded cheddar and add another patty to each. Allow to cook until the cheese has melted.

8.   Repeat until all zucchini patties have been made into sandwiches. Serve while hot.

Did you know?
The word zucchini comes from 'zucca' the Italian word for squash.

Tofu and Bok Choy Salad

INGREDIENTS	Fats	Proteins	Carbs
1/2 cup soft tofu, cubed	4.58 g	8.12 g	2.23 g
1/2 tsp. soy sauce	0.01 g	0.21 g	0.13 g
1 1/2 tsp. sesame oil	6.8 g	0 g	0 g
1 tsp. garlic, chopped	0.01 g	0.18 g	0.93 g
1 tsp. lemon juice	0.01 g	0.02 g	0.35 g
3/4 cups bok choy, cooked	0.2 g	1.98 g	2.26 g
1/2 cup cilantro, chopped	0.04 g	0.17 g	0.29 g
1/4 cup green onions, chopped	0.08 g	0.17 g	1.02 g
2 tbsp. coconut oil	27.2 g	0 g	0 g

1/4 tbsp. soy sauce	0.01 g	0.33 g	0.2 g
1/4 tbsp. peanut butter	1.53 g	1.17 g	1.6 g
1/2 tbsp. lime juice	0.01 g	0.03 g	0.64 g

Nutrition Facts

Amount per 337 g
1 serving (11.9 oz)

Calories 426
From fat 349

Amount	% Daily Value*	Amount	% Daily Value*
Total Fat 40.5g	62%	Total Carbohydrates 10g	3%
Saturated 25.5g	127%	Dietary Fiber 2g	10%
Trans Fat 0g		Sugars 3g	
Cholesterol 0mg	0%	Protein 12g	25%
Sodium 574mg	24%		
Calcium 28% • Iron 18%		Vitamin A 133% • Vitamin C 72%	

* Percent Daily Values are based on 2000 calorie diet. Your Daily Values may be higher or lower depending on your calorie needs.

Directions

1.   In a large container, mix the cubed tofu with the soy sauce, sesame oil, garlic, and lemon juice. Season with salt and pepper. Marinate the tofu in the mixture for at least an hour.

2.   After marinating, pre-heat your oven to 350 F.

3.   Place the tofu cubes on a large baking tray lines with parchment paper. Make sure that the cubes are not in contact with one another to ensure even cooking.

4.   Bake the tofu for 30 to 35 minutes. They should come out golden brown and have a crispy exterior.

5.   In a separate bowl, mix the coconut oil, soy sauce, peanut butter, and lime juice. Mix thoroughly until well-incorporated.

6.   To this bowl, add the chopped cilantro and spring onions. Mix well.
7.   Chop the bok choy into bite-sized strips.

8.   Just before serving, add the dressing to the chopped bok choy.

9.   Once the tofu is cooked, mix the tofu cubes with the bok choy salad.

10.   Serve immediately and enjoy!

Did you know?

Tofu contains all 8 essential amino acids. It is rich in magnesium, phosphorus and selenium too (which helps to trigger happy hormones). Tofu also contains copper, vitamin B1, calcium and iron. It is low in fat but high on nutrition. Research shows that regular tofu eaters get enhanced protection against different kinds of cancer and heart diseases too.

DAY 4

Meal	Recipe	Calories
Breakfast	Feta Cheese Salad with Balsamic Butter	711
Lunch	Mexican Cauliflower Rice	346
Dinner	Pumpkin and Spinach Cannelloni	879

Feta Cheese Salad with Balsamic Butter

INGREDIENTS	Fats	Proteins	Carbs
1/2 cup feta cheese, crumbled	15.96 g	10.66 g	3.07 g
1/8 cup pumpkin seeds	7.5 g	4.57 g	2.25 g
1/4 cup butter	46.07 g	0.48 g	0.03 g
1 tbsp. balsamic vinegar	0 g	0.08 g	2.72 g
1/2 cup baby spinach	0.06 g	0.43 g	0.54 g

Nutrition Facts

Amount per 178 g
1 serving (6.3 oz)

Calories 711
From fat 609

Amount	% Daily Value*	Amount	% Daily Value*
Total Fat 69.6g	107%	Total Carbohydrates 9g	3%
Saturated 41.7g	209%	Dietary Fiber 1g	5%
Trans Fat 1.9g		Sugars 6g	
Cholesterol 189mg	63%	Protein 16g	32%
Sodium 1108mg	46%		
Calcium 41% • Iron 13%		Vitamin A 63% • Vitamin C 8%	

* Percent Daily Values are based on 2000 calorie diet. Your Daily Values may be higher or lower depending on your calorie needs.

Directions

1.   Preheat the oven to 400 °F.

2.   Spread the crumbled feta cheese on a greased baking tray and bake in the oven for 10 minutes.

3.   In a dry frying pan over high heat, toast the pumpkin seeds until they start to pop.

4.   Lower the heat. Add the butter and let simmer until the butter has developed a golden brown color.

5.   Add balsamic vinegar and let simmer for 1 to 2 minutes. Turn off the heat.

6.   Assemble the baby spinach leaves on a dish. Pour the balsamic butter on the baby spinach and top with the feta cheese.

Did you know?
Balsamic vinegar has minerals that prevents bone diseases such as osteoporosis, prevent strokes, treat anemia and fatigue, as well as lower high blood pressure and high cholesterol

Mexican Cauliflower Rice

INGREDIENTS	Fats	Proteins	Carbs
1/2 cup cauliflower, chopped	0.15 g	1.03 g	2.66 g
2 tbsp. olive oil	27 g	0 g	0 g
1 tbsp. onion, chopped	0.01 g	0.11 g	0.93 g
1/2 tbsp. garlic, chopped	0.02 g	0.27 g	1.42 g
1 tbsp jalapeno	0.03 g	0.07 g	0.52 g
1/4 cup tomatoes, chopped	0.07 g	0.33 g	1.45 g
1/4 cup bell peppers, chopped	0.02 g	0.23 g	1.07 g
1 tsp. cumin powder	0.47 g	0.37 g	0.93 g
1/2 tsp. paprika	0.15 g	0.17 g	0.65 g
1/4 cup avocado, sliced	5.35 g	0.73 g	3.11 g

Nutrition Facts

Amount per 191 g
1 serving (6.7 oz)

Calories 346
From fat 291

Amount	% Daily Value*	Amount	% Daily Value*
Total Fat 33.3g	51%	Total Carbohydrates 13g	4%
Saturated 4.7g	23%	Dietary Fiber 5g	21%
Trans Fat 0g		Sugars 4g	
Cholesterol 0mg	0%	Protein 3g	7%
Sodium 28mg	1%		
Calcium 6% • Iron 14%		Vitamin A 24% • Vitamin C 123%	

* Percent Daily Values are based on 2000 calorie diet. Your Daily Values may be higher or lower depending on your calorie needs.

Directions:

1.	Add the chopped cauliflower to a good processor. Pulse until cauliflower has been chopped to small bits, with texture resembling rice.

2.	Heat the olive oil in a pan over medium heat. Add the onions, garlic, and jalapeno. Stir fry until fragrant.

3.   Add the tomatoes, paprika, and cumin powder to the pan. Cook until the tomatoes have softened.
4.   Add the bell peppers and cauliflower tice to the pan. Stir fry until the cauliflower rice is tender which should take about 3 to 4 minutes. Season with salt and pepper, as desired.

5.   Top with the sliced avocado and serve.

Did you know?

Compared to green peppers, red peppers are known to have more vitamins and nutrients and contain the antioxidant lycopene. The level of carotene, like lycopene, is nine times higher in red peppers. Red peppers have twice the vitamin C content of green peppers.

Pumpkin and Spinach Cannelloni

INGREDIENTS	Fats	Proteins	Carbs
1/4 cup pumpkin, cubed	0.03 g	0.29 g	1.89 g
3 slices onion leeks	0.05 g	0.27 g	2.55 g
1/4 cup cauliflower, chopped	0.08 g	0.51 g	1.33 g
1 tsp. fresh thyme	0.01 g	0.04 g	0.2 g
2 tbsp. olive oil	27 g	0 g	0 g
3 tbsp. goat's cheese	8.54 g	7.32 g	0.52 g
1/2 cup spinach	0.06 g	0.43 g	0.54 g
1/4 cup cream cheese	17.16 g	4.26 g	2.1 g
1/4 cup heavy whipping cream	11.1 g	0.62 g	0.84 g

1 tbsp. fresh basil	0.02 g	0.09 g	0.07 g
1 tbsp. Italian style hard cheese, grated	1.39 g	1.42 g	0.7 g
1 egg	4.18 g	5.53 g	0.32 g
1/4 cup cheddar cheese	11.16 g	7.93 g	0.44 g
1/4 tbsp. garlic	0.01 g	0.13 g	0.69 g

Directions:

1.   Preheat the oven to 360 °F.

2.   Place the pumpkin and cauliflower on a baking tray. Sprinkle the thyme over the vegetables and drizzle with olive oil. Bake the vegetables for 35 to 45 minutes until they are soft and caramelized.

3.   Remove from the oven and let cool.

4.   When the vegetables have cooled down, mash them with a fork or potato ricer.

5.   To the mashed vegetables, add the goat's cheese and spinach.

6.   Separate the layers of the sliced leeks. We will only be using the outermost layers in this recipe.

7.   Cook the separated layers in boiling water for 2 to 3 minutes. The goal is to make them slightly tender without being soggy. Once they are soft, remove them from the pot and place in cold water.

8.   Combine the cream cheese and heavy whipping cream. Mix until smooth.

9.   To the cream cheese mixture, add the basil, Italian style hard cheese, garlic, and eggs. Mix until thoroughly combined.

10.   Spread a layer of the cheese mixture on the bottom of the lasagna dish.

11.   In each layer of the leeks, place about three tablespoons of the mashed vegetable mixture. Roll the leek around the filling, ensuring that the filling is well distributed. Place the finished roll on top of the cheese mixture on the lasagna dish.

12.   Repeat previous step until all leek layers or all the mashed vegetable mixture has been consumed.

13.   Pour the remained of the cheese mixture on top of the rolled leeks.

14.   Sprinkle grated cheddar and Italian style hard cheese over the top.

15.   Bake the dish at 360 °F for about 30 minutes, or until the top has browned.

16.   Remove the dish from the oven and let cool before serving.

Did you know?
Each pumpkin has about 500 seeds.

DAY 5

Meal	Recipe	Calories
Breakfast	Spinach Artichoke Breakfast Casserole	462
Lunch	Spaghetti Squash with Creamy Mushroom Sauce	919
Dinner	Cauliflower Macaroni and Cheese	597

Spinach Artichoke Breakfast Casserole

INGREDIENTS	Fats	Proteins	Carbs
1 egg	4.18 g	5.53 g	0.32 g
1/8 cup whole milk	1.04 g	1 g	1.52 g
1/4 cup spinach	0.03 g	0.21 g	0.27 g
1/4 cup artichoke hearts	0.04 g	0.78 g	2.52 g
1/4 tbsp. garlic, chopped	0.01 g	0.13 g	0.69 g
1 tbsp. coconut flour	0.03 g	0.11 g	0.56 g
1/2 tsp. baking powder	0.01 g	0 g	1.17 g
1 tbsp. olive oil	13.5 g	0 g	0 g
1/4 cup feta cheese, crumbled	7.98 g	5.33 g	1.53 g
2 tbsp. unsalted butter	15.43 g	0.92 g	0 g

Nutrition Facts

Amount per 206 g

1 serving (7.3 oz)

Calories 462

From fat 376

Amount	% Daily Value*	Amount	% Daily Value*
Total Fat 42.2g	65%	Total Carbohydrates 9g	3%
Saturated 19.1g	95%	Dietary Fiber 2g	7%
Trans Fat 0g		Sugars 4g	
Cholesterol 230mg	77%	Protein 14g	28%
Sodium 477mg	20%		
Calcium 39% • Iron 12%		Vitamin A 33% • Vitamin C 10%	

* Percent Daily Values are based on 2000 calorie diet. Your Daily Values may be higher or lower depending on your calorie needs.

Directions:

1.   Grease the inside of a deep pan with olive oil. Heat the pan under medium heat.

2.   In a large bowl, whisk together the eggs, milk, spinach, artichoke hearts, feta cheese, butter, and garlic. Season with salt and pepper, if desired. Mix until thoroughly combined.

3.   Add the coconut flour and baking powder to the egg mixture and mix until well combined.

4.   Spread the mixture into the deep pan. Cover and allow to cook for about 7 to 10 minutes, or until the top layer has set.

5.   Allow to cool and serve.

Did you know?

The artichoke is technically a flower bud that has not yet bloomed.

Spaghetti Squash with Creamy Mushroom Sauce

INGREDIENTS	Fats	Proteins	Carbs
1/2 cup spaghetti squash	0.29 g	0.32 g	3.49 g
2 tbsp. olive oil	27 g	0 g	0 g
1/4 cup white mushrooms, sliced	0.06 g	0.54 g	0.57 g
1 tbsp. onions, sliced	0.01 g	0.11 g	0.93 g
1/4 cup butter	46.07 g	0.48 g	0.03 g
1 tsp. Dijon mustard	0.17 g	0.19 g	0.29 g
1 tbsp. sage	0.26 g	0.21 g	1.21 g
1 tsp. thyme	0.01 g	0.04 g	0.2 g
1/4 cup spinach	0.03 g	0.21 g	0.27 g
1/4 cup cheddar, diced	11.16 g	7.93 g	0.44 g
1/4 cup heavy whipping cream	11.1 g	0.62 g	0.84 g

Directions:

1.   Preheat the oven to 375 F.

2.   Place the spaghetti squash on a medium-sized baking tray. Drizzle with olive oil and season with salt and pepper.

3.   Bake the squash for about 60 minutes, or until the flash has been softened enough to be easily pierced with a knife.

4.   Melt the butter in a frying pan over medium heat.

5.   Cook the mushrooms in the butter until they are golden brown.

6.   Add the onions and cook until they are translucent and fragrant.

7.   In a small mixing bowl, combine the Dijon mustard, sage, thyme, cheddar, and heavy whipping cream. Add 2 tbsp. of water and whisk until thoroughly combined.

8.   Add the mixture from step 7 to the cooked mushrooms and onions. Turn the heat down to low and stir until well combined.

9.   Add in the spinach and let the leaves wilt for 1 to 2 minutes.

10.   Remove the cooked squash from the oven and scrape the flesh off to form spaghetti-like strands.

11.   In a bowl, pour the mushroom sauce over the spaghetti squash. Serve and enjoy.

Did you know?

Mushrooms are a fungus, and unlike plants, mushrooms do not require sunlight to make energy for themselves.

Cauliflower Macaroni and Cheese

INGREDIENTS	Fats	Proteins	Carbs
1/2 cup cauliflower, chopped	0.15 g	1.03 g	2.66 g
1/4 cup coconut milk	12.05 g	1.14 g	1.59 g
1 tbsp. desiccated coconut	5.16 g	0.55 g	1.89 g
1 egg	0.06 g	3.6 g	0.24 g
3/4 cup cheddar cheese, diced	33.48 g	23.8 g	1.32 g

Nutrition Facts

Amount per 250 g
1 serving (8.8 oz)

Calories 597
From fat 447

Amount	% Daily Value*	Amount	% Daily Value*
Total Fat 50.9g	78%	Total Carbohydrates 8g	3%
Saturated 34.5g	173%	Dietary Fiber 2g	10%
Trans Fat 1.2g		Sugars 2g	
Cholesterol 101mg	34%	Protein 30g	60%
Sodium 719mg	30%		
Calcium 70% • Iron 14%		Vitamin A 20% • Vitamin C 44%	

* Percent Daily Values are based on 2000 calorie diet. Your Daily Values may be higher or lower depending on your calorie needs.

Directions:

1.   Cook the chopped cauliflower in a steamer until al dente.

2.   In a large skillet, heat up the coconut milk over medium heat. Add the desiccated coconut and allow the mixture to bubble.

3.   Take the coconut mixture off the heat and whisk in the egg. Allow the sauce to thicken.

4.   Spread the cooked cauliflower in a deep baking dish. Pour in the coconut sauce and sprinkle the cheese evenly on the top.

5.   Bake in the oven at 350 °F for 35 to 40 minutes. Broil the top for 3 to 5 minutes to get a brown and crunchy finish.

Did you know?

Cauliflower can grow from 8 to 30 inches both in height and width.

DAY 6

Meal	Recipe	Calories
Breakfast	Keto Yogurt Bowl	330
Lunch	Lettuce and Walnut Salad	774
Dinner	Avocado Walnut Pesto	712

Keto Yogurt Bowl

INGREDIENTS	Fats	Proteins	Carbs
1/2 cup Greek yogurt	0.47 g	12.23 g	4.32 g

	Fats	Proteins	Carbs
2 tbsp. desiccated coconut	11.05 g	0.85 g	3.44 g
1 tbsp. sunflower seeds	4.53 g	1.83 g	1.76 g
1 tbsp. almond butter	8.88 g	3.35 g	3.01 g

Nutrition Facts

Amount per 161 g
1 serving (5.7 oz)

Calories 330
From fat 209

Amount	% Daily Value*	Amount	% Daily Value*
Total Fat 24.9g	38%	Total Carbohydrates 13g	4%
Saturated 11g	55%	Dietary Fiber 2g	10%
Trans Fat 0g		Sugars 5g	
Cholesterol 6mg	2%	Protein 18g	37%
Sodium 51mg	2%		
Calcium 20% • Iron 9%		Vitamin A 0% • Vitamin C 1%	

* Percent Daily Values are based on 2000 calorie diet. Your Daily Values may be higher or lower depending on your calorie needs.

Directions:

1.   In a medium-sized bowl, add the Greek yogurt and drizzle with almond butter.

2.   Top with the desiccated coconut and sunflower seeds. Serve and enjoy.

Did you know?

There two types of sunflower seeds: black and striped Black sunflower seeds are used to make oil and snacks are made out of striped seeds.

Lettuce and Walnut Salad

INGREDIENTS	Fats	Proteins	Carbs
1 tbsp. light sour cream	1.27 g	0.42 g	0.85 g

1 tbsp. mayonnaise	10.33 g	0.13 g	0.08 g
1 tsp. parsley	0.01 g	0.04 g	0.08 g
1 tbsp. milk	0.49 g	0.47 g	0.72 g
1 egg, boiled	4.18 g	5.53 g	0.32 g
1/2 cup cheddar, diced	22.32 g	15.87 g	0.88 g
3/4 cup romaine lettuce	0.11 g	0.43 g	1.16 g
1/4 cup cucumber, cubed	0.05 g	0.18 g	0.64 g
1 tsp. Dijon mustard	0.17 g	0.19 g	0.29 g
1/4 cup walnuts, chopped	19.11 g	4.46 g	4.02 g
1 tbsp. olive oil	13.5 g	0 g	0 g

Nutrition Facts

Amount per 265 g
1 serving (9.3 oz)

Calories 774
From fat 630

Amount	% Daily Value*	Amount	% Daily Value*
Total Fat 71.5g	110%	Total Carbohydrates 9g	3%
Saturated 20.5g	103%	Dietary Fiber 3g	13%
Trans Fat 0.8g		Sugars 3g	
Cholesterol 242mg	81%	Protein 28g	55%
Sodium 652mg	27%		
Calcium 56% • Iron 13%		Vitamin A 84% • Vitamin C 8%	

* Percent Daily Values are based on 2000 calorie diet. Your Daily Values may be higher or lower depending on your calorie needs.

Directions:

1. In a dry frying pan over medium heat, lightly toast the chopped walnuts for about 2 to 3 minutes.

2. Prepare the dressing by mixing together the sour cream, mayonnaise, parsley, Dijon mustard, olive oil, and milk. Whisk together until thoroughly combined.

3. Assemble the salad. Toss together the romaine lettuce, cheddar, slices of the boiled egg, and the toasted walnuts.

4. Mix in the dressing and toss. Serve.

Did you know?

Lettuce provides dietary fibers, vitamins A, B9 and C and minerals such as calcium, iron and copper. Darker varieties provide more nutrients than light green varieties.

Avocado Walnut Pesto

INGREDIENTS	Fats	Proteins	Carbs
1 medium zucchini	0.04 g	0.3 g	0.34 g
1/4 cup avocado, cubed	5.5 g	0.75 g	3.2 g
1 tbsp. basil, chopped	0.02 g	0.09 g	0.07 g
1 tbsp. walnuts, chopped	4.63 g	1.88 g	0.75 g
1 tbsp. garlic, chopped	0.02 g	0.27 g	1.42 g
1 tbsp. lemon juice	0.04 g	0.05 g	1.06 g
1 tbsp. Italian style hard cheese, grated	1.39 g	1.42 g	0.7 g
2 tbsp. olive oil	27 g	0 g	0 g
1/2 cup cheddar cheese, grated	19.11 g	13.58 g	0.75 g
1 tbsp. butter	11.52 g	0.12 g	0.01 g

Nutrition Facts	Amount	% Daily Value*	Amount	% Daily Value*
Amount per 181 g	Total Fat 69.3g	107%	Total Carbohydrates 8g	3%
1 serving (6.4 oz)	Saturated 23.8g	119%	Dietary Fiber 3g	13%
	Trans Fat 1.2g		Sugars 1g	
Calories 712	Cholesterol 92mg	31%	Protein 18g	37%
From fat 610	Sodium 460mg	19%		
	Calcium 45% • Iron 5%		Vitamin A 24% • Vitamin C 26%	

* Percent Daily Values are based on 2000 calorie diet. Your Daily Values may be higher or lower depending on your calorie needs.

Directions:

1.   Cut the zucchini into thin ribbons using a mandolin slicer.

2.   Place the zucchini ribbons in a bowl and sprinkle with some salt. Set aside.

3.   In a food processor, combine the olive oil, butter, Italian style hard cheese, lemon juice, walnuts, avocado, and garlic.

4.   Pulse the food processor until the pesto sauce is smooth and consistent.

5.   Heat some olive oil in a saucepan and sauté the zucchini ribbons just until they start to soften. Remove from heat.

6.   Mix the pesto sauce and zucchini ribbons. Toss until all the zucchini ribbons have been coated.

7.   Top with grated cheddar cheese before serving.

Did you know?

Avocados are one of the only fruits that contain heart-healthy monounsaturated fat (the good-for-you fat) that helps boost good (HDL) cholesterol and lowers bad (LDL) cholesterol

DAY 7

Meal	Recipe	Calories
Breakfast	Brie and Pecan Crepes	738
Lunch	Broccoli and Cheese Soup	509
Dinner	Crunchy Cauliflower and Pine Nut Salad	638

Brie and Pecan Crepes

INGREDIENTS	Fats	Proteins	Carbs
1/2 cup cream cheese	34.32 g	8.52 g	4.2 g
1 egg	4.18 g	5.53 g	0.32 g
1/8 tsp baking soda	0 g	0 g	0 g
1/4 cup pecans, halved	17.85 g	2.27 g	3.44 g
1/4 cup butter	2.92 g	0.03 g	0 g
1/2 tsp. cinnamon powder	0.02 g	0.05 g	1.05 g
1/4 cup brie, diced	9.96 g	7.47 g	0.16 g

Nutrition Facts

Amount per 230 g
1 serving (8.1 oz)

Calories 738
From fat 609

Amount	% Daily Value*	Amount	% Daily Value*
Total Fat 69.3g	107%	Total Carbohydrates 9g	3%
Saturated 32.7g	163%	Dietary Fiber 3g	12%
Trans Fat 0.1g		Sugars 6g	
Cholesterol 315mg	105%	Protein 24g	48%
Sodium 1000mg	42%		
Calcium 21% • Iron 17%		Vitamin A 36% • Vitamin C 1%	

* Percent Daily Values are based on 2000 calorie diet. Your Daily Values may be higher or lower depending on your calorie needs.

Directions:

1.   In a large bowl, combine the ingredients for the batter mix: cream cheese, egg, baking, soda, and salt. Whisk together until smooth.

2.   In a small non-stick pan, melt half of the butter over medium heat.

3.   Ladle the crepe batter into the pan and swirl the pan so that the better is spread thinly and evenly. Let one side cook until the top looks dry and flip gently. Cook the other side only for a few seconds.

4.   Repeat the previous steps until all the batter mix has been consumed.

5.   Melt the remaining butter in a small pan over medium heat and toast the chopped pecans until fragrant. Be careful not to burn them.

6.   Sprinkle the cinnamon powder over the toasted pecans and mix. Set aside to cool.

7.   Assemble the sliced brie cheese on the crepe and top with toasted pecans. Fold or roll up the crepes.

8.   Repeat until all the toppings or crepes have been used. Serve.

Did you know?

The name "pecan" is a Native American word that was used to describe nuts requiring a stone to crack.

Broccoli and Cheese Soup

INGREDIENTS	Fats	Proteins	Carbs
3/4 cup broccoli, chopped	0.15 g	0.95 g	0.86 g
1/2 cup vegetable broth	1.02 g	2.13 g	7.3 g
1/4 cup cheddar, diced	11.16 g	7.93 g	0.44 g
1/4 cup heavy whipping cream	11.1 g	0.62 g	0.84 g
1/8 cup butter	23.93 g	0.25 g	0.02 g
1/4 tsp. mustard powder	0.18 g	0.13 g	0.14 g
1/8 tsp. nutmeg	0.11 g	0.02 g	0.15 g
1/4 tsp. garlic powder	0.01 g	0.13 g	0.58 g
1/4 tsp. onion powder	0.01 g	0.06 g	0.47 g

Nutrition Facts	Amount	% Daily Value*	Amount	% Daily Value*
Amount per 242 g	**Total Fat** 47.7g	73%	**Total Carbohydrates** 11g	4%
1 serving (8.5 oz)	Saturated 28.8g	144%	Dietary Fiber 3g	10%
	Trans Fat 1.4g		Sugars 3g	
Calories 509	**Cholesterol** 138mg	46%	**Protein** 12g	24%
From fat 421	**Sodium** 708mg	30%		
	Calcium 30% • **Iron** 8%		**Vitamin A** 65% • **Vitamin C** 24%	

* Percent Daily Values are based on 2000 calorie diet. Your Daily Values may be higher or lower depending on your calorie needs.

Directions:

1.   Cook the chopped broccoli in a steam for 4 to 5 minutes.

2.   In a blender, combine the cooked broccoli with all other ingredients. Blend until smooth.

3.   Transfer the contents of the blender into a small pot. Simmer the soup over medium heat for about 10 minutes. Season with salt and pepper, if desired.

4.   Serve hot.

Did you know?

Broccoli is also very high in Vitamin A. Vitamin A helps fight cancer within your cells, as well as keep your eyes healthy and stave off glaucoma and other eye degenerative diseases. It also helps to promote healthy skin, break down urinary stones (a big issue with the summer heat and dehydration) and maintain healthy bones and teeth.

Crunchy Cauliflower and Pine Nut Salad

INGREDIENTS	Fats	Proteins	Carbs
1/4 cup cauliflower, chopped	0.08 g	0.51 g	1.33 g
2 tbsp. onion leeks, chopped	0.03 g	0.17 g	1.57 g
1/4 cup pine nuts, chopped	11.55 g	2.31 g	2.21 g
2 tbsp. sour cream	2.54 g	0.84 g	1.7 g
1/2 cup iceberg lettuce, shredded	0.05 g	0.32 g	1.07 g
1/4 cup mayonnaise	41.17 g	0.53 g	0.31 g
1/4 cup feta cheese, crumbled	7.98 g	5.33 g	1.53 g

Nutrition Facts

Amount per 207 g
1 serving (7.3 oz)

Calories 638
From fat 562

Amount	% Daily Value*	Amount	% Daily Value*
Total Fat 63.4g	98%	Total Carbohydrates 10g	3%
Saturated 14.5g	72%	Dietary Fiber 2g	7%
Trans Fat 0.1g		Sugars 4g	
Cholesterol 65mg	22%	Protein 10g	20%
Sodium 727mg	30%		
Calcium 25% • Iron 10%		Vitamin A 13% • Vitamin C 26%	

* Percent Daily Values are based on 2000 calorie diet. Your Daily Values may be higher or lower depending on your calorie needs.

Directions:

1.   In a small pan, toast the pine nut overs medium heat until fragrant.

2.   In a large bowl, combine all the ingredient including the toasted pine nuts.

3.   For best results, refrigerate the salad for at least 2 hours and serve cold.

Did you know?

Pine nuts are one of the calorie-rich edible nuts. 100 g of dry-kernels provide 673 calories. Additionally, they comprise of numerous health promoting phyto-chemicals, vitamins, antioxidants, and minerals.

DAY 8

Meal	Recipe	Calories
Breakfast	Keto Breakfast Muffin	480
Lunch	Thai Soup with Tofu	627
Dinner	Asparagus and Tofu Mash	601

Keto Breakfast Muffin

INGREDIENTS	Fats	Proteins	Carbs
1 egg	23.11 g	30.52 g	1.75 g
1/2 tsp. olive oil	2.3 g	0 g	0 g
1/4 cup spinach	0.03 g	0.21 g	0.27 g
1/4 cup white mushrooms, sliced	0.06 g	0.54 g	0.57 g
1 tbsp. green onion, sliced	0.03 g	0.06 g	0.34 g

1/4 cup Italian style hard cheese, grated	6.96 g	7.11 g	3.48 g

Directions:

1.   Preheat your oven to 350 F.

2.   In a small bowl, crack the egg and whisk. Season with salt, if desired.

3.   Apply olive oil to a muffin pan. In one portion of the pan, add the spinach, mushrooms, green onion, and cheese.

4.   Pour the eggs over the contents of the muffin tin.

5.   Bake for about 20 minutes, or until the top of the egg has set.

6.   Remove from the oven and let the cooked muffin rest for a few minutes. Remove the muffin from the tin using a rubber spatula or by inverting the muffin pan.

7.   Serve immediately.

Did you know?

Extra virgin olive oil comes from the first pressing of the olives with no chemicals used to extract the oil. This means it has a wonderful, fresh, clean taste

Thai Soup with Tofu

INGREDIENTS	Fats	Proteins	Carbs
1 tbsp. bell pepper, diced	0.01 g	0.07 g	0.27 g
1/4 tbsp. white mushrooms, sliced	0.06 g	0.54 g	0.57 g
1/4 tbsp. garlic, chopped	0.01 g	0.13 g	0.69 g
1/4 tbsp. ginger, sliced thinly	0.01 g	0.03 g	0.27 g
1/4 tbsp. chili powder	0.29 g	0.27 g	0.99 g
3/4 cup coconut milk	36.15 g	3.42 g	4.76 g
1/4 cup silky tofu, cubed	2.29 g	4.06 g	1.12 g
1/2 tbsp. soy sauce	0.02 g	0.64 g	0.4 g
1/2 tbsp. lime juice	0.01 g	0.03 g	0.64 g

1/4 tbsp. cilantro	0 g	0.01 g	0.02 g
2 tbsp. coconut oil	27.2 g	0 g	0 g

Nutrition Facts

Amount per 297 g
1 serving (10.5 oz)

Calories 627
From fat 560

	Amount	% Daily Value*	Amount	% Daily Value*
Total Fat 66.1g		102%	**Total Carbohydrates** 10g	3%
Saturated 56g		280%	Dietary Fiber 1g	5%
Trans Fat 0g			Sugars 1g	
Cholesterol 0mg		0%	**Protein** 9g	18%
Sodium 342mg		14%		
Calcium 12% • **Iron** 38%			**Vitamin A** 13% • **Vitamin C** 22%	

* Percent Daily Values are based on 2000 calorie diet. Your Daily Values may be higher or lower depending on your calorie needs.

Directions:

1.   In a medium-sized pot, combine the coconut milk, onion, bell pepper, mushrooms, garlic, ginger, and chili powder.

2.   Bring the coconut mixture to a boil and cook over medium heat for 5 to 7 minutes.

3.   Add the diced tofu to the pot. Mix and cook for another additional 5 minutes.

4.   Remove the pot from heat. Add the soy sauce and lime juice. Stir in the new ingredients.

5.   To serve, scoop the soup onto a bowl and top with fresh cilantro.

Did you know?

When picking out garlic at the grocery store, choose firm, tight, heavy, dry bulbs.

Asparagus and Tofu Mash

INGREDIENTS	Fats	Proteins	Carbs
1/2 cup asparagus, chopped	0.08 g	1.47 g	2.6 g
1 tbsp. spring onion, chopped	0.01 g	0.11 g	0.44 g
4 tbsp. coconut cream	20.81 g	2.18 g	3.99 g
1/2 tbsp. parsley	0.02 g	0.06 g	0.12 g
1 tsp. lemon juice	0.01 g	0.02 g	0.35 g
2 tbsp. coconut oil	27.2 g	0 g	0 g
1 cup silky tofu. cubed	9.15 g	16.24 g	4.46 g

Nutrition Facts

Amount per 415 g
1 serving (14.6 oz)

Calories 601
From fat 486

Amount	% Daily Value*	Amount	% Daily Value*
Total Fat 57.3g	88%	Total Carbohydrates 12g	4%
Saturated 43.3g	217%	Dietary Fiber 4g	14%
Trans Fat 0g		Sugars 3g	
Cholesterol 0mg	0%	Protein 20g	40%
Sodium 26mg	1%		
Calcium 31% • Iron 32%		Vitamin A 15% • Vitamin C 19%	

* Percent Daily Values are based on 2000 calorie diet. Your Daily Values may be higher or lower depending on your calorie needs.

Directions:

1.   Cook the tofu cubes in a steamer for 8 to 10 minutes.

2.   In a pot of boiling water, blanch the chopped asparagus for 2 minutes. Drain immediately.

3.   In a small pan over medium heat, sauté the spring onions in coconut oil.

4.   In a blender, mix together the tofu, asparagus, spring onions, coconut cream, lemon juice, and parsley. Season with salt and pepper, if desired.

5.   Blend the mixture until smooth

6.   Serve while hot.

Did you know?
Asparagus contains NO fat or cholesterol.

DAY 9

Meal	Recipe	Calories
Breakfast	Mediterranean Vegetable Frittata	762
Lunch	Keto Cheese Pizza	553
Dinner	Keto Pasta with Blue Cheese Sauce	749

Mediterranean Vegetable Frittata

INGREDIENTS	Fats	Proteins	Carbs
2 eggs	8.37 g	11.05 g	0.63 g

2 tbsp. butter	23.04 g	0.24 g	0.02 g
1/4 cup heavy cream	11.1 g	0.62 g	0.84 g
1/2 cup cheddar, diced	22.32 g	15.87 g	0.88 g
1 cup spinach	0.12 g	0.86 g	1.09 g
1 tbsp. olives, sliced	0.9 g	0.07 g	0.53 g
1/2 tbsp. garlic, chopped	0.02 g	0.27 g	1.42 g
1/4 cup bell pepper, chopped	3.41 g	0.22 g	1.22 g
1 tbsp. parsley	0.03 g	0.11 g	0.24 g

Nutrition Facts

Amount per 288 g
1 serving (10.1 oz)

Calories 762
From fat 616

Amount	% Daily Value*	Amount	% Daily Value*
Total Fat 69.3g	107%	Total Carbohydrates 7g	2%
Saturated 37.6g	188%	Dietary Fiber 2g	7%
Trans Fat 1.7g		Sugars 2g	
Cholesterol 497mg	166%	Protein 29g	59%
Sodium 837mg	35%		
Calcium 57% • Iron 18%		Vitamin A 111% • Vitamin C 110%	

* Percent Daily Values are based on 2000 calorie diet. Your Daily Values may be higher or lower depending on your calorie needs.

Directions:

1.   Preheat the oven to 350 F.

2.   Coat the bottom and side of a spring form pan with the softened butter.

3.   In a small frying pan, melt a small pat of butter under medium heat.

4.   To the frying pan, add the garlic, olives, and bell pepper. Saute for 2 to 3 minutes until the pepper has softened.

5.   Add the spinach and stir until wilted.

6.   In a large bowl, whisk together the eggs and heavy cream until thoroughly mixed and airy.

7.   Pour the whisked egg on the springform pan.

8.   Drop in the cooked vegetables, spreading them as evenly as possible.

9.   Add diced cheddar to the top.

10.   Bake in the oven for 25 to 30 minutes, or until the top has developed a golden brown color.

11.   Let cool and serve with a garnish of parsley.

Did you know?
Parsley was used in the ancient Rome as ingredient of salads, to eliminate effects of hangover and as ornament in the form of garlands for the head.

Keto Cheese Pizza

INGREDIENTS	Fats	Proteins	Carbs
3/4 cup cauliflower, chopped	0.22 g	1.54 g	3.99 g
1 egg	4.18 g	5.53 g	0.32 g
1 tbsp. coconut flour	5.53 g	0.42 g	1.72 g
1 tbsp. avocado oil	14 g	0 g	0 g
1 tbsp. tomato puree	0.03 g	0.26 g	1.4 g
1 cup mozzarella, shredded	25.03 g	24.83 g	2.45 g

Nutrition Facts

Amount per 274 g
1 serving (9.7 oz)

Calories 603
From fat 430

Amount	% Daily Value*	Amount	% Daily Value*
Total Fat 49g	75%	Total Carbohydrates 10g	3%
Saturated 22.7g	114%	Dietary Fiber 2g	8%
Trans Fat 0g		Sugars 4g	
Cholesterol 252mg	84%	Protein 33g	65%
Sodium 796mg	33%		
Calcium 61% • Iron 12%		Vitamin A 21% • Vitamin C 68%	

* Percent Daily Values are based on 2000 calorie diet. Your Daily Values may be higher or lower depending on your calorie needs.

Directions:

1.   Preheat oven to 405 F.

2.   In a food processor, pulse the chopped cauliflower until a rice-like texture is attained.

3.   Microwave the riced cauliflower on high for 5 minutes.

4.   Pour out the riced cauliflower on a clean kitchen towel and squeeze out as much water as you can. Repeat the process two more times, allowing the cauliflower to rest between cycles

5.   In a large bowl, add the cauliflower paste, egg, coconut flour, and avocado oil. Season with a pinch of salt.

6.   Shape the dough into a pizza crust on top of a baking tray lined with parchment paper. Do not spread the crust thinner than 1/4 inch.

7.   Bake the crust for 25 to 30 minutes until it is has developed a golden brown color with light brown edges.

8.   Take out the crust and allow to cool for 10 minutes.

9.   Spread out the tomato puree on top of the crust as evenly as possible.

10.   Top the pizza with shredded mozzarella.

11.   Return the pizza to the oven and bake for another 5 minutes.

Did you know?

Take out the pizza and slice into 4 parts. Serve while hot. Tomatoes are the fruit of the tomato plant. They originated in the South American Andes around the area of modern day Peru and was first used as a food by the Aztec's in Southern Mexico.

Keto Pasta with Blue Cheese Sauce

INGREDIENTS	Fats	Proteins	Carbs
1 egg	9.64 g	8.97 g	1.02 g
1/8 cup cream cheese	9.93 g	1.72 g	1.18 g
1 tbsp. coconut flour	5.53 g	0.42 g	1.72 g
3 tbsp. cream cheese	12.87 g	3.2 g	1.58 g
1/4 cup blue cheese	9.71 g	7.23 g	0.79 g
1 1/2 tbsp. butter	17.28 g	0.18 g	0.01 g
1 tsp. pine nuts	1.91 g	0.38 g	0.37 g
2 tbsp. Italian style hard cheese, grated	2.78 g	2.84 g	1.39 g

Nutrition Facts

Amount per 220 g
1 serving (7.8 oz)

Calories 749
From fat 614

	Amount	% Daily Value*	Amount	% Daily Value*
Total Fat 69.7g		107%	Total Carbohydrates 8g	3%
Saturated 40.1g		201%	Dietary Fiber 0g	0%
Trans Fat 0.8g			Sugars 3g	
Cholesterol 771mg		257%	Protein 25g	50%
Sodium 977mg		41%		
Calcium 38% • Iron 22%			Vitamin A 44% • Vitamin C	0%

* Percent Daily Values are based on 2000 calorie diet. Your Daily Values may be higher or lower depending on your calorie needs.

Directions:

1.   Preheat oven to 300 F.

2.   Whisk together the eggs, cream cheese, and coconut flour. Season with salt. Let the batter rest for 2 minutes.

3.   Line a baking tray with parchment paper. Spread the batter on the parchment paper. Place another piece of parchment paper on top of the batter

and flatten using a rolling pin. Continue rolling until the batter is about 1 to 2 mm inches in thickness.

4.   Place the baking tray in the oven (still covered with the parchment paper). Bake for 10 to 12 minutes.

5.   Remove the tray from the oven and let cool. Remove the parchment paper cover.

6.   Using a small knife, cut the pasta into thin strips.

7.   Prepare the sauce. In a small saucepan, melt the butter over low heat.

8.   Add in the cream cheese and blue cheese. Stir until smooth. Cook only until all the cheese has been melted.

9.   Mix the sauce with the pasta. Top with pine nuts and grated Italian style hard cheese. Serve immediately.

Did you know?
The coconut comes from the coconut palm tree which grows throughout the tropics and subtropics.

DAY 10

Meal	Recipe	Calories
Breakfast	Chai Yogurt Smoothie	518

| Lunch | Cheesy Cauliflower Bake | 771 |
| Dinner | Keto Salad Nicoise | 544 |

Chai Yogurt Smoothie

INGREDIENTS	Fats	Proteins	Carbs
1/2 tsp. vanilla extract	0 g	0 g	0.27 g
1 cup coconut milk	48.21 g	4.57 g	6.35 g
1 cup brewed chai tea	0 g	0 g	0.71 g

2 tbsp. plain yogurt	0.99 g	1.06 g	1.43 g
1 tbsp. protein powder	1.89 g	5.03 g	2.04 g

Nutrition Facts

Amount per 507 g
1 serving (17.9 oz)

Calories 518
From fat 429

Amount	% Daily Value*	Amount	% Daily Value*
Total Fat 51.1g	79%	Total Carbohydrates 11g	4%
Saturated 43.6g	218%	Dietary Fiber 1g	3%
Trans Fat 0g		Sugars 2g	
Cholesterol 6mg	2%	Protein 11g	21%
Sodium 87mg	4%		
Calcium 13% • Iron 47%		Vitamin A 6% • Vitamin C 10%	

* Percent Daily Values are based on 2000 calorie diet. Your Daily Values may be higher or lower depending on your calorie needs.

Directions:

1. Add all ingredients in a blender, along with 4 ice cubes.

2. Blend until smooth.

3. You may also serve with a pinch of cinnamon or nutmeg, if desired.

Did you know?

The flower that produces the vanilla bean lasts only one day. The beans are hand-picked and then cured, wrapped, and dried in a process that takes 4 to 6 months

Cheesy baked Cauliflower

INGREDIENTS	Fats	Proteins	Carbs
3/4 cup cauliflower, chopped	0.22 g	1.54 g	3.99 g
2 tbsp. butter	23.04 g	0.24 g	0.02 g
1/2 cup heavy cream	22.2 g	1.23 g	1.67 g
1/4 cup cream cheese	19.86 g	3.44 g	2.36 g
1/4 cup cheddar, diced	11.16 g	7.93 g	0.44 g
1 tbsp. green onions, sliced	0.03 g	0.06 g	0.34 g

Directions:

1.   Preheat oven to 350 F.

2.   Boil a pot of water. Blanch the chopped cauliflower for 2 minutes and drain immediately.

3.   In a separate pot, melt the butter over medium heat.

4.   To the butter, add the heavy cream, cream cheese, and half of the cheddar. Season with salt and pepper. Stir until everything has melted and has been well-combined.

5.   On a baking dish, combine the cauliflower and cheese sauce. Top with green onions and the remaining cheddar.

6.   Bake for about 30 minutes, or until the top has turned golden brown.

7.   Remove from oven and serve immediately.

Did you know?
Slicing onions make us cry and we really hate that. But why do we cry while cutting onions? That's because, when we cut onions, sulfur is released by the veggie. This sulfur reaches our eyes and combines with the moisture to produce sulfuric acid.

Keto Salad Nicoise

INGREDIENTS	Fats	Proteins	Carbs
1 large egg	4.76 g	6.28 g	0.36 g

1/2 cup celery, chopped	0.04 g	0.17 g	0.75 g
1/2 snow peas	0 g	0.05 g	0.13 g
2 tbsp. olive oil	27 g	0 g	0 g
1/4 tbsp. garlic, chopped	0.01 g	0.13 g	0.69 g
1 cup romaine lettuce, shredded	0.14 g	0.58 g	1.55 g
1/2 tbsp green onion, chopped	0.01 g	0.03 g	0.17 g
1/2 tbsp olives, chopped	0.45 g	0.04 g	0.26 g
1 tbsp. balsamic vinegar	0 g	0.08 g	2.72 g
1/2 cup feta cheese, crumbled	15.96 g	10.66 g	3.07 g

Nutrition Facts

Amount per 251 g
1 serving (8.9 oz)

Calories 544
From fat 427

Amount	% Daily Value*	Amount	% Daily Value*
Total Fat 48.4g	74%	Total Carbohydrates 10g	3%
Saturated 16.6g	83%	Dietary Fiber 2g	7%
Trans Fat 0g		Sugars 7g	
Cholesterol 253mg	84%	Protein 18g	36%
Sodium 819mg	34%		
Calcium 44% • Iron 13%		Vitamin A 99% • Vitamin C 8%	

* Percent Daily Values are based on 2000 calorie diet. Your Daily Values may be higher or lower depending on your calorie needs.

Directions:

1.   In a small pot, boil the egg until hard. Allow to cool, peel, and cut into wedges.

2.   In a small frying pan, sauté the snow peas, olives, and garlic in 1 tbsp. of olive oil. Cook until the snow peas change color to a bright green.

3.   In a large bowl, combine the romaine lettuce, cooked vegetables, green onion, and celery.

4.   Prepare the dressing. Whisk together the olive oil and balsamic vinegar. Season with salt and pepper, if desired.

5.   Add the dressing to the salad. Add the feta cheese.

6.   Toss until the dressing has been fully incorporated. Serve.

Did you know?

Celery is low-energy vegetable. Due to low level of calories, celery is suitable for diets. Celery contains certain amounts of vitamins C, K, B2 and dietary fibers

DAY 11

Meal	Recipe	Calories
Breakfast	Thai-Style Egg Drop Soup	532
Lunch	Spicy Tofu Tacos	614
Dinner	Greek Salad	594

Thai-Style Egg Drop Soup

INGREDIENTS	Fats	Proteins	Carbs
1 1/2 cup vegetable broth	0 g	0 g	4.51 g
1 tbsp. sesame oil	13.6 g	0 g	0 g

1/2 tbsp. fish sauce	0 g	0.46 g	0.33 g
1 tsp. lemon rind	0.01 g	0.03 g	0.32 g
1/2 tbsp. ginger, grated	0.02 g	0.05 g	0.53 g
1/2 tbsp. green onion	0.01 g	0.03 g	0.17 g
1 egg	4.18 g	5.53 g	0.32 g
1/2 cup coconut milk	24.1 g	2.28 g	3.18 g
1 tbsp. butter	11.52 g	0.12 g	0.01 g

Nutrition Facts

Amount per 553 g
1 serving (19.5 oz)

Calories 532
From fat 461

Amount	% Daily Value*	Amount	% Daily Value*
Total Fat 53.4g	82%	Total Carbohydrates 9g	3%
Saturated 32g	160%	Dietary Fiber 0g	1%
Trans Fat 0.5g		Sugars 4g	
Cholesterol 194mg	65%	Protein 8g	17%
Sodium 2196mg	92%		
Calcium 6% • Iron 26%		Vitamin A 28% • Vitamin C 7%	

* Percent Daily Values are based on 2000 calorie diet. Your Daily Values may be higher or lower depending on your calorie needs.

Directions:

1.   In a medium-sized pot, heat the vegetable broth with the lemon rind and ginger

2.   Bring the water to a simmer for 15 minutes. Strain the broth to remove the ginger and lemon rind.

3.   Return the broth to the pot. Stir in the coconut milk, sesame oil, and fish sauce. Bring the broth to a simmer.

4.   In a small bowl, whisk together the butter and the eggs.

5.   While stirring the broth, gradually pour in the whisked egg.

6. Serve while hot. Garnish with green onions.

Did you know?
Consuming ginger roots is the vital boost to the immunity, Aside from treating nausea and throaty coughs, ginger boosts the immune system to protect against viruses like the flu or the common cold.

Spicy Tofu Tacos

INGREDIENTS	Fats	Proteins	Carbs
1 egg	4.18 g	5.53 g	0.32 g
1/2 cup coconut flour	4.9 g	0.38 g	1.53 g
1 tbsp. avocado oil	14 g	0 g	0 g
1 cup romaine lettuce, shredded	0.11 g	0.43 g	1.16 g
1 tbsp. lime juice	0.01 g	0.06 g	1.27 g
1 tbsp. red onion, chopped	0.01 g	0.11 g	0.93 g
1/2 cup firm tofu	5.49 g	9.94 g	2.69 g
1/4tbsp. paprika	0.44 g	0.48 g	0.92 g
2 tbsp. olive oil	27 g	0 g	0 g
1/8 cup avocado, sliced	2.79 g	0.38 g	1.62 g

Nutrition Facts	Amount	% Daily Value*	Amount	% Daily Value*
	Total Fat 58.7g	90%	**Total Carbohydrates** 10g	3%
Amount per 236 g	Saturated 12.3g	62%	Dietary Fiber 4g	17%
1 serving (8.3 oz)	Trans Fat 0g		Sugars 2g	
	Cholesterol 164mg	55%	**Protein** 17g	34%
Calories 614	**Sodium** 80mg	3%		
From fat 513	**Calcium** 48% • **Iron** 20%		**Vitamin A** 86% • **Vitamin C** 15%	

* Percent Daily Values are based on 2000 calorie diet. Your Daily Values may be higher or lower depending on your calorie needs.

Directions:

1.   Preheat the oven to 350 F.

2.   In a small bowl, toss the tofu cubes in olive oil and paprika. Season with salt and pepper, if desired.

3.   Line a baking tray with parchment paper and spread the tofu cubes evenly. Bake in the oven for 25 to 30 minutes, or until the tofu is firm and crispy.

4.   Remove from the oven and set aside.

5.   Prepare the tortillas. Combine the egg, coconut flour, and avocado oil in a small bowl. Mix thoroughly.

6.   Preheat a small frying pan over medium heat. Coat the pan with some avocado oil.

7.   Pour one spoonful of the batter mixture into the pan. Move the pan around to spread the batter mixture to a diameter of 6 to 8 inches.

8.   Once the top of the tortilla has started to firm up, flip the tortilla and cook the other side for a few more seconds.

9.   Repeat until all the tortilla batter has been used up.

10.   In a large bowl, combine the romaine lettuce, avocado slices, and red onion. Add the cooked tofu.

11.   Add the lime juice to the taco filling. Toss to mix.

12.   Assemble the tacos by placing 3 tbsp. of filling to each tortilla. Fold up the tortilla.

13.   Repeat until all the filling or all the tortillas have been used up. Serve and enjoy!

Did you know?

Limes are high in vitamin C, although not as high as lemons, and they have small quantities of many other vitamins and minerals.

Greek Salad

INGREDIENTS	Fats	Proteins	Carbs
1/4 cup tomato, diced	0.09 g	0.4 g	1.75 g
1/4 cup cucumber, sliced	0.05 g	0.18 g	0.64 g
1/4 cup red onion, sliced	0.03 g	0.3 g	2.57 g
1/4 cup bell pepper, sliced	0.02 g	0.23 g	1.07 g
1/2 cup feta cheese, crumbled	15.96 g	10.66 g	3.07 g
1 tbsp. olives, chopped	0.9 g	0.07 g	0.53 g
3 tbsp. olive oil	40.5 g	0 g	0 g
1/2 tbsp. red wine vinegar	0 g	0 g	0.02 g

Nutrition Facts

Amount per 245 g
1 serving (8.6 oz)

Calories 594
From fat 507

	Amount	% Daily Value*	Amount	% Daily Value*
Total Fat	57.5g	89%	Total Carbohydrates 10g	3%
Saturated	17g	85%	Dietary Fiber 2g	7%
Trans Fat	0g		Sugars 6g	
Cholesterol	67mg	22%	Protein 12g	24%
Sodium	756mg	32%		
Calcium	40% • Iron	8%	Vitamin A 18% • Vitamin C	61%

* Percent Daily Values are based on 2000 calorie diet. Your Daily Values may be higher or lower depending on your calorie needs.

Directions:

1.   In a medium-sized bowl, combine the tomato, bell pepper, cucumber, onion, olives, and feta cheese.

2.   Drizzle in the olive oil and vinegar. Season with salt and pepper, if desired.
3.   Toss until thoroughly mixed, making sure that everything is coated with dressing. Serve and enjoy.

Did you know?

The olive is a fruit, not a vegetable. Can be green, purple, dark brown, black, and even pink color.

DAY 12

Meal	Recipe	Calories
Breakfast	No-Grain Granola	746
Lunch	Bell Pepper Nachos	571
Dinner	Tofu and Broccoli Stir Fry	549

No-Grain Granola

INGREDIENTS	Fats	Proteins	Carbs
1/4 cup desiccated coconut	12.43 g	0.95 g	3.87 g
1 tbsp. sunflower seeds	4.53 g	1.83 g	1.76 g
1 tbsp. pumpkin seeds	3.63 g	2.21 g	1.09 g
1/2 tbsp. flaxseed, ground	4.63 g	1.88 g	0.75 g
1 tbsp. walnuts, chopped	0.01 g	0.03 g	0.56 g

1/4 cup coconut oil	54.5 g	0 g	0 g
1/4 tsp cinnamon powder	0.76 g	0.33 g	0.52 g

Nutrition Facts

Amount per 99 g
1 serving (3.5 oz)

Calories 746
From fat 687

Amount	% Daily Value*	Amount	% Daily Value*
Total Fat 80.5g	124%	Total Carbohydrates 9g	3%
Saturated 59.5g	298%	Dietary Fiber 3g	10%
Trans Fat 0.1g		Sugars 0g	
Cholesterol 0mg	0%	Protein 7g	14%
Sodium 27mg	1%		
Calcium 3% • Iron 12%		Vitamin A 0% • Vitamin C 1%	

* Percent Daily Values are based on 2000 calorie diet. Your Daily Values may be higher or lower depending on your calorie needs.

Directions:

1.   Preheat the oven to 350 F.

2.   In a large baking tray, mix together the desiccated coconut, sunflower seeds, pumpkin seeds, flaxseed, and walnuts.

3.   In a small pan over low heat, melt the coconut oil and mix in the cinnamon powder.

4.   Pour the coconut oil over the granola mix and mix thoroughly. Make sure all the components of the granola mix are coated with the coconut oil

5.   Bake for 20 minutes.

6.   To avoid burning the granola, the mixture needs to be stirred or turned every 3 minutes.

7.   Allow the granola mix to cool to room temperature before serving.

Did you know?

Cinnamon is high in fiber and calcium which helps improve colon health.

Bell Pepper Nachos

INGREDIENTS	Fats	Proteins	Carbs
1 cup bell pepper, sliced	0.16 g	0.79 g	4.27 g
2 tbsp. olive oil	27 g	0 g	0 g
1/4 tsp cumin	0.11 g	0.09 g	0.22 g
1/4 tsp chili powder	0.1 g	0.09 g	0.35 g
1/4 tbsp. jalapeno, sliced	0.04 g	0.09 g	0.65 g
3 tbsp. sour cream	3.82 g	1.26 g	2.56 g
1/4 cup cheddar, shredded	11.16 g	7.93 g	0.44 g
1 tbsp. cilantro	0.01 g	0.02 g	0.04 g
1 tbsp. avocado oil	14 g	0 g	0 g

Directions:

1.   Preheat oven to 350 F.

2.   Place the sliced bell peppers on a baking tray.

3.   Toss the bell peppers with olive oil, avocado oi, cumin, and chili powder. Season with salt, if desired.

4.   Bake the peppers until tender for about 15 to 20 minutes.

5.   Place the cooked bell peppers in a small bowl. Top with shredded cheddar and sliced jalapeno.

6.   Drizzle sour cream over the top and garnish with cilantro. Serve.

Did you know?

Jalapeño peppers are a good source of vitamin C, folate and vitamin A. They are low fat, saturated fat free, cholesterol free, and sodium free.

Tofu and Broccoli StirFry

Nutrition Facts	Amount	% Daily Value*	Amount	% Daily Value*
	Total Fat 49.9g	77%	Total Carbohydrates 9g	3%
	Saturated 6.8g	34%	Dietary Fiber 5g	20%
Amount per 198 g	Trans Fat 0g		Sugars 1g	
1 serving (7 oz)	Cholesterol 0mg	0%	Protein 23g	46%
Calories 549	Sodium 283mg	12%		
From fat 433	Calcium 91% • Iron 25%		Vitamin A 23% • Vitamin C 7%	

* Percent Daily Values are based on 2000 calorie diet. Your Daily Values may be higher or lower depending on your calorie needs.

INGREDIENTS	Fats	Proteins	Carbs
1/2 cup firm tofu cubes	10.99 g	19.88 g	5.38 g
1/2 cup broccoli, chopped	0.1 g	0.63 g	0.57 g
1/2 tbsp. soy sauce	0.02 g	0.61 g	1.08 g
1 tsp sesame seeds	1.65 g	0.55 g	0.32 g
1 tbsp. sesame oil	13.6 g	0 g	0 g
1 1/2 tbsp. olive oil	20.3 g	0 g	0 g
1/2 tsp chili powder	0.2 g	0.19 g	0.7 g
1 tbsp. almond, slivered	3 g	1.27 g	1.29 g

Directions:

1.   Preheat oven to 425 F.

2.   Toss the tofu with 1/2 tbsp. olive oil, salt, and pepper and place on a small baking tray. Make sure the cubes do not touch each other.
3.   Bake the tofu in the oven for 25 to 30 minutes, or until the outsides are firm and crunchy.
4.   Combine the remaining olive oil and sesame oil in a large frying pan and place over high heat.

5.   Add the slivered almonds to the pan and cook for 1 to 2 minutes, or until fragrant.
6.   Add the cooked tofu and stir.
7.   Add the broccoli. Stir while cooking for 4 to 5 minutes, or just until the broccoli has developed a bright green color.
8.   Add in the soy sauce and chili powder. Cook for an additional 1 minutes.
9.   Transfer to a bowl and garnish with sesame seeds. Serve and enjoy.

Did you know?
Almonds help to slow absorption of sugar and carbs

DAY 13

Meal	Recipe	Calories
Breakfast	Cauliflower Toast	524
Lunch	Spicy Tofu and Eggplant	622
Dinner	Sweet and Sour Mushroom Stir Fry	551

Cauliflower Toast

Nutrition Facts	Amount	% Daily Value*	Amount	% Daily Value*
Amount per 212 g	**Total Fat** 44.8g	69%	**Total Carbohydrates** 9g	3%
1 serving (7.5 oz)	Saturated 16.8g	84%	Dietary Fiber 4g	14%
	Trans Fat 0.8g		Sugars 2g	
Calories 524	**Cholesterol** 231mg	77%	**Protein** 24g	47%
From fat 398	**Sodium** 553mg	23%		
	Calcium 49% • **Iron** 8%		**Vitamin A** 19% • **Vitamin C** 49%	

* Percent Daily Values are based on 2000 calorie diet. Your Daily Values may be higher or lower depending on your calorie needs.

INGREDIENTS	Fats	Proteins	Carbs
1 egg	4.18 g	5.53 g	0.32 g
1/2 cup cauliflower, chopped	0.15 g	1.03 g	2.66 g
1/2 cup cheddar, shredded	22.32 g	15.87 g	0.88 g
1 tsp garlic powder	0.02 g	0.61 g	2.25 g
4 tbsp. guacamole	4.58 g	0.63 g	2.71 g
1 tbsp. olive oil	13.5 g	0 g	0 g

Directions:

1.   Cook the chopped cauliflower in a steamer for 10 minutes, or until tender.

2.   Place the cooked cauliflower in food processor and pulse until a very fine texture is achieved.

3.   Wrap the ground cauliflower with a clean kitchen towel and squeeze toe remove excess moisture. Let the ground cauliflower rest for around 10 minutes and squeeze out the excess moisture again. Repeat this process one more time.

4.   In a medium-sized bowl, combine the ground cauliflower, egg, cheddar, and garlic powder. Season with salt and pepper.

5.   In a small frying pan, preheat the olive oil over medium heat.

6.   Place the cauliflower batter into the frying pan and form into the shape of a toast. You may divide the batter into two if there is too much.

7.   Cook on one side until firm and golden brown. Flip and resume cooking on the other side.

8.	Transfer the cooked toast on a plate and top with guacamole. Serve.

Did you know?

Cheese is kept for a period of time before it's ready to eat. Some varieties of cheese, blue cheese, Gorgonzola, and brie are exposed to mold, which helps them age properly.

Spicy Tofu and Eggplant

INGREDIENTS	Fats	Proteins	Carbs
1/2 cup firm tofu cubes	10.99 g	19.88 g	5.38 g
1/4 cup eggplant, diced	0.04 g	0.2 g	1.21 g
1 tbsp. green snap beans	0.04 g	0.11 g	0.41 g
1/2 tbsp. soy sauce	0.05 g	0.63 g	0.71 g
1/2 tsp garlic, chopped	0.01 g	0.09 g	0.46 g
2 tbsp. olive oil	27 g	0 g	0 g
1 1/2 tbsp. sesame oil	20.4 g	0 g	0 g
1 tbsp. red chili, chopped	0.04 g	0.15 g	0.7 g

1/4 tbsp. cider vinegar	0 g	0 g	0.03 g

Nutrition Facts	Amount	% Daily Value*	Amount	% Daily Value*
Amount per 226 g 1 serving (8 oz)	Total Fat 58.6g	90%	Total Carbohydrates 9g	3%
	Saturated 8.2g	41%	Dietary Fiber 4g	16%
	Trans Fat 0g		Sugars 1g	
	Cholesterol 0mg	0%	Protein 21g	42%
Calories 620 From fat 512	Sodium 634mg	26%		
	Calcium 87% • Iron 21%		Vitamin A 6% • Vitamin C 22%	

* Percent Daily Values are based on 2000 calorie diet. Your Daily Values may be higher or lower depending on your calorie needs.

Directions:

1.   Preheat oven to 425 F.

2.   Toss the tofu with 1/2 tbsp. olive oil, salt, and pepper and place on a small baking tray. Make sure the cubes do not touch each other.

3.   Bake the tofu in the oven for 25 to 30 minutes, or until the outsides are firm and crunchy.

4.   In a large frying pan, preheat the remaining olive oil and sesame oil over high heat.

5.   To the frying pan, add the eggplant and garlic. Cook for 5 to 6 minutes, until soft but not mushy.

6.   Add the cooked tofu and stir.

7.   Add the snap beans to the pan and stir.

8.   Add the soy sauce, cider vinegar, and red chili. Cook for another 2 to 3 minutes.

9.   Transfer to a bowl and serve.

Did you know?

Soy sauce is generally made from soybeans, wheat, salt and water, although tamari, a traditional Japanese soy sauce, usually does not include wheat, which makes it suitable for a gluten free diet.

Sweet and Sour Mushroom Stir Fry

INGREDIENTS	Fats	Proteins	Carbs
1/2 tbsp. tomato paste	0.04 g	0.35 g	1.51 g
1/2 cup vegetable broth	0 g	0 g	1.5 g
1/4 tbsp. Apple cider vinegar	0 g	0 g	0.03 g
1/4 tbsp. lime juice	0 g	0.02 g	0.32 g
1/2 tbsp. Stevia	0 g	0 g	2 g
1/4 tbsp. fish sauce	0 g	0.23 g	0.16 g
1/4 tbsp. ginger, sliced	0.01 g	0.03 g	0.27 g
1 cup oyster mushrooms, sliced	0.35 g	2.85 g	5.24 g
2 tbsp. olive oil	27 g	0 g	0 g

1 cup broccoli, sliced	0.2 g	1.27 g	1.14 g
2 tbsp. sesame oil	27.2 g	0 g	0 g
1 tsp sesame seeds	1.65 g	0.55 g	0.32 g
1/2 tbsp. green onion, chopped	0.01 g	0.03 g	0.17 g

Nutrition Facts

Amount per 327 g
1 serving (11.5 oz)

Calories 551
From fat 498

Amount	% Daily Value*	Amount	% Daily Value*
Total Fat 56.5g	87%	Total Carbohydrates 13g	4%
Saturated 7.9g	40%	Dietary Fiber 4g	15%
Trans Fat 0g		Sugars 3g	
Cholesterol 0mg	0%	Protein 5g	11%
Sodium 859mg	36%		
Calcium 6% • Iron 15%		Vitamin A 32% • Vitamin C 19%	

* Percent Daily Values are based on 2000 calorie diet. Your Daily Values may be higher or lower depending on your calorie needs.

Directions:

1. In a medium-sized saucepan, combine the vegetable broth, tomato paste, vinegar, lime juice, fish sauce, Stevia, and ginger. Stir well while heating the mixture to a boil. Boil for 3 minutes, or until thick enough for your liking. Remove from the heat and let cool. Set aside.

2. In a large frying pan, preheat the sesame oil and olive oil.

3. Add the oyster mushrooms to the frying pan and cook for 9 to 10 minutes, or until tender.

4. Add the broccoli and cook for another 4 to 5 minutes, or until the broccoli has turned bright green.

5. Add the sweet and sour sauce and stir thoroughly. Make sure all the pieces of mushroom and broccoli are coated with the sauce.

6. Add in the sesame seeds and green onion. Season with salt and pepper.

7. Turn off the heat and stir thoroughly.

8.   Transfer to a bowl and serve.

9.

Did you know?

Stevia leaves contain potassium, zinc, magnesium and vitamin B3. The Mayo Clinic says stevia and other artificial sweeteners may be attractive to people with diabetes because they make food taste sweet without increasing blood sugar level

DAY 14

Meal	Recipe	Calories
Breakfast	Cauliflower Flatbread with Cheese	592
Lunch	Broccoli and Spinach Curry	603
Dinner	Cheesy Cauliflower Soup	575

Cauliflower Flatbread with Cheese

INGREDIENTS	Fats	Proteins	Carbs
1/2 cup cauliflower, chopped	0.15 g	1.03 g	2.66 g

1 egg	4.18 g	5.53 g	0.32 g
1/4 tbsp. garlic, chopped	0.01 g	0.13 g	0.69 g
1/2 tsp dried oregano	0.04 g	0.08 g	0.62 g
3/4 cup mozzarella, shredded	18.77 g	18.62 g	1.84 g
1/4 cup Italian style hard cheese, grated	6.96 g	7.11 g	3.48 g
1/2 tbsp. parsley	0.02 g	0.06 g	0.12 g
1 1/2 tbsp. butter	17.28 g	0.18 g	0.01 g

Nutrition Facts

Amount per 233 g
1 serving (8.2 oz)

Calories 592
From fat 418

Amount	% Daily Value*	Amount	% Daily Value*
Total Fat 47.4g	73%	Total Carbohydrates 10g	3%
Saturated 27.3g	136%	Dietary Fiber 2g	6%
Trans Fat 0.9g		Sugars 2g	
Cholesterol 297mg	99%	Protein 33g	65%
Sodium 1060mg	44%		
Calcium 70% • Iron 11%		Vitamin A 35% • Vitamin C 48%	

* Percent Daily Values are based on 2000 calorie diet. Your Daily Values may be higher or lower depending on your calorie needs.

Directions:

1.   Preheat the oven to 425 C.

2.   Cook the chopped cauliflower in a steamer for 10 minutes, or until tender.

3.   Place the cooked cauliflower in food processor and pulse until a very fine texture is achieved.

4.   Wrap the ground cauliflower with a clean kitchen towel and squeeze toe remove excess moisture. Let the ground cauliflower rest for around 10 minutes and squeeze out the excess moisture again. Repeat this process one more time.

5.   In a large bowl, combine the ground cauliflower, butter, egg, dried oregano, garlic, mozzarella, and Italian style hard cheese. Season with salt and pepper, if desired. Stir all ingredients until thoroughly combined.

6.	Line a large baking tray with parchment paper and transfer the dough mixture. Pat the dough until it's flat, with a thickness of about quarter of an inch.

7.	Bake in the oven for about 25 minutes or until the top is golden brown.

8.	Remove from the oven and allow to cool before serving.

Did you know?

Oregano is high in antioxidant activity, due to a high content of phenolic acids and flavonoids.

Broccoli and Spinach Curry

INGREDIENTS	Fats	Proteins	Carbs
1/2 cup broccoli, chopped	0.1 g	0.63 g	0.57 g
1 cup spinach	0.12 g	0.86 g	1.09 g
2 tbsp. coconut oil	27.2 g	0 g	0 g
1 tbsp. red onion, chopped	0.01 g	0.11 g	0.93 g
1/4 tbsp. garlic, chopped	0.01 g	0.13 g	0.69 g
1/4 tbsp. ginger, grated	0.01 g	0.03 g	0.27 g
1/4 tbsp. fish sauce	0 g	0.23 g	0.16 g
1/4 tbsp. soy sauce	0.01 g	0.31 g	0.55 g
1/4 tbsp. curry powder	0.88 g	0.9 g	3.52 g
3/4 cup coconut milk	36.15 g	3.42 g	4.76 g

Nutrition Facts	Amount	% Daily Value*	Amount	% Daily Value*
	Total Fat 64.5g	99%	Total Carbohydrates 13g	4%
Amount per 275 g	Saturated 55.7g	279%	Dietary Fiber 5g	19%
1 serving (9.7 oz)	Trans Fat 0g		Sugars 1g	
	Cholesterol 0mg	0%	Protein 7g	13%
Calories 613	Sodium 520mg	22%		
From fat 547	Calcium 12% • Iron 45%		Vitamin A 67% • Vitamin C 26%	

*Percent Daily Values are based on 2000 calorie diet. Your Daily Values may be higher or lower depending on your calorie needs.

Directions:

1.   In a large frying pan, heat up 1 tbsp. of coconut oil over high heat.

2.   Add the broccoli and stir fry just until the broccoli has turned bright green in color, about 3 to 4 minutes. Set aside.

3.   To the same pan, heat the remaining coconut oil.

4.   Add the red onion, garlic, and ginger. Sauté for 2 to 3 minutes or until fragrant.

5.   Add the coconut milk, soy sauce, fish sauce, and curry powder. Stir while the curry mixture heats up.

6.   Allow the curry mixture to boil and lower the heat to a simmer. Simmer for 10 minutes to allow the flavors to develop,

7.   Add the cooked broccoli and stir. Cook for another minute.

8.   Add the spinach leaves. Season with salt and pepper. Stir and allow to cook for another minute.

9.   Turn off the heat and transfer the curry to a bowl. Serve immediately

Did you know?

Curry powder is made primarily of spices, most often turmeric, cumin and coriander, but the mixture also often contains chilli and fenugreek, and sometimes garlic and ginger.

Cheesy Cauliflower Soup

INGREDIENTS	Fats	Proteins	Carbs
2 tbsp. butter	23.04 g	0. 24 g	0.02 g
1/2 tbsp. white onion, chopped	0.01 g	0.06 g	0.47 g
1/2 tbsp. onion leek, chopped	0.01 g	0.04 g	0.4 g
1/2 cup cauliflower, chopped	0.15 g	1.03 g	2.66 g
1/2 cup vegetable broth	0 g	0 g	1.5 g
1/2 cup heavy cream	22.2 g	1.23 g	1.67 g
2tbsp. Italian style hard cheese, grated	2.78 g	2.84 g	1.39 g
1/4 cup feta, crumbled	7.98 g	5.33 g	1.53 g

Nutrition Facts

Nutrition Facts		
Amount per 315 g		
1 serving (11.1 oz)		
Calories 575		
From fat 494		

Amount	% Daily Value*	Amount	% Daily Value*
Total Fat 56.2g	86%	**Total Carbohydrates** 10g	3%
Saturated 35.6g	178%	Dietary Fiber 1g	5%
Trans Fat 1g		Sugars 6g	
Cholesterol 185mg	62%	**Protein** 11g	22%
Sodium 1216mg	51%		
Calcium 33% • **Iron** 3%		**Vitamin A** 43% • **Vitamin C** 45%	

* Percent Daily Values are based on 2000 calorie diet. Your Daily Values may be higher or lower depending on your calorie needs.

Directions:

1.   In a large pot, melt the butter over medium heat.

2.   Add the white onion and onion leek. Stir while cooking until onions are soft.

3.   Add the chopped cauliflower and vegetable broth. Allow to simmer for about 15 minutes, or until the cauliflower becomes very tender.

4.   Transfer the contents of the pot into a blender. Blend until very smooth.

5.   Return the cauliflower soup into the pot.

6.   Add heavy cream and grated Italian style hard cheese. Simmer for another 10 minutes.

7.   Ladle the soup into a bowl and top with crumbled feta before serving.

Did you know?

Imported feta cheese is usually made with goat's or sheep's milk, as is the original Greek feta cheese.

DAY 15

Meal	Recipe	Calories
Breakfast	High-Protein Yogurt Bowl	376
Lunch	Keto Stuffed Mushrooms	733
Dinner	Asian Zucchini Salad	846

High-Protein Yogurt Bowl

Nutrition Facts

Amount per 158 g
1 serving (5.6 oz)

Calories 376
From fat 274

Amount	% Daily Value*	Amount	% Daily Value*
Total Fat 32.6g	50%	Total Carbohydrates 13g	4%
Saturated 13.9g	70%	Dietary Fiber 4g	16%
Trans Fat 0g		Sugars 5g	
Cholesterol 9mg	3%	Protein 13g	27%
Sodium 93mg	4%		
Calcium 27% • Iron 23%		Vitamin A 7% • Vitamin C 8%	

* Percent Daily Values are based on 2000 calorie diet. Your Daily Values may be higher or lower depending on your calorie needs.

INGREDIENTS	Fats	Proteins	Carbs
1/2 cup plain yogurt	1.99 g	2.13 g	2.86 g
1/2 tbsp. sunflower seeds	2.26 g	0.91 g	0.88 g
1 tbsp. walnuts	5.22 g	1.22 g	1.1 g
1/2 tbsp. chia seeds	1.23 g	0.66 g	1.68 g
1 tbsp. almond butter	8.88 g	3.35 g	3.01 g
1 tbsp. protein powder	0.96 g	4 g	1.76 g
1/4 cup coconut milk	12.05 g	1.14 g	1.59 g

Directions:

1.   In a blender, combine the coconut milk, yogurt, and protein powder. Blend until completely combined.

2.   Transfer the contents of the blender into a bowl. Add the sunflower seeds, walnuts, and chia seeds. Mix thoroughly.

3.   Drizzle with almond oil. Serve and enjoy!

Did you know?

Not only is yogurt a delicious and healthy snack option, it contains high levels of lactic acid that promote healthy skin.

Keto Stuffed Mushrooms

INGREDIENTS	Fats	Proteins	Carbs
3 whole white mushrooms	0.18 g	1.67 g	1.76 g
1/2 cup cream cheese	34.32 g	8.52 g	4.2 g
1/4 cup heavy cream	22.02 g	1.22 g	1.66 g
1 1/2 tbsp. butter	17.28 g	0.18 g	0.01 g
1/4 tbsp. garlic, chopped	0.01 g	0.13 g	0.69 g
1/4 tsp cayenne pepper	0.09 g	0.06 g	0.28 g
1/2 tsp onion powder	0.01 g	0.12 g	0.95 g

Nutrition Facts

Amount per 259 g
1 serving (9.1 oz)

Calories 733
From fat 657

Amount	% Daily Value*	Amount	% Daily Value*
Total Fat 73.9g	114%	Total Carbohydrates 10g	3%
Saturated 46.3g	232%	Dietary Fiber 1g	4%
Trans Fat 0.7g		Sugars 7g	
Cholesterol 235mg	78%	Protein 12g	24%
Sodium 687mg	29%		
Calcium 14% • Iron 10%		Vitamin A 57% • Vitamin C 5%	

* Percent Daily Values are based on 2000 calorie diet. Your Daily Values may be higher or lower depending on your calorie needs.

Directions:

1.   Slice off the stems of the mushrooms and carve out the insides from the bottom using a paring knife.

2.   In a medium-sized frying pan, melt the butter over medium heat.

3.   Add the mushroom stems, garlic, cayenne pepper, and onion powder. Cook while stirring for 8 to 9 minutes, or until the mushroom stems are tender.

4.   Add the heavy cream and cream cheese to the pan. Allow the mixture to simmer and thicken to your liking.

5.   Remove the pan from the heat and allow to cool. The filling mixture should thicken even more.

6.   Preheat the oven to 375 F.

7.   Carefully spoon the filling into the cavity of each mushroom.

8.   In a small baking tray, arrange the mushrooms side by side. Bake for 25 to 30 minutes.

9.   Allow to cool before serving.

Did you know?

Cayenne peppers are actually hotter when they are more mature, in their red form.

Asian Zucchini Salad

INGREDIENTS	Fats	Proteins	Carbs
1 medium zucchini	0.04 g	0.3 g	0.34 g
1/2 cup cabbage, shredded	0.04 g	0.57 g	2.58 g

1 1/2 tbsp. sunflower seeds	6.74 g	2.72 g	2.62 g
1/2 tbsp. almonds	0.3 g	0.13 g	0.13 g
3 tbsp. avocado oil	42 g	0 g	0 g
1 1/2 tbsp. sesame oil	20.4 g	0 g	0 g
1 tbsp. white vinegar	0 g	0 g	0.14 g
1/2 cup feta cheese, crumbled	15.96 g	10.66 g	3.07 g

Nutrition Facts

Amount per 222 g
1 serving (7.8 oz)

Calories 846
From fat 752

Amount	% Daily Value*	Amount	% Daily Value*
Total Fat 85.5g	132%	Total Carbohydrates 9g	3%
Saturated 19.6g	98%	Dietary Fiber 2g	10%
Trans Fat 0g		Sugars 5g	
Cholesterol 67mg	22%	Protein 14g	29%
Sodium 698mg	29%		
Calcium 40% • Iron 8%		Vitamin A 8% • Vitamin C 34%	

* Percent Daily Values are based on 2000 calorie diet. Your Daily Values may be higher or lower depending on your calorie needs.

Directions:

1.   In a dry frying pan, toast the almonds until fragrant over low heat.

2.   Slice the zucchini into strands using a spiralizer.

3.   In a large bowl, combine the zucchini, cabbage, sunflower seeds, and almonds.

4.   Whisk together the sesame oil, avocado oil, and white vinegar. Pour the dressing on the salad.

5.   Sprinkle crumbled feta cheese on top of the salad.

6.   Toss the salad together until the dressing has been distributed throughout. Serve.

Did you know?

The term "vinegar" comes from the French word "vin aigre," meaning sour wine.

DAY 16

Meal	Recipe	Calories
Breakfast	Coconut and Walnut Porridge	626
Lunch	Keto Cream of Mushroom Soup	666
Dinner	Pecan Salad with Tahini and Lemon Dressing	555

Coconut and Walnut Porridge

INGREDIENTS	Fats	Proteins	Carbs
1/2 cup coconut milk	24.1 g	2.28 g	3.18 g
1 tbsp. almond butter	8.88 g	3.35 g	3.01 g
3 tbsp. walnuts, crushed	13.88 g	5.63 g	2.24 g
1 1/2 tbsp. desiccated coconut	4.14 g	0.32 g	1.29 g
1/4 tsp cinnamon	0.01 g	0.03 g	0.56 g
1 tbsp. coconut oil	13.6 g	0 g	0 g

Nutrition Facts

Amount per 173 g
1 serving (6.1 oz)

Calories 626
From fat 544

Amount	% Daily Value*	Amount	% Daily Value*
Total Fat 64.6g	99%	Total Carbohydrates 10g	3%
Saturated 38.3g	191%	Dietary Fiber 4g	14%
Trans Fat 0g		Sugars 1g	
Cholesterol 0mg	0%	Protein 12g	23%
Sodium 19mg	1%		
Calcium 10% • Iron 29%		Vitamin A 0% • Vitamin C 3%	

* Percent Daily Values are based on 2000 calorie diet. Your Daily Values may be higher or lower depending on your calorie needs.

112

Directions:

1.   In a saucepan, combine the coconut milk, almond butter, and coconut oil.

2.   Heat the mixture over a stove until boiling.

3.   Add chopped walnuts and desiccated coconut to the saucepan.

4.   Mix thoroughly and remove from heat.

5.   Let the mixture cool down for 5 minutes before transferring to a bowl. Serve.

Did you know?

Coconut oil contain median chain triglycerides which are easy to digest. The oil is source of energy and has an accelerating effect on the metabolism.

Keto Cream of Mushroom Soup

INGREDIENTS	Fats	Proteins	Carbs
1/2 cup cauliflower	0.15 g	1.03 g	2.66 g
1 tbsp. olive oil	13.5 g	0 g	0 g
1 cup white mushroom, sliced	0.24 g	2.16 g	2.28 g
2 tbsp. butter	23.04 g	0.24 g	0.02 g
1/4 tbsp. white onion, chopped	0 g	0.03 g	0.23 g
3/4 cup heavy cream	33.3 g	1.85 g	2.51 g
1/4 cup vegetable broth	0 g	0 g	0.75 g

Nutrition Facts

Amount per 317 g
1 serving (11.2 oz)

Calories 666
From fat 618

Amount	% Daily Value*	Amount	% Daily Value*
Total Fat 70.2g	108%	Total Carbohydrates 8g	3%
Saturated 37.3g	186%	Dietary Fiber 2g	7%
Trans Fat 0.9g		Sugars 6g	
Cholesterol 184mg	61%	Protein 5g	11%
Sodium 472mg	20%		
Calcium 8% • Iron 4%		Vitamin A 43% • Vitamin C 47%	

* Percent Daily Values are based on 2000 calorie diet. Your Daily Values may be higher or lower depending on your calorie needs.

Directions:

1.   In a large pot, combine the cauliflower, vegetable broth, and heavy cream.

2.   Bring to a boil and lower the heat to a simmer. Allow to cook for 7 to 8 minutes, or until the cauliflower is tender.

3.   Transfer the contents of the pot into a blender. Blend the mixture until smooth.

4.   In a large saucepan, melt the butter over high heat. Add the olive oil.

5.   Add the white onions. Stir while cooking until the onions are translucent.

6.   Add the white mushroom and cook while stirring until the mushrooms have turned a light brown, or about 9 to 10 minutes.

7. Add the cauliflower puree to the mushrooms. Stir thoroughly.

8. Allow to cook for an additional 10 minutes.

9. Ladle the soup into a bowl and serve while hot.

Did you know?

There are more amino acids in mushrooms than in corn, peanuts, or soybeans.

Pecan Salad with Tahini and Lemon Dressing

INGREDIENTS	Fats	Proteins	Carbs
1/4 tbsp. tahini	2.04 g	0.65 g	0.81 g
1/4 tbsp. lemon juice	0.01 g	0.01 g	0.26 g
1/2 tbsp. Dijon mustard	0.26 g	0.29 g	0.45 g
1/4 tbsp. garlic, chopped	0 g	0.04 g	0.23 g
1 1/2 tbsp. olive oil	20.3 g	0 g	0 g
1/4 tbsp. rosemary leaves	0.02 g	0.01 g	0.08 g
1 cup romaine lettuce, shredded	0.14 g	0.58 g	1.55 g
2 tbsp. pecans, crushed	11.52 g	1.47 g	2.22 g
1/4 cup celery, sliced	0.04 g	0.17 g	0.75 g
1 tbsp. olives, sliced	0.9 g	0.07 g	0.53 g
1/4 cup gouda, crumbled	16.46 g	14.96 g	1.33 g

Nutrition Facts	Amount	% Daily Value*	Amount	% Daily Value*
Amount per 194 g 1 serving (6.8 oz)	**Total Fat** 51.7g	80%	**Total Carbohydrates** 8g	3%
	Saturated 14.8g	74%	Dietary Fiber 4g	16%
	Trans Fat 0g		Sugars 3g	
Calories 555	**Cholesterol** 68mg	23%	**Protein** 18g	37%
From fat 449	**Sodium** 668mg	28%		
	Calcium 49% • **Iron** 11%		**Vitamin A** 92% • **Vitamin C** 8%	

* Percent Daily Values are based on 2000 calorie diet. Your Daily Values may be higher or lower depending on your calorie needs.

Directions:

1.   Prepare the dressing. In a blender, combine the tahini, lemon juice, Dijon mustard, garlic, olive oil, and rosemary leaves

2.   Blend until smooth. Set aside.

3.   In large bowl, combine the lettuce, celery, pecans, olives, and gouda.

4.   Drizzle the salad with the dressing.

5.   Toss the salad until the dressing is well-distributed.

6.   Serve and enjoy.

Did you know?

It has 20% complete protein, making it a higher protein source than most nuts.

DAY 17

Meal	Recipe	Calories
Breakfast	High Protein Chocolate Smoothie	543
Lunch	Corned Tofu with Cabbage	595
Dinner	Keto Shepherd's Pie	688

High Protein Chocolate Smoothie

INGREDIENTS	Fats	Proteins	Carbs
1/2 cup coconut milk	24.1 g	2.28 g	3.18 g
2 tbsp. avocado, cubed	2.35 g	0.32 g	1.36 g
1/2 tbsp. cacao powder, unsweetened	1.71 g	0.31 g	1.84 g
1/4 tsp cinnamon powder	0.01 g	0.03 g	0.56 g
1/4 tsp vanilla extract	0 g	0 g	0.14 g
1 1/2 tbsp. coconut oil	20.4 g	0 g	0 g
2 tbsp. milk-based protein powder	3.77 g	10.06 g	4.07 g

Directions:

1.   Combine all ingredients in a blender. Add 3 ice cubes.

2.   Blend until smooth.
3.   Serve!

Did you know?

It takes 5 years for a cocoa tree to produce its first seed pods.

Corned Tofu with Cabbage

INGREDIENTS	Fats	Proteins	Carbs
1/4 cup firm tofu, diced	5.49 g	9.94 g	2.69 g
1/4 cup vegetable broth	0 g	0 g	0.75 g
1/2 tbsp. soy sauce	0.05 g	0.65 g	0.39 g
1/4 tbsp. yellow mustard	0.13 g	0.15 g	0.23 g
1/4 tbsp. coriander	0 g	0 g	0 g
1/4 tbsp. ginger, grated	0 g	0.01 g	0.09 g
2 tbsp. olive oil	27 g	0 g	0 g
1/2 cup cabbage, chopped	0.07 g	0.64 g	3.28 g
1/4 tbsp. green onion, chopped	0.01 g	0.01 g	0.09 g
2 tbsp. sesame oil	27.2 g	0 g	0 g

Directions:

1.   In a small bowl, mix together the vegetable broth, sesame oil, soy sauce, yellow mustard, coriander, and ginger.

2.   Transfer the contents of the bowl into a resealable plastic bag. Add the tofu cubes into the bag.

3.   Place the bag in the refrigerator and allow to marinate for at least 2 hours.

4.   After marinating, remove the tofu cubes from the marinade. Set aside the marinade solution.

5.   Preheat the oven to 425 F.

6.   Line a baking tray with parchment paper and spread the tofu cubes evenly. Bake in the oven for 25 to 30 minutes, or until the tofu is firm and crispy.

7.   Remove from the oven and set aside.

8.   In a large saucepan, heat the olive oil over high heat.

9.   Add the cabbage to the saucepan. Add 2 tbsp. of the marinade solution to the cabbage. Stir while cooking until the cabbage turn bright green but is still crispy.

10.   Toss in the green onions. Stir and remove from heat.

11.   Serve the tofu with the cabbage on the side.

Did you know?

Mustard is made from the ground seeds of a mustard plant, water, vinegar, and optionally some flavorings and spices

Keto Shepherd's Pie

INGREDIENTS	Fats	Proteins	Carbs
1/4 cup cauliflower, chopped	0.08 g	0.51 g	1.33 g
2 1/2 tbsp. olive oil	33.8 g	0 g	0 g
1/4 tbsp. green onion, chopped	0.01 g	0.01 g	0.09 g
1/4 tbsp. celery, chopped	0 g	0.01 g	0.06 g
1/4 tbsp. garlic	0.01 g	0.13 g	0.69 g
1/4 cup oyster mushrooms, chopped	0.09 g	0.71 g	1.31 g
1/2 tbsp. tomato paste	0.04 g	0.35 g	1.51 g
1/2 cup vegetable broth	0 g	0 g	1.5 g
1/4 tbsp. mustard	0.13 g	0.15 g	0.23 g
1/2 tsp thyme	0.01 g	0.02 g	0.1 g
1/4 cup white mushrooms, chopped	0.06 g	0.54 g	0.57 g
1 egg	4.18 g	5.53 g	0.32 g
2 tbsp. butter	23.04 g	0.24 g	0.02 g
1/4 tsp nutmeg	0.22 g	0.04 g	0.3 g
1/4 cup Italian style hard cheese, shredded	5.47 g	7.57 g	0.68 g

Nutrition Facts	Amount	% Daily Value*	Amount	% Daily Value*
Amount per 328 g 1 serving (11.6 oz)	Total Fat 67.1g	103%	Total Carbohydrates 9g	3%
	Saturated 24.3g	122%	Dietary Fiber 2g	8%
	Trans Fat 1g		Sugars 4g	
Calories 688 From fat 592	Cholesterol 239mg	80%	Protein 16g	32%
	Sodium 1118mg	47%		
	Calcium 30% • Iron 11%		Vitamin A 32% • Vitamin C 28%	

* Percent Daily Values are based on 2000 calorie diet. Your Daily Values may be higher or lower depending on your calorie needs.

Directions:

1. Preheat the oven to 400 F.

2. Cook the chopped cauliflower in a steamer for 10 minutes, or until tender.

3. Place the cooked cauliflower in food processor and pulse until a very fine texture is achieved.

4. Wrap the ground cauliflower with a clean kitchen towel and squeeze toe remove excess moisture. Let the ground cauliflower rest for around 10 minutes and squeeze out the excess moisture again. Repeat this process one more time.

5. In a food processor, combine the ground cauliflower, 2 tbsp. olive oil, mustard, thyme, Italian style hard cheese, and nutmeg. Season with salt and pepper, if desired. Blend until smooth. Set aside.

6. In a large saucepan, melt the butter over high heat. Add the remaining olive oil.

7. Add the oyster mushrooms and the white mushrooms to the saucepan. Cook while stirring for 12 to 13 minutes.

8. Add the garlic and celery. Cook for an additional 4 to 5 minutes.

9.   Add the vegetable broth and celery. Allow to boil and simmer for 15 minutes, or until the volume of the stock has reduced by half.

10.   Add the green onions and stir. Remove the saucepan from the heat.

11.   Assemble the shepherd's pie. Spoon the mushroom stew into a ramekin and top with the cauliflower mash.

12.   Bake the shepherd's pie in the oven for 20 minutes, or until the top has turned a light brown.

13.   Allow to cool for a few minutes before serving.

Did you know?

Thyme was used for soothing of the wounds and for the prevention of infections in the past. It was also used in a treatment of cough, congestion, stomach pain and gout.

DAY 18

Meal	Recipe	Calories
Breakfast	Cauliflower and Italian style hard cheese Hash Browns	573
Lunch	Coconut Curry Soup	556
Dinner	Cauliflower and Green Tea Soup	750

Cauliflower and Italian style hard cheese Hash Browns

INGREDIENTS	Fats	Proteins	Carbs
1/2 cup cauliflower, chopped	0.15 g	1.03 g	2.66 g
2 tbsp. coconut oil	27.2 g	0 g	0 g
1/2 tbsp. chickpea flour	0.19 g	0.65 g	1.68 g
1/2 tbsp. cornstarch	0 g	0.01 g	3.65 g
1 egg	4.18 g	5.53 g	0.32 g
1 1/2 tbsp. butter	17.28 g	0.18 g	0.01 g
4 tbsp. Italian style hard cheese, shredded	5.47 g	7.57 g	0.68 g

Nutrition Facts

Amount per 173 g
1 serving (6.1 oz)

Calories 573
From fat 475

	Amount	% Daily Value*	Amount	% Daily Value*
	Total Fat 54.5g	84%	Total Carbohydrates 9g	3%
	Saturated 39.4g	197%	Dietary Fiber 1g	6%
	Trans Fat 0.8g		Sugars 2g	
	Cholesterol 224mg	75%	Protein 15g	30%
	Sodium 422mg	18%		
	Calcium 29% • Iron 7%		Vitamin A 19% • Vitamin C 43%	

* Percent Daily Values are based on 2000 calorie diet. Your Daily Values may be higher or lower depending on your calorie needs.

Directions:

1. Preheat the oven to 400 F.

2. Cook the chopped cauliflower in a steamer for 10 minutes, or until tender.

3. Place the cooked cauliflower in food processor and pulse until a very fine texture is achieved.

4. Wrap the ground cauliflower with a clean kitchen towel and squeeze toe remove excess moisture. Let the ground cauliflower rest for around 10 minutes and squeeze out the excess moisture again. Repeat this process one more time.

5.   In a large bowl, combine the ground cauliflower, chickpea flour, cornstarch, egg, Italian style hard cheese, coconut oil. Mix thoroughly until well-combined.

6.   Line a baking tray with parchment paper. Scoop a portion of the cauliflower mash into the baking tray and shape into roughly an oval shape. Repeat this until all the cauliflower mash has been consumed.

7.   Bake the patties for 40 minutes or until golden brown and firm. Flip all the patties and bake for another 4 to 5 minutes on the other side.

8.   Place a pat of butter on top of each patty and return to the oven for another 4 to 5 minutes.

9.   Allow to cool for a few minutes before serving.

Did you know?
Chickpea is rich source of dietary fibers and proteins. It contains vitamins B6 and B9 and minerals such as iron and magnesium.

Coconut Curry Soup

INGREDIENTS	Fats	Proteins	Carbs
2 tbsp. coconut oil	27.2 g	0 g	0 g
1/4 tbsp. red onion, chopped	0 g	0.03 g	0.23 g
1/4 tbsp. garlic, chopped	0.01 g	0.13 g	0.69 g
1/4 tbsp. ginger, sliced	0.01 g	0.03 g	0.27 g
1/2 tbsp. curry powder	0.45 g	0.46 g	1.79 g
1/2 cup vegetable broth	0 g	0 g	1.5 g
1/4 cup coconut milk	12.05 g	1.14 g	1.59 g
1/2 tbsp. bell pepper, sliced	0.01 g	0.08 g	0.38 g
1/4 cup white mushrooms, whole	0.08 g	0.74 g	0.78 g
1/2 tbsp. fish sauce	0 g	0.46 g	0.33 g
1/4 tbsp. cilantro	0 g	0.01 g	0.01 g
1/2 medium-sized zucchini	0.02 g	0.15 g	0.17 g
1/2 soft tofu, cubes	4.58 g	8.12 g	2.23 g
1/ tbsp. butter	11.52 g	0.12 g	0.01 g

Nutrition Facts

Amount per 392 g
1 serving (13.8 oz)

Calories 556
From fat 480

Amount	% Daily Value*	Amount	% Daily Value*
Total Fat 55.9g	86%	Total Carbohydrates 10g	3%
Saturated 42.2g	211%	Dietary Fiber 2g	10%
Trans Fat 0.5g		Sugars 3g	
Cholesterol 31mg	10%	Protein 11g	23%
Sodium 1200mg	50%		
Calcium 18% • Iron 23%		Vitamin A 14% • Vitamin C 23%	

* Percent Daily Values are based on 2000 calorie diet. Your Daily Values may be higher or lower depending on your calorie needs.

Directions:

1.   In a large saucepan, melt the coconut oil over high heat. Add the red onion, ginger, garlic, and curry paste. Cook for 3 to 4 minutes until fragrant.

2.   Add the white mushrooms. Stir while cooking for 9 to 10 minutes, or until the mushrooms have developed a light brown color.

3.   Add the vegetable broth and coconut milk. Allow to boil and simmer for 20 minutes.

4.   Add the bell peppers and tofu. Stir and continue simmering for an additional 5 minutes.

5.   Meanwhile, slice the zucchini into thin strip using a spiralizer. Place the zucchini strips in a medium-sized bowl.

6.   Add butter to the curry and stir in to melt. Cook for an additional 2 to 3 minutes.

7.   Ladle the curry over the zucchini. Garnish with some cilantro. Serve while hot.

Did you know?
Cilantro is rich in several vitamins like A, C and K. Vitamin A is an antioxidant and is important for healthy eyes, teeth and skin as well as cell growth and a strong immune system. Vitamin C, a powerful antioxidant, helps boost your immune system, keeps your skin healthy, and is essential for tissue repair and wound healing. Vitamin K is essential for normal blood clotting and is important for bone health

Cauliflower and Green Tea Soup

INGREDIENTS	Fats	Proteins	Carbs
1/4 cup cauliflower, chopped	0.08 g	0.51 g	1.33 g
1 tbsp. leeks, chopped	0.02 g	0.08 g	0.79 g
1/4 tbsp. garlic, chopped	0.01 g	0.13 g	0.69 g
1 tbsp. celery, chopped	0.01 g	0.05 g	0.22 g
1 cup brewed green tea	0 g	0 g	0.47 g
1/4 cup heavy cream	11.1 g	0.62 g	0.84 g
1/2 tbsp. thyme	0.02 g	0.07 g	0.29 g
1/2 tbsp. lemon juice	0.02 g	0.03 g	0.52 g
2 1/2 tbsp. coconut oil	34 g	0 g	0 g
1 tbsp. butter	23.04 g	0.24 g	0.02 g
2 tbsp. almonds, slivered	7.99 g	3.38 g	3.45 g
1/4 cup soft tofu, cubes	2.29 g	4.06 g	1.12 g

Nutrition Facts

Amount per 458 g
1 serving (16.2 oz)

Calories 750
From fat 680

Amount	% Daily Value*	Amount	% Daily Value*
Total Fat 78.6g	121%	Total Carbohydrates 10g	3%
Saturated 51.9g	260%	Dietary Fiber 3g	12%
Trans Fat 1g		Sugars 3g	
Cholesterol 102mg	34%	Protein 9g	18%
Sodium 38mg	2%		
Calcium 16% • Iron 11%		Vitamin A 27% • Vitamin C 33%	

* Percent Daily Values are based on 2000 calorie diet. Your Daily Values may be higher or lower depending on your calorie needs.

Directions:

1.	In a large saucepan, melt the coconut oil and butter over high heat.

2.	Add the leeks and garlic and sauté for 5 minutes.

3.	Add the celery, tofu, cauliflower, and lemon juice. Sauté for another 5 minutes.

4.	Add in the green tea and the cream. Sprinkle with thyme and stir.

5.	Bring to a boil and simmer the soup for 20 minutes.

6.   Transfer the contents of the pot to a blender. Puree until smooth.

7.   Ladle to a bowl and top with slivered almonds. Serve while warm.

Did you know?
Lemons are a hybrid between a sour orange and a citron.

DAY 19

Meal	Recipe	Calories
Breakfast	Baked Eggs in Avocado	572
Lunch	Pesto Roasted Cabbage and Mushrooms	576
Dinner	Broccoli in Creamy Blue Cheese Sauce	642

Baked Eggs in Avocado

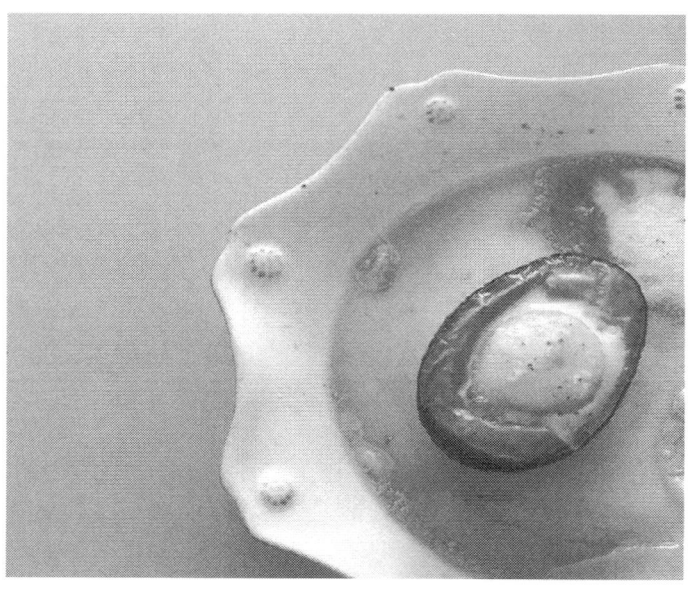

INGREDIENTS	Fats	Proteins	Carbs
1/2 avocado	14.73 g	2.01 g	8.57 g
1 egg	4.18 g	5.53 g	0.32 g
1/2 cup cheddar, shredded	19.11 g	13.58 g	0.75 g
1 tbsp. olive oil	13.5 g	0 g	0 g

Nutrition Facts

Amount per 215 g
1 serving (7.6 oz)

Calories 572
From fat 452

Amount	% Daily Value*	Amount	% Daily Value*
Total Fat 51.5g	79%	Total Carbohydrates 10g	3%
Saturated 16.3g	82%	Dietary Fiber 7g	27%
Trans Fat 0.7g		Sugars 1g	
Cholesterol 221mg	74%	Protein 21g	42%
Sodium 434mg	18%		
Calcium 42% • Iron 8%		Vitamin A 19% • Vitamin C 17%	

* Percent Daily Values are based on 2000 calorie diet. Your Daily Values may be higher or lower depending on your calorie needs.

Directions:

1.   Preheat the oven to 425 C.

2.   Remove the pit from the half avocado.

3.   Carve out just enough of the insides of the avocado to form a crevice for the egg.

4.   Drizzle the open face of the avocado with olive oil and spread it around as much as possible.

5.   Crack open the egg into the avocado.

6.   Sprinkle shredded cheddar on top.

7.   Bake in the oven for 15 to 16 minutes, depending on your desired consistency of the egg.

8.   Serve immediately.

DID YOU KNOW? Avocado trees do not self-pollinate; they need another avocado tree close by in order to grow

Pesto Roasted Cabbage and Mushrooms

INGREDIENTS	Fats	Proteins	Carbs
3/4 cup cabbage, shredded	0.11 g	0.96 g	4.92 g
2 tbsp. pesto sauce	17.6 g	3.13 g	1.28 g
2 tbsp. Italian style hard cheese, grated	2.78 g	2.84 g	1.39 g
1/4 cup feta, crumbled	7.98 g	5.33 g	1.53 g
1 tbsp. basil, chopped	0.02 g	0.09 g	0.07 g
2 tbsp. olive oil	27 g	0 g	0 g
1/4 cup white mushrooms, chopped	0.06 g	0.54 g	0.57 g

Nutrition Facts

Amount per 192 g
1 serving (6.8 oz)

Calories 576
From fat 488

Amount	% Daily Value*	Amount	% Daily Value*
Total Fat 55.6g	85%	Total Carbohydrates 10g	3%
Saturated 13.9g	69%	Dietary Fiber 2g	8%
Trans Fat 0.1g		Sugars 5g	
Cholesterol 47mg	16%	Protein 13g	26%
Sodium 832mg	35%		
Calcium 38% • Iron 10%		Vitamin A 30% • Vitamin C 67%	

* Percent Daily Values are based on 2000 calorie diet. Your Daily Values may be higher or lower depending on your calorie needs.

Directions:

1.   Preheat the oven to 375 F.

2.   Place the cabbage and chopped mushrooms on a baking tray. Drizzle with olive oil and toss together, ensuring that every piece is coated with oil.

3.	Slather the top with pesto sauce, distributing the sauce as evenly as possible.

4.	Sprinkle grated Italian style hard cheese over the top.

5.	Bake in the oven for 20 minutes.

6.	Remove from the oven and sprinkle feta and basil over the top. Serve hot.

Did you know?
Fresh basil's flavor has a clove accent while dried basil has a curry-like flavor

Broccoli in Creamy Blue Cheese Sauce

INGREDIENTS	Fats	Proteins	Carbs
1/4 cup avocado, diced	5.5 g	0.75 g	3.2 g
1/2 tbsp. avocado oil	7 g	0 g	0 g
1 tsp lemon juice	0.01 g	0.02 g	0.35 g
1/4 tsp garlic powder	0.01 g	0.13 g	0.58 g
1/4 tsp tarragon	0.01 g	0.05 g	0.1 g
1 tbsp. heavy cream	5.55 g	0.31 g	0.42 g
1/2 cup broccoli	0.1 g	0.63 g	0.57 g
1 tbsp. olive oil	13.5 g	0 g	0 g
1 tbsp. butter	11.52 g	0.12 g	0.01 g
1/2 cup blue cheese, crumbled	19.4 g	14.45 g	1.58 g

Nutrition Facts	Amount	% Daily Value*	Amount	% Daily Value*
Amount per 181 g 1 serving (6.4 oz)	**Total Fat** 62.6g	96%	**Total Carbohydrates** 7g	2%
	Saturated 26.8g	134%	Dietary Fiber 3g	13%
	Trans Fat 0.5g		Sugars 1g	
Calories 642	**Cholesterol** 102mg	34%	**Protein** 16g	33%
From fat 549	**Sodium** 791mg	33%		
	Calcium 40% • **Iron** 6%		**Vitamin A** 33% • **Vitamin C** 17%	

* Percent Daily Values are based on 2000 calorie diet. Your Daily Values may be higher or lower depending on your calorie needs.

Directions:

1.   Prepare the sauce. In a food processor, combine the avocado, avocado oil, butter, lemon juice, heavy cream, garlic powder, blue cheese, and tarragon. Season with salt and pepper, if desired.

2.   Blend until smooth.

3.   In a small flying pan, preheat the olive oil over medium heat.

4.   Add the broccoli florets and stir while cooking for 6 to 7 minutes, or until the broccoli is tender but not soft.

5.   Remove the broccoli from heat. Combine with the creamy avocado sauce and serve while hot.

Did you know?

Leaves of tarragon have sharp, peppery, anise-like flavor. They are rich source of vitamins A and C and minerals such as iodine, calcium, manganese and iron.

DAY 20

Meal	Recipe	Calories
Breakfast	Mushroom Omelet	599
Lunch	Cauliflower Curry Soup with Tofu	638
Dinner	Keto Pesto Gnocchi	672

Mushroom Omelet

INGREDIENTS	Fats	Proteins	Carbs
1 egg	4.18 g	5.53 g	0.32 g
1 1/2 tbsp. butter	17.28 g	0.18 g	0.01 g
1/2 cup cheddar	22.32 g	15.87 g	0.88 g
1 tbsp. green onion, chopped	0.03 g	0.06 g	0.34 g
1/4 cup white mushroom, chopped	0.16 g	1.48 g	1.56 g
2 tbsp. heavy cream	11.1 g	0.62 g	0.84 g

Nutrition Facts

Amount per 215 g

1 serving (7.6 oz)

Calories 599

From fat 490

Amount	% Daily Value*	Amount	% Daily Value*
Total Fat 55.1g	85%	Total Carbohydrates 4g	1%
Saturated 32g	160%	Dietary Fiber 1g	2%
Trans Fat 1.5g		Sugars 2g	
Cholesterol 318mg	106%	Protein 24g	47%
Sodium 639mg	27%		
Calcium 50% • Iron 6%		Vitamin A 42% • Vitamin C 3%	

* Percent Daily Values are based on 2000 calorie diet. Your Daily Values may be higher or lower depending on your calorie needs.

Directions:

1.   In a small bowl, whisk together the egg and heavy cream. Season with salt and pepper, if desired

2.   In a small pan, melt the 1/2 tbsp. butter over medium heat.

3.   Add the white mushroom to the pan. Cook with continuous stirring until the mushroom has turned light brown, about 7 minutes.

4.   To the same pan, add the whisked egg mixture

5.   Add the shredded cheddar and stir.

6.   To keep the omelet runny, stir the mixture as soon as the bottom starts to get firm. Repeat this step until you achieve your desired consistency.

7.   Garnish with green onions before serving.

Did you know?

Butter has a melting temperature of 98.6°F, exactly the same temperature inside the mouth (at least for 99.7% of us). This is what gives butter its rich, creamy feel in the mouth.

Cauliflower Curry Soup with Tofu

INGREDIENTS	Fats	Proteins	Carbs
1/4 cup cauliflower, chopped	0.08 g	0.51 g	1.33 g
1/2 tsp cumin	0.24 g	0.2 g	0.49 g
1/2 tsp paprika	0.15 g	0.17 g	0.65 g
1/2 tsp curry powder	0.14 g	0.14 g	0.56 g
1/2 tsp garlic powder	0.01 g	0.26 g	1.16 g
1 1/2 tbsp. olive oil	20.3 g	0 g	0 g
1 1/2 tbsp. butter	17.28 g	0.18 g	0.01 g
1/2 cup heavy cream	22.2 g	1.23 g	1.67 g
1/2 cup soft tofu, diced	4.58 g	8.12 g	2.23 g

Nutrition Facts

Amount per 257 g
1 serving (9.1 oz)

Calories 638
From fat 570

Amount	% Daily Value*	Amount	% Daily Value*
Total Fat 65g	100%	Total Carbohydrates 8g	3%
Saturated 28.3g	142%	Dietary Fiber 2g	8%
Trans Fat 0.7g		Sugars 3g	
Cholesterol 128mg	43%	Protein 11g	22%
Sodium 48mg	2%		
Calcium 21% • Iron 16%		Vitamin A 41% • Vitamin C 23%	

* Percent Daily Values are based on 2000 calorie diet. Your Daily Values may be higher or lower depending on your calorie needs.

Directions:

1.   Preheat the oven to 425 F.

2.   In a small bowl, toss together the chopped cauliflower, paprika, cumin, curry powder, garlic powder, and olive oil.

3.   Place the seasoned cauliflower on a large baking tray and bake in the oven for about 20 minutes.

4. Remove from the oven and allow to cool.

5. Place the cauliflower inside the food processor and pulse until you get a rice-like texture. Set aside.

6. In a large saucepan, heat the heavy cream with the butter.

7. Add the riced cauliflower and stir. Allow the mixture to boil and simmer for 5 minutes.

8. Add the tofu and stir. Simmer for an additional 10 minutes.

9. Ladle the soup into a bowl and serve while hot.

Did you know?

Cumin is the second most popular spice in the world (black pepper is number one).

Keto Pesto Gnocchi

INGREDIENTS	Fats	Proteins	Carbs
2 egg yolks	9.02 g	5.39 g	1.22 g

1 cup mozzarella, shredded	0 g	35.82 g	3.96 g
1 tsp garlic powder	0.02 g	0.51 g	2.25 g
1 tbsp. butter	11.52 g	0.12 g	0.01 g
1 tbsp. olive oil	13.5 g	0 g	0 g
2 tbsp. pesto sauce	17.6 g	3.13 g	1.28 g

Nutrition Facts

Amount per 208 g
1 serving (7.3 oz)

Calories 672
From fat 456

	Amount	% Daily Value*		Amount	% Daily Value*
Total Fat 51.7g		79%	**Total Carbohydrates** 9g		3%
Saturated 15.4g		77%	Dietary Fiber 3g		10%
Trans Fat 0.5g			Sugars 2g		
Cholesterol 425mg		142%	**Protein** 45g		90%
Sodium 1238mg		52%			
Calcium 121% • **Iron** 12%			**Vitamin A** 35% • **Vitamin C** 2%		

* Percent Daily Values are based on 2000 calorie diet. Your Daily Values may be higher or lower depending on your calorie needs.

Directions:

1.   Melt the mozzarella in the microwave.

2.   Combine the egg yolks, melted mozzarella, and garlic powder. Mix until a dough-like consistency is achieved.

3.   Divide the dough into 2 portions.

4.   Chill the dough in the refrigerator for 10 minutes.

5.   Line a baking tray with parchment paper. Lightly grease the surface with some olive oil.

6.   Roll out each dough into 1/2-inch thick logs.

7.   Slice each log into 1-inch pieces.

8.   In a large pot, bring some salted water to a boil. Drop the gnocchi pieces into the boiling water.

9.   You will know that the gnocchi are done cooking when they float, which should take about 2 to 3 minutes. Strain the cooked gnocchi using a colander.

10. In a large frying pan, melt the butter in the olive oil over medium heat.

11. Add the gnocchi and sauté for about 2 to 3 minutes, or until they turn golden brown.

12. Top with pesto sauce and serve.

Did you know?
Gnocchi is Italian for dumplings. Gnocchi with tomato sauce is known as strangolapreti or strangoloprevete, meaning priest stranglers, because a local priest liked them so much, and ate them so fast, that he choked on them.

DAY 21

Meal	Recipe	Calories
Breakfast	Crust less Spinach Quiche	561
Lunch	Creamy Mustard Greens and Spinach Soup	725
Dinner	Roasted Vegetables Salad	722

Crust less Spinach Quiche

INGREDIENTS	Fats	Proteins	Carbs
1 cup spinach	0.12 g	0.86 g	1.09 g
1 egg	4.18 g	5.53 g	0.32 g
1/2 cup cheddar, shredded	19.11 g	13.58 g	0.75 g
1/4 cup blue cheese, crumbled	9.71 g	7.23 g	0.79 g
1 tbsp. white onion, chopped	0.01 g	0.06 g	0.6 g
1/2 tbsp. garlic, chopped	0.02 g	0.27 g	1.42 g
1 tbsp. butter	11.52 g	0.12 g	0.01 g
1/4 cup whole milk	1.99 g	1.92 g	2.92 g

Nutrition Facts

Amount per 252 g
1 serving (8.9 oz)

Calories 567
From fat 416

	Amount	% Daily Value*	Amount	% Daily Value*
	Total Fat 46.7g	72%	Total Carbohydrates 8g	3%
	Saturated 27.1g	135%	Dietary Fiber 1g	3%
	Trans Fat 1.1g		Sugars 4g	
	Cholesterol 283mg	94%	Protein 30g	59%
	Sodium 867mg	36%		
	Calcium 70% • Iron 11%		Vitamin A 86% • Vitamin C 17%	

* Percent Daily Values are based on 2000 calorie diet. Your Daily Values may be higher or lower depending on your calorie needs.

Directions:

1. Preheat the oven to 375 F.

2. Grease a muffin pan with butter.

3. In a large bowl, combine the egg, spinach, cheddar, blue cheese, white onion, garlic, and milk. Whisk together until completely mixed.

4. Pour the mixture into the muffin pan.

5. Bake for about 30 minutes, or unit the edges start to turn brown.

6. Remove from the oven and allow to cool before serving.

Did you know?

Blue cheeses are semisoft cheeses that are marbled with delicate veins of blue-green mold. The blue mold in these cheeses is due to mold spores from Penicillium roqueforti or Penicillium glaucum, etc.

Creamy Mustard Greens and Spinach Soup

INGREDIENTS	Fats	Proteins	Carbs
3 tbsp. olive oil	40.5 g	0 g	0 g
1/2 tsp cumin	0.24 g	0.2 g	0.49 g
1 tsp coriander	0 g	0.01 g	0.01 g
1/4 tsp turmeric	0.03 g	0.08 g	0.54 g
1/2 tsp paprika	0.15 g	0.17 g	0.65 g
1/2 tbsp. white onion, chopped	0.01 g	0.06 g	0.47 g
1/2 tbsp. ginger, chopped	0.02 g	0.05 g	0.53 g
1/4 tbsp. garlic, chopped	0.01 g	0.13 g	0.69 g
1/2 tbsp. jalapeno, chopped	0.01 g	0.04 g	0.26 g
1/2 cup mustard greens	0.12 g	0.8 g	1.31 g
1 cup spinach	0.12 g	0.86 g	1.09 g
3/4 cup coconut milk	36.15 g	3.42 g	4.76 g

Nutrition Facts

Amount per 286 g
1 serving (10.1 oz)

Calories 725
From fat 667

	Amount	% Daily Value*		Amount	% Daily Value*
	Total Fat 77.4g	119%		Total Carbohydrates 11g	4%
	Saturated 37.7g	189%		Dietary Fiber 3g	10%
	Trans Fat 0g			Sugars 1g	
	Cholesterol 0mg	0%		Protein 6g	12%
	Sodium 56mg	2%			
	Calcium 11% • Iron 48%			Vitamin A 87% • Vitamin C 60%	

* Percent Daily Values are based on 2000 calorie diet. Your Daily Values may be higher or lower depending on your calorie needs.

Directions:

1.   In a medium-sized pot, heat 1 tbsp. of olive oil over medium heat.

2.   Add the cumin, coriander, and turmeric. Let the spices brown for 1 to 2 minutes.

3.   Add the white onion and sauté until translucent. Add the ginger, garlic, and jalapeno. Stir while cooking for an additional 1 to 2 minutes.

4.   Add the spinach and mustard green. Sauté until the leaves have wilted, which should take 8 to 10 minutes.

5.   Add the coconut milk and stir. Cook for an additional minute.

6.   Transfer the contents of the pot into a blender. Blend until smooth.

7.   Transfer the soup into a bowl.

8.   In a frying pan, heat some olive oil and add in the remaining garlic and paprika. Stir for a few minutes.

9.   Drizzle the seasoned olive oil over the soup. Serve while hot.

Did you know?
Leaves of coriander (also known as cilantro in North and South America) have fresh, grassy, lemony taste, while seed have sweet, nutty, warm and orange-like flavor.

Roasted Vegetables Salad

INGREDIENTS	Fats	Proteins	Carbs
1/2 tbsp. poppy seeds	1.83 g	0.79 g	1.24 g
1/2 tbsp. sesame seeds	2.45 g	0.82 g	0.47 g

1/4 tsp red onion, chopped	0 g	0.03 g	0.23 g
1/2 tsp garlic, chopped	0.01 g	0.09 g	0.46 g
3/4 cup cheddar, shredded	28.68 g	20.39 g	1.13 g
1/2 cup bell pepper, chopped	0.13 g	0.64 g	3.46 g
1/4 cup white mushrooms, chopped	0.08 g	0.74 g	0.78 g
1 cup arugula	0.13 g	0.52 g	0.73 g
1 tbsp. avocado oil	14 g	0 g	0 g
1 tbsp. olive oil	13.5 g	0 g	0 g

Nutrition Facts

Amount per 243 g
1 serving (8.6 oz)

Calories 664
From fat 540

Amount	% Daily Value*	Amount	% Daily Value*
Total Fat 60.8g	94%	Total Carbohydrates 9g	3%
Saturated 20.5g	103%	Dietary Fiber 3g	13%
Trans Fat 1g		Sugars 3g	
Cholesterol 86mg	29%	Protein 24g	48%
Sodium 559mg	23%		
Calcium 68% • Iron 9%		Vitamin A 32% • Vitamin C 107%	

* Percent Daily Values are based on 2000 calorie diet. Your Daily Values may be higher or lower depending on your calorie needs.

Directions:

1.   In a small bowl, toss together the bell pepper, white mushroom, and olive oil. Ensure that all pieces are covered in oil.

2.   In a small frying pan over high heat, char the bell pepper and mushrooms. Do this just until the skin of the pepper starts to turn black and the pepper becomes tender.

3.   Remove from the heat and set aside.

4.   To the same pan, toast the poppy seeds and sesame seeds. Cook for 1 to 2 minutes, or until fragrant.

5.   In a large bowl combine the arugula, garlic, and onions.

6.   Add the cooked mushrooms and bell peppers.

7.   Sprinkle with the toasted poppy seeds and sesame seeds. Top with cheddar cheese.

8.   Drizzle with avocado oil. Season with salt and pepper, if desired.

9.   Toss the salad and serve

Did you know?

Poppy seeds are excellent source B-complex vita metabolism, especially fat and carbohydrates inside the human body. mins such as thiamin, pantothenic acid, pyridoxine, riboflavin, niacin, and folic acid. Many of these vitamins functions as co-factors in the substrate

DAY 22

Meal	Recipe	Calories
Breakfast	Keto Buttermilk Pancakes	774
Lunch	Four Cheese Pesto Zoodles	787
Dinner	Keto Summer Salad	327

Keto Buttermilk Pancakes

Nutrition Facts

Amount per 351 g
1 serving (12.4 oz)

Calories 774
From fat 604

Amount	% Daily Value*	Amount	% Daily Value*
Total Fat 69.3g	107%	**Total Carbohydrates** 8g	3%
Saturated 44.8g	224%	Dietary Fiber 1g	4%
Trans Fat 0.6g		Sugars 1g	
Cholesterol 934mg	311%	**Protein** 33g	66%
Sodium 450mg	19%		
Calcium 22% • **Iron** 38%		**Vitamin A** 33% • **Vitamin C** 1%	

* Percent Daily Values are based on 2000 calorie diet. Your Daily Values may be higher or lower depending on your calorie needs.

INGREDIENTS	Fats	Proteins	Carbs
1 egg	23.11 g	30.52 g	1.75 g
1/4 cup coconut milk	12.05 g	1.14 g	1.59 g
1/2 tbsp. apple cider vinegar	0 g	0 g	0.07 g
1 1/2 tbsp. coconut flour	8.29 g	0.64 g	2.58 g
1/4 tbsp. flaxseed, ground	0.76 g	0.33 g	0.52 g
1/4 tsp cinnamon, ground	0.01 g	0.03 g	0.56 g
1/4 tsp baking powder	0.01 g	0 g	0.61 g
1 tbsp. butter, melted	11.52 g	0.12 g	0.01 g
1 tbsp. coconut oil	13.6 g	0 g	0 g

Directions:

1.   Add the apple cider vinegar to the coconut milk and set aside.

2.   In a separate bowl, combine the dry ingredients: coconut flour, flaxseed, cinnamon, and baking powder. Add a pinch of salt.

3.   Whisk the egg until frothy. Combine the whisked egg with the coconut milk and melted butter.

4.   Fold in the dry ingredients with the wet ingredients. Mix only until there are no more lumps. Do not overmix.

5.   Brush a small frying pan with coconut oil and place over medium heat.

6.   Place on spoonful of the pancake batter into the frying pan. Cook until bubbles break into the surface. Flip and cook on the other side for a few more seconds.

7.   Repeat until all the batter has been used.

8.   Serve while hot.

Did you know?
Coconut Water Can Be Used as a Substitute for Blood Plasma

Four Cheese Pesto Zoodles

INGREDIENTS	Fats	Proteins	Carbs
1 large zucchini	0.06 g	0.43 g	0.5 g
1/2 cup pesto sauce	68.05 g	12.1 g	4.95 g
1/8 tsp nutmeg	0.11 g	0.02 g	0.15 g
1/2 tbsp. Italian style hard cheese, grated	0.7 g	0.71 g	0.35 g
1/8 cup mozzarella, shredded	3.26 g	3.24 g	0.32 g
1/8 cup feta, crumbled	4.15 g	2.77 g	0.8 g
1/2 tbsp. blue cheese	1.15 g	0.86 g	0.09 g

Nutrition Facts	Amount	% Daily Value*	Amount	% Daily Value*
Amount per 173 g	**Total Fat** 77.5g	119%	**Total Carbohydrates** 7g	2%
1 serving (6.1 oz)	Saturated 17.5g	87%	Dietary Fiber 1g	6%
	Trans Fat 0g		Sugars 2g	
Calories 787	**Cholesterol** 54mg	18%	**Protein** 20g	40%
From fat 676	**Sodium** 1478mg	62%		
	Calcium 51% • **Iron** 15%		**Vitamin A** 33% • **Vitamin C** 17%	

* Percent Daily Values are based on 2000 calorie diet. Your Daily Values may be higher or lower depending on your calorie needs.

Directions:

1. Using a spiralizer, cut the zucchini into strands.

2. With a clean kitchen towel, squeeze out as much moisture as you can from the zucchini noodles. Set aside.

3. In a microwave-safe bowl, combine the Italian style hard cheese, mozzarella, feta and blue cheese. Microwave on high for 20 to 30 seconds, or just until the cheese has melted.

4. In a large bowl, combine the zucchini noodles, pesto sauce, and the melted cheese. Season with salt and pepper, if desired. Toss together until thoroughly mixed.

5. Serve immediately.

Did you know?

The active principles in nutmeg have many therapeutic applications in many traditional medicines as anti-fungal, anti-depressant, aphrodisiac, digestive, and carminative functions.

Keto Summer Salad

INGREDIENTS	Fats	Proteins	Carbs
1 cup romaine lettuce	0.14 g	0.58 g	1.55 g
1/2 cup arugula	0.07 g	0.26 g	0.37 g
1/4 cup celery, chopped	5.35 g	0.73 g	3.11 g
1/4 cup avocado, sliced	0.04 g	0.17 g	0.75 g
1/4 cup cucumber, chopped	0.05 g	0.18 g	0.64 g
1 tbsp. olive oil	13.5 g	0 g	0 g
1/2 tbsp. balsamic vinegar	0 g	0.04 g	1.36 g
1 tbsp. avocado oil	14 g	0 g	0 g

Nutrition Facts

Amount per 184 g
1 serving (6.5 oz)

Calories 327
From fat 290

Amount	% Daily Value*	Amount	% Daily Value*
Total Fat 33.2g	51%	Total Carbohydrates 8g	3%
Saturated 4.3g	22%	Dietary Fiber 4g	17%
Trans Fat 0g		Sugars 3g	
Cholesterol 0mg	0%	Protein 2g	4%
Sodium 32mg	1%		
Calcium 5% • Iron 6%		Vitamin A 90% • Vitamin C 15%	

* Percent Daily Values are based on 2000 calorie diet. Your Daily Values may be higher or lower depending on your calorie needs.

Directions:

1.	In a large bowl, combine the lettuce, arugula, celery, cucumber, and avocado.

2.	Drizzle with olive oil, balsamic vinegar, and avocado oil. Season with salt and pepper, if desired.

3.	Toss to mix thoroughly. Serve immediately.

you eat cucumber slices before going to bed, you will wake up feeling fresh and headache free!

DAY 23

Meal	Recipe	Calories
Breakfast	Eggs with Mayonnaise and Roasted Vegetables	429
Lunch	Collard Greens in Coconut Stew	687
Dinner	Zoodles Alfredo	696

Eggs with Mayonnaise and Roasted Vegetables

INGREDIENTS	Fats	Proteins	Carbs
2 eggs	8.37 g	11.05 g	0.63 g
1 tbsp. mayonnaise	10.33 g	0.13 g	0.08 g
3 spears asparagus	0.06 g	1.06 g	1.86 g
1 1/2 tbsp. olive oil	20.3 g	0 g	0 g
1 cup eggplant, diced	0.15 g	0.8 g	4.82 g

Nutrition Facts

	Amount	% Daily Value*	Amount	% Daily Value*
Total Fat 39.2g		60%	**Total Carbohydrates** 7g	2%
Saturated 7.2g		36%	Dietary Fiber 4g	14%
Trans Fat 0.1g			Sugars 4g	
Cholesterol 333mg		111%	**Protein** 13g	26%
Sodium 216mg		9%		
Calcium 7% • **Iron** 16%			**Vitamin A** 17% • **Vitamin C** 8%	

Amount per 252 g
1 serving (8.9 oz)

Calories 429
From fat 350

* Percent Daily Values are based on 2000 calorie diet. Your Daily Values may be higher or lower depending on your calorie needs.

Directions:

1.   Preheat the oven to 425 F.

2.   Boil the eggs. Cooking time may vary according to your desired doneness.

3.   On a small baking tray, toss the asparagus and eggplant in olive oil. Season with salt and pepper.

4.   Bake for 18 to 20 minutes, or until the asparagus is tender.

5.   Serve the boiled eggs topped with mayonnaise and a side of the roasted vegetables!

Did you know?

An egg contains 2/3 of your recommended cholesterol intake, but it turns out this isn't a big deal. Studies show that regular egg consumption does not increase risk of heart disease.

Collard Greens in Coconut Stew

INGREDIENTS	Fats	Proteins	Carbs
1 cup collard greens, chopped	0.22 g	1.09 g	1.95 g

1/2 cup coconut milk	24.1 g	2.28 g	3.18 g
1/2 cup vegetable broth	0 g	0 g	1.5 g
1/2 tbsp. lime juice	0.01 g	0.03 g	0.64 g
1 tbsp. tahini	8.06 g	2.55 g	3.18 g
3 tbsp. coconut oil	40.8 g	0 g	0 g
1/2 tbsp. ginger, grated	0.02 g	0.05 g	0.53 g
1/2 tbsp. garlic	0.01 g	0.09 g	0.46 g

Nutrition Facts

Amount per 334 g
1 serving (11.8 oz)

Calories 687
From fat 623

Amount	% Daily Value*	Amount	% Daily Value*
Total Fat 73.2g	113%	Total Carbohydrates 11g	4%
Saturated 57.8g	289%	Dietary Fiber 3g	12%
Trans Fat 0.1g		Sugars 1g	
Cholesterol 0mg	0%	Protein 6g	12%
Sodium 509mg	21%		
Calcium 17% • Iron 30%		Vitamin A 41% • Vitamin C 28%	

* Percent Daily Values are based on 2000 calorie diet. Your Daily Values may be higher or lower depending on your calorie needs.

Directions:

1.   Melt the coconut oil over medium heat. Add the ginger and garlic and sauté for 5 minutes.

2.   Add the collard greens and stir for 1 to 2 minutes, or until they have started to wilt.

3.   Add the vegetable broth, coconut milk, and lime juice. Allow to boil and lower the heat to a simmer. Add the tahini and stir the soup.

4.   Cook for an additional 15 minutes. Season with salt and pepper, if desired.

5.   Serve while hot.

Did you know?

Collard greens is rich source of dietary fibers, vitamin B9, C, A, K and minerals such as iron, calcium, copper, manganese and selenium. 100 g of collard greens contains only 30 calories.

Zoodles Alfredo

INGREDIENTS	Fats	Proteins	Carbs
1 medium zucchini	0.04 g	0.3 g	0.34 g
2tbsp.butter	23.04 g	0.24 g	0.02 g
1 tbsp. cream cheese	4.96 g	0.86 g	0.59 g
1 tbsp. sour cream	1.27 g	0.42 g	0.85 g
1 cup heavy cream	44.4 g	2.46 g	3.35 g
1/2 tbsp. Italian style hard cheese, grated	0.7 g	0.71 g	0.35 g

Nutrition Facts

	Amount	% Daily Value*	Amount	% Daily Value*
Amount per 188 g	**Total Fat** 74.4g	114%	**Total Carbohydrates** 6g	2%
1 serving (6.6 oz)	Saturated 46.2g	231%	Dietary Fiber 0g	0%
	Trans Fat 1g		Sugars 4g	
Calories 696	**Cholesterol** 248mg	83%	**Protein** 5g	10%
From fat 654	**Sodium** 157mg	7%		
	Calcium 14% • **Iron** 1%		**Vitamin A** 56% • **Vitamin C** 8%	

* Percent Daily Values are based on 2000 calorie diet. Your Daily Values may be higher or lower depending on your calorie needs.

Directions:

1. Using a spiralizer, cut the zucchini into strands.

2. With a clean kitchen towel, squeeze out as much moisture as you can from the zucchini noodles. Set aside.

3. In a small saucepan, melt the butter over medium heat.

4. Add the heavy cream, cream cheese, Italian style hard cheese, and sour cream. Simmer until all the cheese has melted.

5. Pour the cheese sauce over the zucchini noodles. Season with salt and pepper, if desired. Toss to mix thoroughly.

Did you know?

Sour Cream (cultured sour cream) is the product resulting from adding lactic acid bacteria to pasteurized cream at least 18% milk fat.

DAY 24

Meal	Recipe	Calories
Breakfast	Mini Eggplant Pizzas	418
Lunch	Sesame Tofu Salad	668
Dinner	Keto Falafel with Tahini Sauce	687

Mini Eggplant Pizzas

INGREDIENTS	Fats	Proteins	Carbs
1/4 eggplant	0.12 g	0.67 g	4.03 g
1 egg	4.18 g	5.53 g	0.32 g
2 tbsp. Italian style hard cheese, grated	2.78 g	2.84 g	1.39 g
2 tbsp. mozzarella, crumbled	3.58 g	3.55 g	0.35 g
1 tbsp. olives, chopped	0.9 g	0.07 g	0.53 g
2 tbsp. olive oil	27 g	0 g	0 g

Nutrition Facts

Amount per 174 g
1 serving (6.1 oz)

Calories 418
From fat 341

Amount	% Daily Value*	Amount	% Daily Value*
Total Fat 38.6g	59%	Total Carbohydrates 7g	2%
Saturated 8.9g	44%	Dietary Fiber 2g	9%
Trans Fat 0.1g		Sugars 3g	
Cholesterol 185mg	62%	Protein 13g	25%
Sodium 407mg	17%		
Calcium 21% • Iron	8%	Vitamin A 10% • Vitamin C	3%

* Percent Daily Values are based on 2000 calorie diet. Your Daily Values may be higher or lower depending on your calorie needs.

Directions:

1.   Preheat the oven to 425 C.

2.   Slice the eggplant into 1/2-inch thick rounds.

3.   In a small bowl, combine the egg, olive oil, olives Italian style hard cheese, and mozzarella. Whisk together until thoroughly combined.

4.   Top the eggplant slices with the egg mixture.

5.   Arrange the eggplant slices on a baking tray, taking care not to have them touch each other.

6.   Bake for 18 to 20 minutes, or until the toppings have turned golden brown.

7.   Serve while hot.

Did you know?

There are more than 2000 varieties of cheese available worldwide, mozzarella is the favorite around the globe, and the most consumed. That's quite impressive!

Sesame Tofu Salad

INGREDIENTS	Fats	Proteins	Carbs
1 cup collard greens, chopped	0.22 g	1.09 g	1.95 g
1/2 tbsp. tahini	4.03 g	1.28 g	1.59 g

1/4 cup firm tofu, diced	5.49 g	9.94 g	2.69 g
1 tbsp. sesame seeds	4.9 g	1.64 g	0.94 g
3 tbsp. sesame oil	40.8 g	0 g	0 g
1/2 tbsp. soy sauce	0.05 g	0.65 g	0.39 g
2 tbsp. walnuts, chopped	10.43 g	2.44 g	2.19 g

Nutrition Facts

Amount per 179 g
1 serving (6.3 oz)

Calories 668
From fat 571

Amount	% Daily Value*	Amount	% Daily Value*
Total Fat 65.9g	101%	**Total Carbohydrates** 10g	3%
Saturated 8.9g	44%	Dietary Fiber 6g	23%
Trans Fat 0g		Sugars 1g	
Cholesterol 0mg	0%	**Protein** 17g	34%
Sodium 467mg	19%		
Calcium 57% • **Iron** 20%		**Vitamin A** 39% • **Vitamin C** 22%	

* Percent Daily Values are based on 2000 calorie diet. Your Daily Values may be higher or lower depending on your calorie needs.

Directions:

1.	In a bowl, combine the 2 tbsp. sesame oil, soy sauce, and tahini.

2.	Mix in the tofu cubes. Place the marinade mixture in an airtight container and marinate in the refrigerator for at least 2 hours.

3.	In a small frying pan, toast the walnuts over low heat until fragrant, which should take 2 to 3 minutes.

4.	After the tofu cubes have been marinated, arrange them on a parchment-lined baking tray.

5.	Bake in a 425 F preheated oven for 24 to 25 minutes, or until the tofu has turned golden brown with a firm texture.

6.	In a large bowl, combine the collard greens, cooked tofu, and walnuts. Toss and serve.

Did you know?

Sesame doesn't contain gluten, it's perfect for celiacs and those who would like to avoid eating gluten.

Keto Falafel with Tahini Sauce

INGREDIENTS	Fats	Proteins	Carbs
1/4 cup cauliflower, chopped	0.08 g	0.51 g	1.33 g
2 tbsp. almonds, slivered	7.99 g	3.38 g	3.45 g
1/4 tbsp. cumin	0.33 g	0.27 g	0.66 g
1/4 tbsp. coriander	0 g	0.01 g	0.01 g
1/2 tsp garlic, chopped	0.01 g	0.09 g	0.46 g
1/2 tbsp. parsley, chopped	0.02 g	0.06 g	0.12 g
1 egg	4.18 g	5.53 g	0.32 g
1/2 tbsp. coconut flour	2.76 g	0.21 g	0.86 g
1/2 tbsp. tahini	4.03 g	1.28 g	1.59 g
1/2 tbsp. lemon juice	0.02 g	0.03 g	0.52 g
2 tbsp. olive oil	27 g	0 g	0 g
2 tbsp. butter	23.04 g	0.24 g	0.02 g

Nutrition Facts

Amount per 166 g
1 serving (5.9 oz)

Calories 687
From fat 606

Amount	% Daily Value*	Amount	% Daily Value*
Total Fat 69.5g	107%	Total Carbohydrates 9g	3%
Saturated 23.4g	117%	Dietary Fiber 4g	14%
Trans Fat 1g		Sugars 2g	
Cholesterol 225mg	75%	Protein 12g	23%
Sodium 88mg	4%		
Calcium 13% • Iron 20%		Vitamin A 23% • Vitamin C 32%	

* Percent Daily Values are based on 2000 calorie diet. Your Daily Values may be higher or lower depending on your calorie needs.

Directions:

1.   In a food processor, combine the cauliflower and almonds. Pulse until a fine powder-like consistency is achieved.

2.   Add the cumin, coriander, garlic, egg, coconut flour, butter, and parsley. Pulse again until everything has been well incorporated.

3.   Form the batter into 1/2-inch thick patties.

4.   Heat the olive oil in a small frying pan over medium heat.

5.   Cook the patties on one side 4 to 5 minutes, ensuring that it has turned a golden brown color. Flip to the other side and cook for another 4 to 5 minutes.

6.   Repeat until all the batter and the patties have been cooked.

7.   For the tahini sauce, combine the tahini and lemon juice and mix until well-incorporated.

8.   Serve the falafels with the tahini sauce on the side.

Did you know?

Olive oil has a higher proportion of monounsaturated fats than animal fat, which is often high in saturated fat. Studies have indicated that if you replace saturated fats with monounsaturated fats, you can lower your risk of coronary heart disease.

DAY 25

Meal	Recipe	Calories
Breakfast	Pumpkin Breakfast Porridge	629
Lunch	Mediterranean Cauliflower Pizza	641

Dinner	Roasted Asparagus with Buttermilk Dressing	559

Pumpkin Breakfast Porridge

INGREDIENTS	Fats	Proteins	Carbs
1 tbsp. peanut flour	0.83 g	1.28 g	1.19 g
1/2 tbsp. flaxseed, ground	1.48 g	0.64 g	1.01 g
1/4 tsp pumpkin spice	0.05 g	0.02 g	0.28 g
1 egg	4.18 g	5.53 g	0.32 g
1/4 tsp vanilla extract	0 g	0 g	0.14 g
2 tbsp. canned pumpkin	0.09 g	0.34 g	2.48 g
1 cup heavy cream	44.4 g	2.46 g	3.35 g
1 tbsp. butter	11.52 g	0.12 g	0.01 g

Nutrition Facts	Amount	% Daily Value*	Amount	% Daily Value*
Amount per 218 g	**Total Fat** 62.6g	96%	**Total Carbohydrates** 9g	3%
1 serving (7.7 oz)	Saturated 36.6g	183%	Dietary Fiber 3g	10%
	Trans Fat 0.5g		Sugars 5g	
Calories 629	**Cholesterol** 359mg	120%	**Protein** 10g	21%
From fat 550	**Sodium** 202mg	8%		
	Calcium 13% • **Iron** 9%		**Vitamin A** 142% • **Vitamin C** 4%	

*Percent Daily Values are based on 2000 calorie diet. Your Daily Values may be higher or lower depending on your calorie needs.

Directions:

1.   In a small pot, combine the peanut flour, flaxseed, pumpkin spice, heavy cream, canned pumpkin, and butter.

2.   Boil the mixture over high heat, then lower the heat to a simmer.

3.   Whisk the egg in a small bowl. Slowly add the whisked egg into the soup while continuously stirring. Continue cooking the soup while stirring until it thickens up.

4.   Add the vanilla extract and flaxseed. Cook for another 5 minutes.

5.   Ladle the soup into a bowl. Serve while hot

Did you know?

Flaxseed oil can heal inflamed skin areas in cases of acne, rosacea, and eczema. The topical application of this oil heals sunburns effectively.

Mediterranean Cauliflower Pizza

INGREDIENTS	Fats	Proteins	Carbs
1/4 cup cauliflower, chopped	0.08 g	0.51 g	1.33 g

2 tbsp. Italian style hard cheese, grated	2.78 g	2.84 g	1.39 g
1/2 tbsp. almond paste	1.11 g	0.36 g	1.91 g
1/4 tsp garlic powder	0.01 g	0.13 g	0.58 g
1 egg	4.18 g	5.53 g	0.32 g
1/4 tsp dried oregano	0.01 g	0.03 g	0.21 g
1//2 tbsp. tomato paste	0.04 g	0.35 g	1.51 g
1 tbsp. olives, sliced	0.9 g	0.07 g	0.53 g
1 tbsp. basil	0.02 g	0.09 g	0.07 g
2 tbsp. olive oil	27 g	0 g	0 g
3/4 cup mozzarella	18.77 g	18.62 g	1.84 g

Nutrition Facts

Amount per 216 g
1 serving (7.6 oz)

Calories 641
From fat 484

Amount	% Daily Value*	Amount	% Daily Value*
Total Fat 54.9g	84%	Total Carbohydrates 10g	3%
Saturated 18g	90%	Dietary Fiber 2g	6%
Trans Fat 0.1g		Sugars 4g	
Cholesterol 239mg	80%	Protein 29g	57%
Sodium 846mg	35%		
Calcium 57% • Iron 13%		Vitamin A 24% • Vitamin C 26%	

* Percent Daily Values are based on 2000 calorie diet. Your Daily Values may be higher or lower depending on your calorie needs.

Directions:

1.   Preheat the oven to 450 F.

2.   Place the cauliflower in a food processor and pulse until a rice-like texture is achieved.

3.   Place the riced cauliflower in a microwave safe bowl. Microwave on high for about 7 to 8 minutes.

4.   In a small bowl, combine the cooked cauliflower, Italian style hard cheese, almond paste, garlic powder, and egg. Season with salt. Mix thoroughly until a homogenous batter is formed.

5.   Place the batter on a baking tray lined with parchment paper. Spread the batter to form the shape of a pizza crust.

6.   Bake the pizza crust in the oven for 14 to 15 minutes.

7.   Remove the crust from the oven and assemble the pizza.

8.   Spread the tomato paste evenly over the pizza. Tops with sliced olives and mozzarella.

9.   Put the pizza back on the oven and bake for an addition 2 or 3 minutes, just until the cheese has melted.

10.   Serve hot.

Did you know?
There are more than 450 varieties of garlic.

Roasted Asparagus with Buttermilk Dressing

INGREDIENTS	Fats	Proteins	Carbs
1/2 tsp. garlic, crushed	0.01 g	0.09 g	0.46 g
2 tbsp. buttermilk	1.01 g	0.98 g	1.49 g
1 tbsp. distilled vinegar	0 g	0 g	0.01 g
2 1/2 tbsp. olive oil	33.8 g	0 g	0 g

4 spears asparagus	0.08 g	1.41 g	2.48 g
1 tbsp. cilantro, chopped	0.01 g	0.02 g	0.04 g
1/2 tbsp. sunflower seeds	2.26 g	0.91 g	0.88 g
1/2 cup feta, crumbled	15.96 g	10.66 g	3.07 g

Nutrition Facts

Amount per 225 g
5 servings (7.9 oz)

Calories 559
From fat 468

Amount	% Daily Value*	Amount	% Daily Value*
Total Fat 53.1g	82%	Total Carbohydrates 8g	3%
Saturated 16.7g	83%	Dietary Fiber 2g	7%
Trans Fat 0g		Sugars 6g	
Cholesterol 70mg	23%	Protein 14g	28%
Sodium 723mg	30%		
Calcium 43% • Iron 13%		Vitamin A 18% • Vitamin C 7%	

* Percent Daily Values are based on 2000 calorie diet. Your Daily Values may be higher or lower depending on your calorie needs.

Directions:

1.   Preheat the oven to 425 F.

2.   On a baking tray, toss the asparagus with 2 tbsp olive oil, garlic, and sunflower seeds.

3.   Bake the asparagus in the oven for 19 to 20 minutes, or until the asparagus is tender.

4.   Remove the asparagus from the oven and place on a small bowl.

5.   Drizzle the asparagus with the buttermilk, vinegar, and the remaining olive oil. Add the cilantro and feta. Toss the salad completely before serving.

Did you know?

You can use full strength white distilled vinegar to kill grass on sidewalks and driveways.

DAY 26

Meal	Recipe	Calories
Breakfast	Grain-Free Overnight Oats	586
Lunch	Cucumber Salad with Wasabi Dressing	657
Dinner	Roasted Cauliflower and Tofu	658

Grain-Free Overnight Oats

INGREDIENTS	Fats	Proteins	Carbs
1/2 cup coconut milk	24.1 g	2.28 g	3.18 g
1/4 tbsp. chia seeds	0.61 g	0.33 g	0.84 g
1 tbsp. desiccated coconut	0.03 g	0.11 g	0.56 g
1 tsp sunflower seeds	1.49 g	0.6 g	0.58 g
1/2 tsp vanilla extract	0 g	0 g	0.27 g
1 tbsp. almonds, slivered	3.99 g	1.69 g	1.72 g
2 tbsp. coconut oil	27.2 g	0 g	0 g
1 1/2 tbsp. protein powder	1.44 g	6 g	2.64 g

Nutrition Facts

Amount per 182 g
1 serving (6.4 oz)

Calories 586
From fat 500

Amount	% Daily Value*	Amount	% Daily Value*
Total Fat 58.9g	91%	Total Carbohydrates 10g	3%
Saturated 45.6g	228%	Dietary Fiber 2g	9%
Trans Fat 0.1g		Sugars 2g	
Cholesterol 1mg	0%	Protein 11g	22%
Sodium 61mg	3%		
Calcium 21% • Iron 32%		Vitamin A 8% • Vitamin C 11%	

* Percent Daily Values are based on 2000 calorie diet. Your Daily Values may be higher or lower depending on your calorie needs.

Directions:

1.   In a blender, combine the coconut milk, protein powder, coconut oil, and vanilla extract. Blend until smooth.

2.   Transfer the contents of the blender into an airtight container. Add the chia seeds, desiccated coconut, and sunflower seeds. Mix thoroughly and cover. Leave overnight.

3.   The following day, add the slivered almonds before serving.

Did you know?
The word chia originated from the Aztecs word for oily, chian.

Cucumber Salad With Wasabi Dressing

INGREDIENTS	Fats	Proteins	Carbs
1/4 cup cucumber, sliced	0.08 g	0.3 g	1.09 g
3/4 cup romaine lettuce, shredded	0.11 g	0.43 g	1.16 g

1 tsp sesame seeds	1.65 g	0.55 g	0.32 g
2 tbsp. avocado, diced	2.35 g	0.32 g	1.36 g
1 tbsp. green onion, sliced	0.03 g	0.06 g	0.34 g
1 tbsp. lime juice	0.01 g	0.06 g	1.27 g
1/2 tbsp. wasabi powder	0.03 g	0.19 g	0.94 g
2 tbsp. avocado oil	28 g	0 g	0 g
2 tsp vinegar	0 g	0 g	0.09 g
2 tbsp. olive oil	27 g	0 g	0 g
8 tbsp. walnuts	10.43 g	2.44 g	2.19 g

Nutrition Facts

Amount per 210 g
1 serving (7.4 oz)

Calories 657
From fat 609

Amount	% Daily Value*	Amount	% Daily Value*
Total Fat 69.7g	107%	Total Carbohydrates 9g	3%
Saturated 8.6g	43%	Dietary Fiber 4g	16%
Trans Fat 0g		Sugars 2g	
Cholesterol 0mg	0%	Protein 4g	9%
Sodium 9mg	0%		
Calcium 5% • Iron 8%		Vitamin A 68% • Vitamin C 20%	

* Percent Daily Values are based on 2000 calorie diet. Your Daily Values may be higher or lower depending on your calorie needs.

Directions:

1.   Prepare the dressing by combining the lime juice, wasabi powder, avocado oil, vinegar, and olive oil. Whisk together until well combined.

2.   In a large bowl, combine the sliced cucumber, romaine lettuce, avocado, green onion, walnuts, and sesame seeds.

3.   Drizzle with the dressing and toss to combine. Serve immediately.

Did you know?

Wasabi or Japanese horseradish is a plant of the Brassicaceae family, which includes cabbages, horseradish, and mustard.

Roasted Cauliflower and Tofu

INGREDIENTS	Fats	Proteins	Carbs
1/2 cup cauliflower, sliced	0.15 g	1.03 g	2.66 g
1/4 cup firm tofu, diced	5.49 g	9.94 g	2.69 g
3/4 tbsp. tahini	6.07 g	1.92 g	2.39 g
2 tbsp. olive oil	27 g	0 g	0 g
1/4 tbsp. Italian style hard cheese, grated	0.36 g	0.37 g	0.18 g
2 tbsp. sesame oil	27.2 g	0 g	0 g
1/2 tbsp. lemon juice	0.02 g	0.03 g	0.52 g

Nutrition Facts

Amount per 191 g
1 serving (6.7 oz)

Calories 658
From fat 581

	Amount	% Daily Value*	Amount	% Daily Value*
Total Fat	66.3g	102%	Total Carbohydrates 8g	3%
Saturated	9.5g	48%	Dietary Fiber 4g	14%
Trans Fat	0g		Sugars 1g	
Cholesterol	1mg	0%	Protein 13g	27%
Sodium	62mg	3%		
Calcium 50% • Iron 17%			Vitamin A 3% • Vitamin C 48%	

* Percent Daily Values are based on 2000 calorie diet. Your Daily Values may be higher or lower depending on your calorie needs.

Directions:

1.   Preheat the oven to 425 F.

2.   In a baking tray, toss the cauliflower and tofu with the tahini, sesame oil, and olive oil.

3.   Bake in the oven for 24 to 25 minutes, or until the tofu is crispy and the cauliflower is tender.

4.   Remove from the oven and transfer to a bowl.

5.   Spritz the lemon juice over the salad and top with Italian style hard cheese. Serve while hot.

Did you know?
Tofu is one of the oldest foods in the world: It is said that almost 2000 years ago, tofu was discovered accidentally by a Chinese cook, who curdled soy milk using nigari seaweed. It was then introduced to Japan and called okabe.

DAY 27

Meal	Recipe	Calories
Breakfast	Egg and Avocado Salad	598
Lunch	Jalapeno and Cauliflower Casserole	755
Dinner	Indian Egg Curry	607

Egg and Avocado Salad

INGREDIENTS	Fats	Proteins	Carbs

3 eggs	12.55 g	16.58 g	0.95 g
1/2 cup avocado, diced	11 g	1.5 g	6.4 g
1/2 tbsp. mayonnaise	5.16 g	0.07 g	0.04 g
1/2 tsp mustard	0.08 g	0.09 g	0.15 g
1 tsp lemon juice	0.01 g	0.02 g	0.35 g
1/4 tsp dill	0.02 g	0.07 g	0.14 g
1/4 tsp parsley	0 g	0.01 g	0.02 g
2 tbsp. olive oil	27 g	0 g	0 g

Nutrition Facts

Amount per 215 g
1 serving (7.6 oz)

Calories 572
From fat 452

Amount	% Daily Value*	Amount	% Daily Value*
Total Fat 51.5g	79%	Total Carbohydrates 10g	3%
Saturated 16.3g	82%	Dietary Fiber 7g	27%
Trans Fat 0.7g		Sugars 1g	
Cholesterol 221mg	74%	Protein 21g	42%
Sodium 434mg	18%		
Calcium 42% • Iron 8%		Vitamin A 19% • Vitamin C 17%	

* Percent Daily Values are based on 2000 calorie diet. Your Daily Values may be higher or lower depending on your calorie needs.

Directions:

1.   Boil the eggs until your desired doneness. After cooking, submerge the eggs immediately into ice water.

2.   Peel the eggs and mash using a fork.

3.   In a separate container, mash the avocados.

4.   Combine the eggs, mashed avocado, mayonnaise, mustard, lemon juice, dill, parsley, and olive oil. Mix thoroughly.

5. Chill for at least 30 minutes before serving.

Did you know?

Dill can be used in treatment of digestive problems, lack of appetite and jaundice. It reduces flatulence and can be used as a cure for hiccups. Dill stimulates lactation in breastfeeding women and alleviates colic in babies. It can be also used to calm babies and help them fall asleep during teething.

Jalapeno and Cauliflower

Casserole

INGREDIENTS	Fats	Proteins	Carbs
1/4 cup cauliflower, chopped	0.08 g	0.51 g	1.33 g
1/2 cup heavy cream	22.2 g	1.23 g	1.67 g
1 tbsp. butter	11.52 g	0.12 g	0.01 g
1/4 cup cheddar, shredded	9.57 g	6.8 g	0.38 g
1/4 cup, jalapeno	0.08 g	0.2 g	1.46 g
1/2 tsp garlic powder	0.01 g	0.26 g	1.16 g
1/4 cup cheddar, shredded	9.57 g	6.8 g	0.38 g
1/4 cup cream cheese	19.86 g	3.44 g	2.36 g

Nutrition Facts	Amount	% Daily Value*	Amount	% Daily Value*
Amount per 240 g	**Total Fat** 72.9g	112%	**Total Carbohydrates** 9g	3%
1 serving (8.5 oz)	Saturated 43.3g	217%	Dietary Fiber 1g	5%
	Trans Fat 1.1g		Sugars 5g	
Calories 755	**Cholesterol** 234mg	78%	**Protein** 19g	39%
From fat 645	**Sodium** 700mg	29%		
	Calcium 49% • **Iron** 3%		**Vitamin A** 56% • **Vitamin C** 67%	

* Percent Daily Values are based on 2000 calorie diet. Your Daily Values may be higher or lower depending on your calorie needs.

Directions:

1.   Preheat the oven to 375 F.

2.   Place the chopped cauliflower in a microwave-safe bowl and microwave on high for 10 minutes. Check to see if the cauliflower is tender; if not, then microwave for an additional 5 minutes.

3.   Place the cooked cauliflower in a blender and add the heavy cream, 1/4 cup cheddar, jalapeno, butter, and garlic powder. Season with salt and pepper, if desired. Blend until smooth.

4.   Transfer the contents of the blender to an oven-safe dish. Spread the cream cheese over the top, and sprinkle with the remaining cheddar.
5.   Bake the cauliflower casserole in the oven for 20 minutes, or until the cheese on top has melted and browned.

6.   Allow to cool for a few minutes before serving.

Did you know?

The psychological term for fear of garlic is Alliumphobia.

Indian Egg Curry

INGREDIENTS	Fats	Proteins	Carbs
1 egg	4.18 g	5.53 g	0.32 g
1/4 cup snap beans	0.18 g	0.43 g	1.65 g
1/2 tsp green onion, chopped	0 g	0.01 g	0.06 g
1/4 tsp garlic, chopped	0 g	0.04 g	0.23 g
1/4 tsp turmeric	0.03 g	0.08 g	0.54 g
1/2 tsp ginger, grated	0.01 g	0.02 g	0.18 g
1/2 tsp cumin	0.24 g	0.2 g	0.49 g
1/2 tsp coriander	0 g	0g	0.01 g
1/2 tbsp. tomato paste	0.04 g	0.35 g	1.51 g
1/2 cup coconut milk	24.1 g	2.28 g	3.18 g
1/2 tbsp. cilantro	0 g	0.01 g	0.02 g
1/2 tbsp. lime juice	0.01 g	0.03 g	0.64 g
2 tbsp. coconut oil	27.2 g	0 g	0 g
1/2 tbsp. red chili, crushed	0.02 g	0.07 g	0.35 g
1/2 tbsp. sesame oil	6.8 g	0 g	0 g

Nutrition Facts

Amount	**% Daily Value***		**Amount**		**% Daily Value***
Total Fat 62.8g	97%		**Total Carbohydrates** 9g		3%
Saturated 47.3g	237%		Dietary Fiber 2g		6%
Trans Fat 0.1g			Sugars 2g		
Cholesterol 164mg	55%		**Protein** 9g		18%
Sodium 86mg	4%				
Calcium 8% • **Iron** 36%			**Vitamin A** 13% • **Vitamin C** 21%		

Amount per 254 g
1 serving (9 oz)

Calories 607
From fat 538

* Percent Daily Values are based on 2000 calorie diet. Your Daily Values may be higher or lower depending on your calorie needs.

Directions:

1. Boil the egg in water until the desired doneness. After cooking, submerge the egg immediately in ice water and peel.

2. Melt the coconut oil in a large frying pan over medium heat. Add the sesame oil.

3. To the frying pan, add the garlic, ginger, and red chili. Cook for around 3 minutes.

4. Add the turmeric, cumin, and coriander. Cook for another 3 minutes.

5. Add the tomato paste. Stir and cook for another 3 minutes

6. Add the coconut milk and bring it to a boil. Lower the heat down to a simmer, and simmer for 10 minutes.

7. Add the boiled egg and the snap beans to the curry. Cook for an additional 8 minutes.

8. Drizzle the lime juice over the curry and sprinkle with coriander. Serve while hot.

Did you know?

Turmeric paste is a home remedy for sunburn and it is also an ingredient in many commercial sunscreens.

DAY 28

Meal	Recipe	Calories
Breakfast	Creamy Coconut Porridge	602
Lunch	Blue Cheese Coleslaw	531
Dinner	Fried Zucchini Cakes	790

Creamy Coconut Porridge

INGREDIENTS	Fats	Proteins	Carbs
1/2 cup coconut milk	24.1 g	2.28 g	3.18 g
2 tbsp. coconut oil	27.2 g	0 g	0 g
1/2 tbsp. desiccated coconut	2.76 g	0.21 g	0.86 g
1 tsp flaxseed, ground	1.05 g	0.46 g	0.72 g
1/2 tsp chia seeds	1.23 g	0.66 g	1.68 g
1/4 tsp vanilla extract	0 g	0 g	0.14 g
1/4 tsp nutmeg	0.22 g	0.04 g	0.3 g
1 1/2 tbsp. walnuts, chopped	7.83 g	1.83 g	1.65 g

Nutrition Facts

Amount	% Daily Value*	Amount	% Daily Value*
Total Fat 64.4g	99%	Total Carbohydrates 9g	3%
Saturated 48.5g	242%	Dietary Fiber 3g	12%
Trans Fat 0.1g		Sugars 1g	
Cholesterol 0mg	0%	Protein 5g	11%
Sodium 18mg	1%		
Calcium 7% • Iron 26%		Vitamin A 0% • Vitamin C 2%	

Amount per 164 g
1 serving (5.8 oz)

Calories 602
From fat 546

* Percent Daily Values are based on 2000 calorie diet. Your Daily Values may be higher or lower depending on your calorie needs.

Directions:

1.   In a saucepan, toast the desiccated coconut over high heat for 4 to 5 minutes. Keep stirring so that the coconut does not burn.

2.   Add the coconut milk and coconut oil bring to a boil.

3.   Add the flaxseed, chia seeds, nutmeg, and vanilla extract. Simmer for an additional 5 minutes.

4.   Transfer to a bowl and top with walnuts. Serve while hot.

Did you know?

The smell of vanilla is known to directly impact the brain and induce calmness.

Blue Cheese Coleslaw

INGREDIENTS	Fats	Proteins	Carbs
1/2 cup red cabbage, shredded	0.06 g	0.5 g	2.58 g
1 tbsp. green onion, chopped	0.03 g	0.06 g	0.34 g
1/2 tbsp. celery, chopped	0.01 g	0.03 g	0.11 g
1/4 cup buttermilk	0.54 g	2.03 g	2.94 g
1/2 cup blue cheese, crumbled	19.4 g	14.45 g	1.58 g
1 1/2 tbsp. butter	17.28 g	0.18 g	0.01 g
1/2 cup green cabbage, shredded	0.04 g	0.45 g	2.03 g
1 tbsp. mayonnaise	10.33 g	0.13 g	0.08 g

Nutrition Facts

Amount per 244 g
1 serving (8.6 oz)

Calories 531
From fat 421

Amount	% Daily Value*	Amount	% Daily Value*
Total Fat 47.7g	73%	Total Carbohydrates 10g	3%
Saturated 25.5g	128%	Dietary Fiber 2g	7%
Trans Fat 0.7g		Sugars 6g	
Cholesterol 105mg	35%	Protein 18g	36%
Sodium 1000mg	42%		
Calcium 47% • Iron 4%		Vitamin A 35% • Vitamin C 57%	

* Percent Daily Values are based on 2000 calorie diet. Your Daily Values may be higher or lower depending on your calorie needs.

Directions:

1.   In a microwave-safe bowl, combine the buttermilk, blue cheese, and butter. Microwave on medium setting for 3 minutes, or until the cheese has melted. Mix the blue cheese mixture immediately after.

2.   In a large bowl, combine the red cabbage, green cabbage, celery, green onion, mayonnaise and the cheese mixture. Season with salt and pepper, if desired.

3.   Toss the coleslaw together.

4.   Chill in the refrigerator for at least 30 minutes before serving.

Did you know?

Cabbage is an excellent source of vitamin K, vitamin C and vitamin B6. It is also a very good source of manganese, dietary fiber, potassium, vitamin B1, folate and copper. Additionally, cabbage is a good source of choline, phosphorus, vitamin B2, magnesium, calcium, selenium, iron, pantothenic acid, protein and niacin.

Fried Zucchini Cakes

INGREDIENTS	Fats	Proteins	Carbs
4 large baby zucchini	0.26 g	1.73 g	1.99 g
1 egg	4.18 g	5.53 g	0.32 g
2 tbsp. desiccated coconut	11.05 g	0.85 g	3.44 g
1/2 tsp garlic powder	0.01 g	0.26 g	1.16 g
1/2 tsp cumin	0.24 g	0.2 g	0.49 g
2 tbsp. butter	23.04 g	0.24 g	0.02 g
1/4 tbsp. sesame seeds	1.22 g	0.41 g	0.23 g
2 tbsp. olive oil	27 g	0 g	0 g
3 tbsp. Italian style hard cheese, grated	4.18 g	4.26 g	2.09 g
1 tbsp. pesto sauce	8.8 g	1.56 g	0.64 g

Nutrition Facts

Amount per 208 g
1 serving (7.3 oz)

Calories 790
From fat 694

Amount	% Daily Value*	Amount	% Daily Value*
Total Fat 79.4g	122%	Total Carbohydrates 10g	3%
Saturated 33.3g	167%	Dietary Fiber 1g	5%
Trans Fat 1.1g		Sugars 0g	
Cholesterol 218mg	73%	Protein 14g	29%
Sodium 664mg	28%		
Calcium 22% • Iron 18%		Vitamin A 31% • Vitamin C 38%	

* Percent Daily Values are based on 2000 calorie diet. Your Daily Values may be higher or lower depending on your calorie needs

Directions:

1.   Using a mandolin slicer, slice the zucchini into very fine strips.

2.   Place the zucchini strips on a clean kitchen towel and squeeze as much excess water as possible. Set aside.

3.   In a large bowl, combine the zucchini strips, egg, desiccated coconut, garlic powder, butter, Italian style hard cheese, cumin, and sesame seeds. Toss together until thoroughly mixed.

4.   Divide the batter into patties of about 3 inches in diameter.

5.   Heat the olive oil in a small frying pan over medium heat.

6.   Put the patties into the frying pan. Cook one side for 6 to 7 minutes, or until it turns a golden brown. Flip and cook on the other side for the same length of time.

7.   Repeat until all patties have been cooked.

8.   Top with pesto sauce. Serve while hot.

Did you know?

Biggest is NOT best. The most flavorful zucchinis are small- to medium-sized and the darker the skin, the richer the nutrients.

DAY 29

Meal	Recipe	Calories
Breakfast	High Protein Green Smoothie	570
Lunch	Simple Greek Salad	675
Dinner	Pesto and Sun-Dried Tomatoes Mug Cake	650

High Protein Green Smoothie

INGREDIENTS	Fats	Proteins	Carbs
1/2 cup spinach	0.06 g	0.43 g	0.54 g
1/4 cup avocado, cubed	5.5 g	0.75 g	3.2 g
2 tbsp. coconut oil	27.2 g	0 g	0 g
1 tsp vanilla extract	0 g	0 g	0.53 g
1/4 cup coconut milk	12.05 g	1.14 g	1.59 g
1/4 cup heavy cream	11.1 g	0.62 g	0.84 g
1 tbsp. protein powder	1.89 g	5.03 g	2.04 g

Nutrition Facts

Amount per 181 g
1 serving (6.4 oz)

Calories 570
From fat 496

Amount	% Daily Value*	Amount	% Daily Value*
Total Fat 57.8g	89%	Total Carbohydrates 9g	3%
Saturated 42.1g	211%	Dietary Fiber 4g	14%
Trans Fat 0g		Sugars 2g	
Cholesterol 43mg	14%	Protein 8g	16%
Sodium 70mg	3%		
Calcium 10% • Iron 19%		Vitamin A 44% • Vitamin C 20%	

* Percent Daily Values are based on 2000 calorie diet. Your Daily Values may be higher or lower depending on your calorie needs.

Directions:

1.   In a blender, combine all the ingredients and add 4 to 5 ice cubes.

2.   Blend until smooth.

3.   Serve and enjoy!

Did you know?

Spinach is best eaten fresh. It loses nutritional properties with each passing day. Although refrigeration slows the deterioration, half of the major nutrients are lost by the eighth day after harvest. (For long term storage, freeze while fresh.) When fresh, it has crisp leaves. As they deteriorate, the leaves turn limp.

Simple Greek Salad

INGREDIENTS	Fats	Proteins	Carbs
1/2 cup cucumber, diced	0.1 g	0.35 g	1.29 g
3/4 cup feta, crumbled	23.94 g	15.99 g	4.6 g
1 tbsp. dill	0.09 g	0.28 g	0.56 g
3 tbsp. olive oil	40.5 g	0 g	0 g
1/4 cup cherry tomatoes	0.07 g	0.33 g	1.45 g
1/2 cup arugula	0.07 g	0.26 g	0.37 g

Nutrition Facts

Amount per 268 g
1 serving (9.4 oz)

Calories 675
From fat 571

Amount	% Daily Value*	Amount	% Daily Value*
Total Fat 64.8g	100%	Total Carbohydrates 8g	3%
Saturated 22.4g	112%	Dietary Fiber 1g	5%
Trans Fat 0g		Sugars 7g	
Cholesterol 100mg	33%	Protein 17g	34%
Sodium 1043mg	43%		
Calcium 60% • Iron 10%		Vitamin A 34% • Vitamin C 26%	

* Percent Daily Values are based on 2000 calorie diet. Your Daily Values may be higher or lower depending on your calorie needs.

Directions:

1.   Combine the cucumber, dill, feta, cherry tomatoes, and arugula in a bowl.

2.   Drizzle with olive oil. Season with salt and pepper, if desired.

3.   Toss lightly and serve.

Did you know?

Because the tomato has seeds and grows from a flowering plant botanically it is classed as a fruit not a vegetable.

Pesto and Sun-Dried Tomatoes Mug Cake

INGREDIENTS	Fats	Proteins	Carbs
1 egg	4.18 g	5.53 g	0.32 g
2 tbsp. butter	23.04 g	0.24 g	0.02 g
1/2 tbsp. almond meal	1.11 g	0.36 g	1.91 g
1/2 tsp baking powder	0.01 g	0 g	1.17 g
4 tbsp. pesto sauce	35.2 g	6.26 g	2.56 g
1/2 tbsp. sun dried tomato	0.48 g	0.17 g	0.79 g
1 tbsp. peanut flour	0.02 g	1.98 g	1.32 g

Nutrition Facts		Amount	% Daily Value*	Amount	% Daily Value*
Amount per 146 g		Total Fat 64g	99%	Total Carbohydrates 8g	3%
1 serving (5.2 oz)		Saturated 22.1g	110%	Dietary Fiber 2g	6%
		Trans Fat 0.9g		Sugars 2g	
Calories 650		Cholesterol 235mg	78%	Protein 15g	29%
From fat 561		Sodium 841mg	35%		
		Calcium 31% • Iron 13%		Vitamin A 34% • Vitamin C 10%	

* Percent Daily Values are based on 2000 calorie diet. Your Daily Values may be higher or lower depending on your calorie needs.

Directions:

1.   In a mug, combine the egg, almond meal, butter, pesto sauce, sun dried tomato, peanut flour and baking powder. Add a pinch of salt, if desired.

2.   Whisk everything together.

3.   Microwave the mug on the highest setting for exactly 75 seconds.

4.   Invert the mug on top of a plate and tap the bottom of the bug until the cake falls off.

5.   Serve while hot.

Did you know?
There are more than 7500 tomato varieties grown around the world.

DAY 30

Meal	Recipe	Calories
Breakfast	Tofu and Mushroom Scramble	688
Lunch	Broccoli and Cauliflower Salad	685
Dinner	Avocado and Lime Coleslaw	524

Tofu and Mushroom Scramble

INGREDIENTS	Fats	Proteins	Carbs
3 tbsp. olive oil	40.5 g	0 g	0 g
1/4 cup firm tofu, diced	5.49 g	9.94 g	2.69 g
1/2 tbsp. green onion, chopped	0.01 g	0.03 g	0.17 g
1/4 cup white mushrooms, chopped	0.08 g	0.74 g	0.78 g
1/4 cup bell pepper, sliced	0.02 g	0.23 g	1.07 g

1/2 cup spinach	0.06 g	0.43 g	0.54 g
1/2 tsp garlic, chopped	0.01 g	0.09 g	0.46 g
1/2 tsp turmeric	0.05 g	0.15 g	1.01 g
1 egg	4.18 g	5.53 g	0.32 g
3 tbsp. heavy cream	16.65 g	0.92 g	1.26 g

Nutrition Facts

Amount per 249 g
1 serving (8.8 oz)

Calories 688
From fat 590

	Amount	% Daily Value*	Amount	% Daily Value*
Total Fat 67.1g		103%	Total Carbohydrates 8g	3%
Saturated 18.2g		91%	Dietary Fiber 3g	10%
Trans Fat 0g			Sugars 3g	
Cholesterol 225mg		75%	Protein 18g	36%
Sodium 104mg		4%		
Calcium 51% • Iron 23%			Vitamin A 53% • Vitamin C 56%	

* Percent Daily Values are based on 2000 calorie diet. Your Daily Values may be higher or lower depending on your calorie needs.

Directions:

1.   In a medium-sized frying pan, heat 2 tbsp. olive oil over high heat.

2.   Add the tofu and white mushrooms to the pan. Cook for 9 to 10 minutes while stirring or until the tofu is firm and the mushrooms has turned light brown. Set aside.

3.   In a small bowl, whisk together the egg and heavy cream. Set aside.

4.   In a medium-sized frying pan, heat the remaining olive oil. Pour in the egg mixture.

5.   Add the turmeric, bell pepper, tofu, and mushrooms. Stir the eggs continuously for a minute.

6.   Add the spinach and green onion. Stir and cook for another minute.

7.   Season with salt and pepper, if desired.

8.   Remove from heat and serve immediately.

Did you know?

The scientific name for bell peppers is Capsicum annum

Broccoli and Cauliflower Salad

INGREDIENTS	Fats	Proteins	Carbs
1 1/4 cup broccoli, chopped	0.25 g	1.59 g	1.43 g
1/2 cup cauliflower, chopped	0.15 g	1.03 g	2.66 g
1/2 tbsp. red onion, chopped	0.01 g	0.06 g	0.47 g
1 tbsp. mayonnaise	10.33 g	0.13 g	0.08 g
1/2 tbsp. red wine vinegar	0 g	0 g	0.02 g
1/2 cup Monterey jack, diced	19.98 g	16.16 g	0.45 g
1 tbsp. olive oil	13.5 g	0 g	0 g
1/2 cup feta, crumbled	15.96 g	10.66 g	3.07 g

Nutrition Facts	Amount	% Daily Value*	Amount	% Daily Value*
Amount per 284 g 1 serving (10 oz)	Total Fat 60.2g	93%	Total Carbohydrates 8g	3%
	Saturated 27.4g	137%	Dietary Fiber 3g	10%
	Trans Fat 0g		Sugars 5g	
Calories 685	Cholesterol 131mg	44%	Protein 30g	59%
From fat 532	Sodium 1205mg	50%		
	Calcium 93% • Iron 13%		Vitamin A 43% • Vitamin C 61%	

*Percent Daily Values are based on 2000 calorie diet. Your Daily Values may be higher or lower depending on your calorie needs.

Directions:

1. Prepare a pot of boiling salted water.

2. Blanch the broccoli and cauliflower for exactly 1 minute. Submerge them immediately in ice water after. Strain on a colander and set aside.

3. In a large bowl, combine the broccoli, cauliflower, red onion, Monterey jack, feta, olive oil, and red vinegar. Sprinkle the feta on top of the salad.

4. Toss the salad thoroughly. Serve immediately.

Did you know?

Broccoli rabe may reduce the number of visits to your derm. The phytochemicals and antioxidants found in green veggies like broccoli rabe can help protect your skin against UV damage by countering free radicals in your body to lessen the deterioration of skin's vital components like collagen and elastin. Say hello to greens and say hello to gorgeous skin!

Avocado and Lime Coleslaw

INGREDIENTS	Fats	Proteins	Carbs
1/4 cup red cabbage, shredded	0.04 g	0.32 g	1.64 g
1/4 cup green cabbage, shredded	0.02 g	0.29 g	1.29 g
1/4 cup cilantro	0.02 g	0.09 g	0.15 g
1/4 cup avocado, sliced	5.35 g	0.73 g	3.11 g
1 tbsp. lime juice	0.01 g	0.06 g	1.27 g
1/4 tbsp. garlic, chopped	0 g	0.04 g	0.23 g
1 tbsp. mayonnaise	4.77 g	0.89 g	0.46 g
1 1/2 tbsp. avocado oil	21 g	0g	0 g
1 tbsp. buttermilk	0.13 g	0.51 g	0.73 g
1 tbsp. blue cheese, crumbled	2.3 g	1.71 g	0.19 g
1 1/2 tbsp. olive oil	20.3 g	0 g	0 g

Nutrition Facts

Amount per 181 g
1 serving (6.4 oz)

Calories 524
From fat 475

	Amount	% Daily Value*	Amount	% Daily Value*
	Total Fat 54g	83%	Total Carbohydrates 9g	3%
	Saturated 8g	40%	Dietary Fiber 4g	15%
	Trans Fat 0g		Sugars 3g	
	Cholesterol 7mg	2%	Protein 5g	9%
	Sodium 252mg	11%		
	Calcium 10% • Iron 4%		Vitamin A 13% • Vitamin C 51%	

* Percent Daily Values are based on 2000 calorie diet. Your Daily Values may be higher or lower depending on your calorie needs.

Directions:

1.   In a microwave-safe bowl, combine the buttermilk and blue cheese. Microwave the mixture on high for 20 seconds.

2.   To the same bowl, add the avocado oil, olive oil, garlic, lime juice, and mayonnaise. Whisk together until thoroughly mixed.

3.   Add the avocado and mash it in with a fork.

4.   In a large bowl, combine the red cabbage, green cabbage, and cilantro.

5.   Drizzle the dressing all over the salad and toss to mix.

6.   Serve immediately.

Did you know?

Avocados contain more fat than any other fruit or vegetable. Also, the trees contain enzymes that prevent the fruit from ever ripening on the tree, allowing farmers to use the trees as storage devices for up to 7 months after they reach full maturity, allowing avocados to always be in season

BOOK 2

KETO VEGETARIAN COOKBOOK

Desserts

COLLECTION OF 90 DELICIOUS DESSERT RECIPES FOR BEGINNERS

INTRODUCTION

KETO VEGETARIAN DESSERTS

In this section of the book, you can learn 90 creative and simple ketogenic vegetarian desserts recipes that will surely satisfy your sweet tooth. 90 delicious and easy recipes in which the macros are indicated for each recipe and respective ingredient, so you will not have a problem following the ketogenic diet. You just have to personalize the recipes according to the calories and macros you need. 90 recipes with ingredients that are easy to source from your preferred groceries store. Very easy step to follow that even someone who don't love cooking will be able to execute. Every ingredients here are mostly plant based that no animals were harm. So happy cooking and enjoy!

Just in case you will need a conversions chart for the ingredients weight

Metric Conversion Chart

Volume Measurements		Weight Measurements		Temperature Conversion	
U.S.	Metric	U.S.	Metric	Fahrenheit	Celsius
1 teaspoon	5 ml	½ ounce	15 g	250	120
1 tablespoon	15 ml	1 ounce	30 g	300	150
¼ cup	60 ml	3 ounces	90 g	325	160
⅓ cup	75 ml	4 ounces	115 g	350	180
½ cup	125 ml	8 ounces	225 g	375	190
⅔ cup	150 ml	12 ounces	350 g	400	200
¾ cup	175 ml	1 pound	450 g	425	220
1 cup	250 ml	2¼ pounds	1 kg	450	230

Equivalents are not exact; figures have been rounded up or down for easier measuring.

By weight, a cup is not the same for all ingredients. Volume equivalents, above, apply to liquids only. Dry ingredients should be weighed and scaled using the following approximate equivalents for 1 cup: all-purpose flour, spooned and leveled (approximately 4½ ounces, 130 g), granulated sugar (approximately 7 ounces, 200 g), packed light brown sugar (approximately 7⅔ ounces, 215 g).

Erin Mira

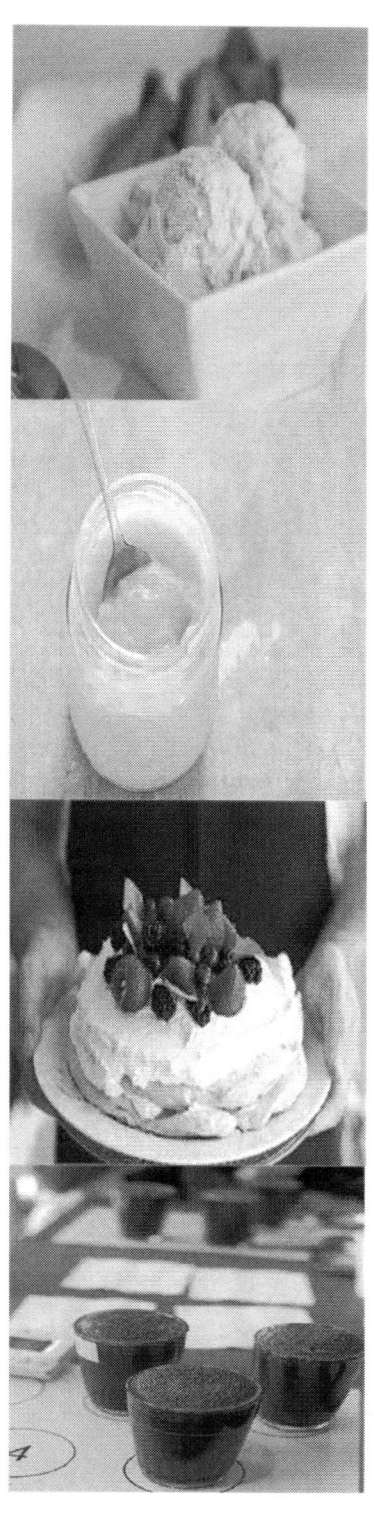

LACTO
OVO

Low-Carb Chocolate

Chip Cookies

INGREDIENTS	Fats	Proteins	Carbs
0.5 cup almond flour	23.72 g	10.05 g	10.24 g
1/4 cup walnuts, chopped	19.11 g	4.46 g	4.02 g
1/2 cup butter	92.06 g	0.96 g	0.07 g
2 eggs	8.37 g	11.05 g	0.63 g
1/8 tsp Stevia (powder)	0 g	0 g	2 g
1 tbsp dark chocolate chips	6.82 g	1.25 g	7.34 g
1/2 tsp salt	0 g	0 g	0 g
1/2 tbsp baking soda	0 g	0 g	0 g
1 tbsp vanilla extract	0.01 g	0.01 g	1.64 g

Total calories: 1536 kcal
Servings: 12

Nutrition Facts

Nutrition Facts	Amount	% Daily Value*	
Amount per 27 g	Total Fat 12.5g	19%	
1 serving (0.9 oz)	Saturated 5.7g	29%	
	Trans Fat 0.3g		
Calories 128	Cholesterol 48mg	16%	
From fat 109	Sodium 266mg	11%	

Amount	% Daily Value*
Total Carbohydrates 2g	1%
Dietary Fiber 1g	3%
Sugars 1g	
Protein 2g	5%

Calcium 2% • Iron 3%   Vitamin A 6% • Vitamin C 0%

* Percent Daily Values are based on a 2000 calorie diet. Your Daily Values may be higher or lower depending on your calorie needs.

Instructions:

1. Preheat oven to 350 F
2. In a medium-sized mixing bowl, combine the almond flour, baking soda, salt and Stevia. Mix thoroughly.
3. In a separate bowl, melt the butter and mix in the vanilla extract, eggs, walnuts, and dark chocolate chips.
4. Fold in the wet ingredients into the dry ingredients. Mix thoroughly until a cohesive dough is formed.
5. Using an ice cream scoop, scoop out six portions of the dough and place flat onto a cookie sheet. Make sure to leave enough allowance between each portion. Flatten out the dough if needed.
6. Bake for 9 to 10 minutes, or until the edges of the cookies have turned brown.
7. Remove from the oven and allow to cool to room temperature on a cooling rack.
8. Serve and enjoy.

No-Bake Mint and

Chocolate Pie

INGREDIENTS	Fats	Proteins	Carbs
1 cup almond flour	47.43 g	20.09 g	20.47 g
1 tbsp cocoa powder	0.71 g	0.98 g	3.15 g
1/4 tsp Stevia (powder)	0 g	0 g	4 g
3 1/2 tbsp butter	40.31 g	0.42 g	0.03 g
1 cup heavy cream	44.4 g	2.46 g	3.35 g
1/2 tbsp vodka, 80 proof	0 g	0 g	0 g

2 tsp gelatin, dry mix	0 g	0.14 g	1.6 g
1/2 tsp peppermint extract	0 g	0.01 g	0.04 g
1 tbsp Stevia	0 g	0 g	4 g
6 large egg yolks	27.07 g	16.18 g	3.66 g

Total calories: 1680 kcal
Servings: 12

Nutrition Facts

Amount per 33 g
1 serving (1.2 oz)

Calories 140
From fat 116

Amount	% Daily Value*	Amount	% Daily Value*
Total Fat 13.3g	20%	**Total Carbohydrates** 3g	1%
Saturated 5.6g	28%	Dietary Fiber 1g	4%
Trans Fat 0.1g		Sugars 1g	
Cholesterol 115mg	38%	**Protein** 3g	7%
Sodium 9mg	0%		
Calcium 4% • **Iron** 3%		**Vitamin A** 7% • **Vitamin C** 0%	

* Percent Daily Values are based on 2000 calorie diet. Your Daily Values may be higher or lower depending on your calorie needs.

Instructions

1. To make the crust, mix together the almond flour, cocoa powder, and 1/4 tsp Stevia.
2. Add in the melted butter and stir until thoroughly combined.
3. Transfer the mixture into a glass or ceramic pie pan. Press into the bottom and sides to form a pie crust.
4. Refrigerate until the filling has been made.
5. Combine the heavy cream and peppermint extract in a medium-sized saucepan. Over medium heat, allow the mixture to simmer.
6. Remove the saucepan from heat and cover with a lid. Set aside.
7. Whisk together the vodka and gelatin in a saucepan. Let stand for one minute, then add the heavy cream mixture. Whisk the gelatin mixture over medium heat until the gelatin is completely dissolved.
8. In a separate bowl, whisk together the egg yolks and 1 tbsp Stevia. While continuing to whisk, slowly pour in 1 cup of the hot cream mixture. When thoroughly mixed, whisk in the egg yolk mixture into the rest of the hot cream. Whisk in medium heat until the mixture slightly thickens, or until a temperate of 160° F is reached.
9. Refrigerate the mixture until cool and a pudding-like consistency has been achieved. To avoid clumps, whisk the mixture after every few minutes while it is cooling.

10. Spread the cooled filling mixture in the prepared crust. Refrigerate the pie for at least 3 hours.

Healthy Vegetarian Cheesecake

INGREDIENTS	Fats	Proteins	Carbs
2 cups cream cheese	158.87 g	27.52 g	18.88 g
1 cup plain yogurt	7.96 g	8.5 g	11.42 g
2 1/2 tsp vanilla extract	0.01 g	0.01 g	1.33 g
2 tbsp lemon juice	0.07 g	0.11 g	2.1 g
1/4 tbsp Stevia (powder)	0 g	0 g	4 g
1 egg	4.18 g	5.53 g	0.32 g

Total calories: 1836 kcal
Servings: 12

Nutrition Facts	Amount	% Daily Value*	Amount	% Daily Value*
	Total Fat 14.3g	22%	Total Carbohydrates 3g	1%
Amount per 67 g	Saturated 8g	40%	Dietary Fiber 0g	0%
1 serving (2.3 oz)	Trans Fat 0g		Sugars 2g	
	Cholesterol 59mg	20%	Protein 3g	7%
Calories 153	Sodium 156mg	7%		
From fat 125	Calcium 7% • Iron 1%		Vitamin A 11% • Vitamin C 2%	

* Percent Daily Values are based on 2000 calorie diet. Your Daily Values may be higher or lower depending on your calorie needs.

Instructions:
1. Preheat oven to 350 F.

2. Fill a baking pan halfway with water and place it on the oven's lower rack.
3. In a large bowl, combine the cream cheese, yogurt, egg, vanilla extract, lemon juice, and Stevia sweetener.
4. Using a hand blender, beat all the ingredients just until smooth. Be careful not to overbeat so you do not add unnecessary air into the mixture.
5. Transfer the cheesecake mix into a 9-inch springform pan. Smooth the top with a spatula.
6. Bake the cheesecake in the oven (place on middle tray) for 30 minutes, making sure not to open the oven door.
7. Leave in the open for an additional 5 minutes with the oven door still closed.
8. Remove the cheesecake from the oven and let cool for 20 minutes.
9. Cool the cheesecake in the fridge for at least 6 hours before serving.

Vanilla Keto Ice Cream

INGREDIENTS	Fats	Proteins	Carbs
4 whole eggs	16.74 g	22.11 g	1.27 g

1/4 tsp lemon juice	0 g	0 g	0.09 g
1/4 tbsp Stevia (powder)	0 g	0 g	4 g
1 1/4 cup heavy whipping cream	55.5 g	3.08 g	4.19 g
1 tbsp vanilla extract	0.01 g	0.01 g	1.64 g

Total calories: 810 kcal
Servings: 6

Nutrition Facts

Amount per 57 g
1 serving (2 oz)

Calories 135
From fat 107

Amount	% Daily Value*	Amount	% Daily Value*
Total Fat 12g	19%	Total Carbohydrates 2g	1%
Saturated 6.7g	33%	Dietary Fiber 0g	0%
Trans Fat 0g		Sugars 1g	
Cholesterol 143mg	48%	Protein 4g	8%
Sodium 51mg	2%		
Calcium 3% • Iron 3%		Vitamin A 11% • Vitamin C	0%

* Percent Daily Values are based on 2000 calorie diet. Your Daily Values may be higher or lower depending on your calorie needs.

Instructions

1. Separate the egg whites from the egg yolks.

2. Whisk the egg white and slowly add in the lemon juice.

3. When the egg white has started to stiffen, add the Stevia.

4. Continue whisking until you get stiff peaks.

5. In a separate bowl, start whisking the heavy whipping cream.
6. Continue whisking until you get soft peaks.
7. In another bowl, combine the egg yolks and the vanilla extract.
8. Gradually fold the whisked egg whites into the whipped cream. Add the egg yolk mixture and gently fold the whole mixture until it is well-combined.
9. Transfer the mixture into a freezer-friendly container and freeze for 2 to 4 hours.
10. The ice cream is ready to serve. It can be kept in the freezer up to 3 months.

No-Crust Cream Cheese Pie

INGREDIENTS	Fats	Proteins	Carbs
1 1/2 cup cream cheese	119.16 g	20.64 g	14.16 g
4 eggs	16.74 g	22.11 g	1.27 g
1/2 tsp Stevia	0 g	0 g	4 g
1 tbsp vanilla extract	0.01 g	0.01 g	1.64 g
1/4 tsp lemon juice	0 g	0 g	0.09 g
1 1/2 cup plain yogurt	11.94 g	12.75 g	17.13 g
1 tsp vanilla extract	0 g	0 g	0.53 g
1/4 tsp nutmeg, ground	0.73 g	0.12 g	0.99 g
1/4 tsp Stevia (powder)	0 g	0 g	4 g

Total calories: 1728 kcal
Servings: 12

Nutrition Facts

Amount per 77 g
1 serving (2.7 oz)

Calories 144
From fat 109

Amount	% Daily Value*	Amount	% Daily Value*
Total Fat 12.4g	19%	Total Carbohydrates 4g	1%
Saturated 6.7g	34%	Dietary Fiber 0g	0%
Trans Fat 0g		Sugars 3g	
Cholesterol 90mg	30%	Protein 5g	9%
Sodium 141mg	6%		
Calcium 7% • Iron 2%		Vitamin A 10% • Vitamin C 0%	

* Percent Daily Values are based on 2000 calorie diet. Your Daily Values may be higher or lower depending on your calorie needs.

Instructions:
1. Preheat oven to 325 F.

2. In a medium-sized bowl, whisk the cream cheese until smooth. Add the Stevia and 1 egg and mix again.

3. Add the remaining eggs one at a time while continuing mixing, ensuring that the eggs are well-incorporated at every step.

4. Add 1 tbsp vanilla extract and 1/4 tsp lemon juice and mix again.
5. Continue mixing until all ingredients are well-incorporated.

6. Coat the bottom of a pie plate with baking spray and pour in the cream cheese mixture.

7. Bake for 30 minutes.
8. Remove the pie from the oven and let cool for 30 minutes.
9. To make the topping, combine the yogurt, 1 tsp vanilla extract, and 1/4 tsp Stevia in a medium-sized bowl.
10. Mix all ingredients together until they are well-incorporated.
11. Spread on top of the cream cheese base. Sprinkle freshly grated nutmeg on top of the pie.
12. Put the pie back into the oven and bake for an additional 15 to 20 minutes, or until the topping has set.
13. Remove the pie from the oven and cool at room temperature for 30 minutes.
14. Chill the pie in the refrigerator overnight. Serve the next day.

Quick and Easy Coffee Pudding

INGREDIENTS	Fats	Proteins	Carbs
1 cup cream cheese	79.44 g	13.76 g	9.44 g
1/4 cup butter	46. 07 g	0.48 g	0.03 g
1 tbsp espresso powder	0.02 g	0.37 g	2.26 g
4 eggs	16.74 g	22.11 g	1.27 g
1/2 tsp Stevia (powder)	0 g	0 g	4 g

Total calories: 1450 kcal
Servings: 10

Nutrition Facts	Amount	% Daily Value*	Amount	% Daily Value*
Amount per 47 g 1 serving (1.7 oz)	**Total Fat** 14.2g	22%	**Total Carbohydrates** 2g	1%
	Saturated 7.9g	40%	Dietary Fiber 0g	0%
	Trans Fat 0.2g		Sugars 1g	
Calories 146 From fat 125	**Cholesterol** 103mg	34%	**Protein** 4g	7%
	Sodium 110mg	5%		
	Calcium 3% • **Iron** 2%		**Vitamin A** 11% • **Vitamin C** 0%	

*Percent Daily Values are based on 2000 calorie diet. Your Daily Values may be higher or lower depending on your calorie needs.

Instructions

1. Separate the egg whites and the egg yolks.

2. In a saucepan, melt together the cream cheese and butter on low heat.

3. Gradually whisk in the espresso powder and the egg yolks.
4. Continue cooking on low heat while stirring occasionally until the custard thickens.

5. Remove the custard from heat and add the Stevia powder.

6. In a separate bowl, beat the egg whites until stiff peaks form.

7. Fold the egg whites into the custard mix.

8. Chill the custard for at least 2 hours before serving. Cloud

Cake with Espresso Buttercream Filling

INGREDIENTS	Fats	Proteins	Carbs
2 eggs	8.37 g	11.05 g	0.63 g
1 cup cream cheese	79.44 g	13.76 g	9.44 g
1/4 tbsp vanilla extract	0 g	0 g	0.42 g
1/4 tsp Stevia (powder)	0 g	0 g	4 g
1/2 tsp salt	0 g	0 g	0 g
2 tbsp butter	23.04 g	0.24 g	0.02 g
1/2 cup cream cheese	39.72 g	6.88 g	4.72 g
1/4 tsp Stevia (powder)	0 g	0 g	4 g
1/2 tbsp espresso powder	0.01 g	0.18 g	1.13 g

Total calories: 1536 kcal
Servings: 12

Nutrition Facts	Amount	% Daily Value*	Amount	% Daily Value*
Amount per 40 g 1 serving (1.4 oz)	**Total Fat** 12.6g	19%	**Total Carbohydrates** 2g	1%
	Saturated 7g	35%	Dietary Fiber 0g	0%
	Trans Fat 0.1g		Sugars 1g	
Calories 128 From fat 110	**Cholesterol** 64mg	21%	**Protein** 3g	5%
	Sodium 165mg	7%		
	Calcium 3% • Iron 1%		Vitamin A 10% • Vitamin C 0%	

* Percent Daily Values are based on 2000 calorie diet. Your Daily Values may be higher or lower depending on your calorie needs

Instructions
1. Preheat oven to 300 F.
2. Line a baking pan with parchment paper.
3. Separate the egg whites from the egg yolks.
4. In a medium-sized bowl, combine 1 cup of cream cheese with 1/2 tsp Stevia, salt, and the egg yolks. Blend with an electric mixer until thoroughly combined.
5. In a separate bowl, whisk the egg whites until you get stiff peaks.
6. Gradually fold the egg whites into the egg yolk mixture. Do not overmix as you want to preserve the volume of the egg whites.
7. Divide the mixture into 4 portions and spoon each portion in the baking pan. Flatten each mound using the back of a spoon.
8. Bake in the oven for about 25 minutes.
9. Transfer the cloud cakes to a cooling rack and allow to cool for the rest of the day.
10. To make the frosting, whip the remaining cream cheese, Stevia, and espresso powder together in a small mixing bowl until fluffy.
11. Assemble the cake by frosting the top of each layer and stacking them on top of one another.
12. Garnish on top some fruits (optional)
13. Slice into individual portions and serve.

Keto Gingerbread Cookies

INGREDIENTS	Fats	Proteins	Carbs
1 egg	8.37 g	11.05 g	0.63 g

1/2 cup butter	92.06 g	0.96 g	0.07 g
2 tbsp desiccated coconut	22.11 g	1.70 g	6.89 g
1/4 cup almond flour	11.88 g	5.03 g	5.13 g
1 tbsp baking powder	0.06 g	0.02 g	7.04 g
1/4 tsp allspice, ground	0.04 g	0.03 g	0.36 g
1/4 tbsp Stevia (powder)	0 g	0 g	4 g
1 tsp ginger, grated	0.02 g	0.04 g	0.36 g
1/2 tsp cinnamon powder	0.02 g	0.05 g	1.05 g
1/4 tsp nutmeg, ground	0.22 g	0.04 g	0.30 g
1 egg yolk	4.51 g	2.7 g	0.61 g

Total calories: 1368 kcal
Servings: 12

Nutrition Facts

Amount per 25 g
1.33 serving (0.9 oz)

Calories 114
From fat 101

Amount	% Daily Value*	Amount	% Daily Value*
Total Fat 11.6g	18%	Total Carbohydrates 2g	1%
Saturated 6.9g	35%	Dietary Fiber 0g	2%
Trans Fat 0.3g		Sugars 0g	
Cholesterol 63mg	21%	Protein 2g	4%
Sodium 14mg	1%		
Calcium 7% • Iron 3%		Vitamin A 6% • Vitamin C 0%	

* Percent Daily Values are based on 2000 calorie diet. Your Daily Values may be higher or lower depending on your calorie needs.

Directions:
1. In a medium-sized bowl, combine the butter, Stevia and 1 whole egg. Whisk together until well-combined.
2. In a separate bowl, mix together the desiccated coconut, almond flour, baking powder, allspice, ginger, cinnamon, and nutmeg. Mix the dry ingredients until uniform in composition. Add the egg yolk and mix lightly.
3. Add the butter mixture into the dry ingredients. Mix lightly using a spatula. Pour the mixture into a sheet of plastic wrap and close tightly.
4. Refrigerate the cookie batter for 1 hour.
5. Preheat the oven to 335 F.
6. Take the cookie batter out of the refrigerator and roll out using a rolling pin until thickness is reduced to about 5 mm.
7. Cut out individual cookies using your cookie cutter of choice. You should have enough batter to make 15 to 18 cookies.

8. Place the cookies on a baking tray lined with parchment paper and bake in the oven for 10-12 minutes. The cookies should be firm but not dry.
9. Allow the cookies to cool on a cooling rack before serving

Keto Lemon Curd

INGREDIENTS	Fats	Proteins	Carbs
3 eggs	12.55 g	16.58 g	0.95 g
1 egg yolk	4.51 g	2.7 g	0.61 g
4 lemons	0.46 g	0.67 g	13.25 g
1/4 tbsp Stevia (powder)	0 g	0 g	4 g
1/2 cup butter	92.06 g	0.96 g	0.07 g

Total calories: 1104 kcal
Servings: 12

Nutrition Facts	Amount	% Daily Value*	Amount	% Daily Value*
	Total Fat 9.1g	14%	Total Carbohydrates 2g	1%
Amount per 38 g	Saturated 5.3g	27%	Dietary Fiber 0g	0%
1 serving (1.3 oz)	Trans Fat 0.3g		Sugars 0g	
	Cholesterol 77mg	26%	Protein 2g	3%
Calories 92	Sodium 17mg	1%		
From fat 81	Calcium 1% • Iron 1%		Vitamin A 6% • Vitamin C 10%	

* Percent Daily Values are based on 2000 calorie diet. Your Daily Values may be higher or lower depending on your calorie needs.

Directions:

1. Squeeze the lemons into a medium-sized glass or stainless-steel bowl. Zest the skin and add to the lemon juice.

2. Add in the Stevia and butter.

3. Set the bowl over a pot of simmering water. Make sure that the bowl does not come into contact with the water surface.

4. Stir the mixture until the butter has completely melted.

5. In a separate bowl, whisk together all the eggs along with the egg yolk.

6. While whisking the lemon mixture, gradually add in the eggs. Keep stirring until all the eggs have been added.

7. Continue whisking for about 10 minutes or until the mixture is thick enough to coat the back of a spoon.

8. Remove from the heat and transfer the lemon curd into airtight sterilized jars.

9. Cool the lemon curd in the refrigerator. It will keep for up to 2 weeks.

Low-Carb Cinnamon Donuts

INGREDIENTS	Fats	Proteins	Carbs
1/4 cup heavy whipping cream	11.1 g	0.62 g	0.84 g
1/4 cup sour cream	6.1 g	2.01 g	4.08 g
4 eggs	16.74 g	22.11 g	1.27 g
1/2 cup desiccated coconut	13.82 g	1.06 g	4.3 g
1/4 tsp baking soda	0 g	0 g	0 g
1/4 tsp Stevia (powder)	0 g	0 g	4 g
1/4 tsp nutmeg	0.22 g	0.04 g	0.3 g
1/4 tsp salt	0 g	0 g	0 g
1/4 tsp Stevia	0 g	0 g	4 g
1 tsp cinnamon	0.03 g	0.1 g	2.1 g
1/2 cup coconut oil	109 g	0 g	0 g

Total calories: 1170 kcal
Servings: 10

Nutrition Facts	Amount	% Daily Value*	Amount	% Daily Value*
Amount per 42 g 1 serving (1.5 oz)	Total Fat 12g	18%	Total Carbohydrates 2g	1%
	Saturated 9.2g	46%	Dietary Fiber 0g	1%
	Trans Fat 0g		Sugars 0g	
Calories 117	Cholesterol 60mg	20%	Protein 2g	4%
From fat 104	Sodium 112mg	5%		
	Calcium 2% • Iron 2%		Vitamin A 3% • Vitamin C 1%	

* Percent Daily Values are based on 2000 calorie diet. Your Daily Values may be higher or lower depending on your calorie needs.

Directions:

1. Preheat the oven to 355 F.

2. In a large bowl, combine the heavy whipping cream, sour cream, eggs, and vanilla extract.

3. While continuously mixing, gradually add in the dry ingredients – desiccated coconut, baking soda, 1/4 tsp Stevia, nutmeg, and salt.

4. Pour the batter into a donut pan, filling up only each mold is 3/4 full.

5. Bake the donuts in the oven for 10 to 15 minutes, or until the donuts develop a firm exterior.

6. Remove the donuts from the oven and allow to cool for about 15 minutes

7. In a frying pan, heat the coconut oil over high heat.

8. Fry each donut on the coconut oil for 2 minutes on each side.

9. In a shallow plate, combine the cinnamon and 1/4 tsp Stevia.

10. Roll the fried donuts in the cinnamon mixture. You may coat only one or both sides of each donut depending on preference.

High Protein French Toast Cookies

INGREDIENTS	Fats	Proteins	Carbs
1 cup almond flour	47.43 g	20.09 g	20.47 g
1/2 cup butter	92.06 g	0.96 g	0.07 g
2 eggs	8.37 g	11.05 g	0.63 g
1/4 tsp Stevia (powder)	0 g	0 g	4 g
1/2 tsp baking soda	0 g	0 g	0 g
1/4 tsp salt	0 g	0 g	0 g
1 tsp vanilla extract	0 g	0 g	0.53 g
1 tsp cinnamon	0.03 g	0.1 g	2.1 g
1 tbsp walnuts, chopped	4.63 g	2.44 g	2.19 g
1 1/2 scoops protein powder	4.5 g	18.75 g	8.25 g

Total calories: 1712 kcal
Servings: 16

Nutrition Facts	Amount	% Daily Value*	Amount	% Daily Value*
Amount per 22 g	**Total Fat** 9.8g	15%	**Total Carbohydrates** 2g	1%
1 serving (0.8 oz)	Saturated 4.1g	20%	Dietary Fiber 1g	4%
	Trans Fat 0.2g		Sugars 0g	
Calories 107	**Cholesterol** 36mg	12%	**Protein** 3g	7%
From fat 85	**Sodium** 127mg	5%		
	Calcium 5% • **Iron** 4%		**Vitamin A** 6% • **Vitamin C** 2%	

* Percent Daily Values are based on 2000 calorie diet. Your Daily Values may be higher or lower depending on your calorie needs.

Directions:

1. Preheat the oven to 355 F.

2. Place the butter on a microwave-safe bowl and melt in the microwave for 30 seconds.

3. In a large mixing bowl, combine the melted butter with the Stevia. Add the vanilla extract and eggs. Mix until just well-combined.

4. Add the almond baking, baking soda, and salt. Mix until well-combined.

5. Cool the batter in the refrigerator for 20 minutes.

6. Remove the batter from the fridge and divide into 12 equal portions. Roll each portion into a ball and roll each ball on the powdered cinnamon.

7. Place the balled dough into a baking tray, leaving enough space for expansion during baking.

8. Bake the cookies for 10 minutes.

9. Remove from the oven and place on a cooling rack. Let the cookies cool for at least 10 minutes before serving. They can also be kept in an airtight container and refrigerated.

High-Protein Peanut and Chocolate Cookies

INGREDIENTS	Fats	Proteins	Carbs
3/4 cup peanut flour	0.25 g	23.49 g	15.62 g
1/4 cup chunky peanut butter	33.2 g	16.81 g	11.41 g
4 egg whites	0.22 g	14.39 g	0.96 g
2 1/2 scoops protein powder	7.5 g	31.25 g	13.75 g
1 tsp vanilla extract	0 g	0 g	0.53 g
1/4 tsp Stevia (powder)	0 g	0 g	4 g
2 tbsp dark chocolate chips	13.64 g	2.49 g	14.69 g
1 cup butter	184.12 g	1.93 g	0.14 g

Total calories: 2680 kcal
Servings: 20

Nutrition Facts	Amount	% Daily Value*	Amount	% Daily Value*
	Total Fat 12g	18%	**Total Carbohydrates** 3g	1%
Amount per 29 g	Saturated 6.5g	33%	Dietary Fiber 1g	3%
1 serving (1 oz)	Trans Fat 0.4g		Sugars 1g	
	Cholesterol 25mg	8%	**Protein** 5g	9%
Calories 134	**Sodium** 36mg	2%		
From fat 105	**Calcium** 5% • **Iron** 7%		**Vitamin A** 10% • **Vitamin C** 2%	

* Percent Daily Values are based on 2000 calorie diet. Your Daily Values may be higher or lower depending on your calorie needs.

Directions:

1. Preheat the oven at 350 F.

2. In a large bowl, combine the peanut flour, Stevia, and protein powder. Mix well.

3. In a separate bowl, combine the butter, vanilla extract, egg whites, and chunky peanut butter. Whisk together until smooth.

4. Combine the wet ingredients into the dry ingredients. Mix until well-combined.

5. Gently fold in the dark chocolate chips into the dough.

6. Prepare a baking tray by lining with parchment paper.

7. Drop spoon full of dough into the cookies sheet. Slightly flatten the dough, making sure to leave space for the cookie to expand.

8. Bake for 10 minutes or until the outside of the cookies have become firm.

9. Remove from the oven and transfer to a cooling rack.

10. Cool for at least 20 minutes before serving.

Easy Vanilla Mug Cake

INGREDIENTS	Fats	Proteins	Carbs
1 egg	23.11 g	30.52 g	1.75 g
1/4 cup almond flour	11.88 g	5.03 g	5.13 g
2 tbsp desiccated coconut	0.06 g	0.22 g	1.11 g
1 1/2 tbsp butter	17.28 g	0.18 g	0.01 g
1/4 tsp baking powder	0.01 g	0 g	0.61 g
1 tsp vanilla extract	0 g	0 g	0.53 g
1/4 tsp Stevia (powder)	0 g	0 g	4 g

Total calories: 987 kcal

Servings: 3

Nutrition Facts

Amount per   164 g
1 serving (5.8 oz)

Calories   329
From fat   230

Amount	% Daily Value*	Amount	% Daily Value*
Total Fat 26.2g	40%	Total Carbohydrates 7g	2%
Saturated 9.7g	49%	Dietary Fiber 2g	7%
Trans Fat 0.4g		Sugars 2g	
Cholesterol 475mg	158%	Protein 18g	36%
Sodium 258mg	11%		
Calcium 14% • Iron 15%		Vitamin A 18% • Vitamin C 1%	

* Percent Daily Values are based on 2000 calorie diet. Your Daily Values may be higher or lower depending on your calorie needs.

Directions:
1. Combine all the ingredients in a blender. Blend together until smooth.
2. Transfer the mixture into microwaveable mugs, filling each one halfway. Microwave on high for 90 seconds.

Healthy Carrot Cake with High-Protein Frosting

INGREDIENTS	Fats	Proteins	Carbs
1 medium-sized carrot, grated	0.15 g	0.15 g	5.84 g
1/4 tsp Stevia (powder)	0 g	0 g	4 g

1 tsp baking powder	0.02 g	0.01 g	2.35 g
1/4 tsp salt	0 g	0 g	0 g
1 cup coconut milk	48.21 g	4.57 g	6.35 g
1 egg	4.18 g	5.53 g	0.32 g
1 tsp vanilla extract	0 g	0 g	0.53 g
1 cup butter	184.12 g	1.93 g	0.14 g
2 scoops protein powder	6 g	25 g	11 g
1 1/2 tbsp butter	17.28 g	0.18 g	0.01 g
1/4 tsp Stevia (powder)	0 g	0 g	4 g
1/2 cup coconut milk	24.1 g	2.28 g	3.18 g

Total calories: 2748 kcal
Servings: 12

Nutrition Facts

Amount per 63 g
1 serving (2.2 oz)

Calories 229
From fat 206

Amount	% Daily Value*	Amount	% Daily Value*
Total Fat 23.7g	36%	Total Carbohydrates 3g	1%
Saturated 16.1g	81%	Dietary Fiber 0g	1%
Trans Fat 0.7g		Sugars 0g	
Cholesterol 59mg	20%	Protein 3g	7%
Sodium 85mg	4%		
Calcium 8% • Iron 9%		Vitamin A 31% • Vitamin C 4%	

* Percent Daily Values are based on 2000 calorie diet. Your Daily Values may be higher or lower depending on your calorie needs

Directions:
1. Preheat the oven to 350 F.
2. In a small bowl, whisk together 1 cup coconut milk, vanilla extract, 1 cup butter, and egg.
3. In a separate bowl, combine the grated carrots, 1/4 tsp Stevia, salt, and baking powder. Mix until well-combined.
4. Gradually add the wet ingredients into the dry ingredients while mixing continuously. Continue to mix the batter until all components have been thoroughly combined.
5. Prepare a deep baking tray by lining it with parchment paper.
6. Pour the batter into the baking tray.
7. Bake in the oven for 25 to 30 minutes, or until a toothpick stuck into the center comes out clean.
8. Meanwhile, prepare the frosting by combining the protein powder, remaining butter, remaining Stevia, and 1/2 cup coconut milk. Whisk this mixture until its volume has somewhat increased.
9. Refrigerate the frosting for at least an hour.

10. Remove the carrot cake from the oven and allow to cool for at least an hour.
11. When the cake has completely cooled, apply the frosting at the top using a spatula. Serve immediately.

Keto Pumpkin Cake

INGREDIENTS	Fats	Proteins	Carbs
2 tbsp butter	23.04 g	0.24 g	0.02 g
2 scoops protein powder	6 g	25 g	11 g
1 tsp baking powder	0.02 g	0.01 g	2.35 g
1/4 tsp Stevia (powder)	0 g	0 g	4 g
2 eggs	8.37 g	11.05 g	0.63 g
1 tsp vanilla extract	0 g	0 g	0.53 g
1 cup pumpkin puree	0.23 g	2.32 g	15.08 g
1/2 tsp cinnamon	0.02 g	0.05 g	1.05 g
1/4 tsp allspice	0.04 g	0.03 g	0.36 g
1/4 tsp nutmeg	0.22 g	0.04 g	0.3 g
1/4 tsp salt	0 g	0 g	0 g
1/4 tsp ginger	0 g	0.01 g	0.09 g
1 1/2 cups almond flour	71.15 g	30.14 g	30.71 g

Total calories: 1560 kcal
Servings: 12

Nutrition Facts		
Amount per 47 g 1 serving (1.6 oz)		
Calories 120 From fat 78		

Amount	% Daily Value*	Amount	% Daily Value*
Total Fat 9.1g	14%	Total Carbohydrates 6g	2%
Saturated 2g	10%	Dietary Fiber 2g	7%
Trans Fat 0.1g		Sugars 1g	
Cholesterol 33mg	11%	Protein 6g	11%
Sodium 85mg	4%		
Calcium 11% • Iron 7%		Vitamin A 38% • Vitamin C 6%	

* Percent Daily Values are based on 2000 calorie diet. Your Daily Values may be higher or lower depending on your calorie needs.

Directions:
1. In a large bowl, combine the protein powder, baking powder, Stevia, cinnamon, allspice, nutmeg, salt, ginger, and almond flour. Stir thoroughly until all ingredients are well-distributed.
2. In a separate bowl, combine butter, eggs, vanilla extract, and pumpkin puree. Stir thoroughly.
3. Add the wet ingredients to the dry ingredients. Stir until there are no more lumps and the batter is uniform in texture and composition.
4. Transfer the batter to a deep microwave-safe dish.
5. Microwave on high for 4 minutes.
6. Remove from the microwave and let the cake cool for at least 10 minutes.
7. Slice into individual portions and serve while still warm.

Bulletproof Hot Chocolate

INGREDIENTS	Fats	Proteins	Carbs
1/2 cup coconut milk	24.1 g	2.28 g	3.18 g
1 tbsp unsweetened cocoa powder	11.93 g	3.03 g	9.05 g
1 tsp vanilla extract	0 g	0 g	0.14 g
1/16 tsp Stevia (powder)	0 g	0 g	2 g
1 tbsp heavy cream	5.55 g	0.31 g	0.42 g
2 tbsp coconut oil	27.2 g	0 g	0 g
2 scoops protein powder	6 g	25 g	11g

Total calories: 828 kcal
Servings: 4

Nutrition Facts

Amount per 58 g
1 serving (2.1 oz)

Calories 207
From fat 160

Amount	% Daily Value*	Amount	% Daily Value*
Total Fat 18.7g	29%	Total Carbohydrates 6g	2%
Saturated 13.8g	69%	Dietary Fiber 1g	6%
Trans Fat 0g		Sugars 1g	
Cholesterol 6mg	2%	Protein 8g	15%
Sodium 37mg	2%		
Calcium 16% • Iron 15%		Vitamin A 10% • Vitamin C 9%	

* Percent Daily Values are based on 2000 calorie diet. Your Daily Values may be higher or lower depending on your calorie needs.

Directions:

1. In a blender, combine the cocoa powder, coconut oil, coconut milk, vanilla extract, Stevia, and protein powder. Add 1 cup of hot water.

2. Blend until smooth

3. Pour the hot chocolate into individual cups.

4. In a small bowl, whip the heavy cream until its volume has increased.

5. Top the hot chocolate with the heavy whipped cream. Serve while hot.

217

Keto Chocolate Torte

INGREDIENTS	Fats	Proteins	Carbs
5 eggs	20.92 g	27.63 g	1.58 g
1 1/2 cups unsweetened baking chocolate	103.57 g	28.35 g	56.27 g
12 tbsp butter	138.21 g	1.45 g	0.1 g
1/2 tsp Stevia (powder)	0 g	0 g	8 g
1/4 tsp salt	0 g	0 g	0 g
1 tsp vanilla extract	0 g	0 g	0.53 g
2 scoops protein powder	6 g	25 g	11 g

Total calories: 3012 kcal
Servings: 12

Nutrition Facts

Amount per 54 g
1 serving (1.9 oz)

Calories 251
From fat 199

	Amount	% Daily Value*	Amount	% Daily Value*
Total Fat 22.4g		34%	Total Carbohydrates 6g	2%
Saturated 13.2g		66%	Dietary Fiber 3g	11%
Trans Fat 0.5g			Sugars 0g	
Cholesterol 99mg		33%	Protein 7g	14%
Sodium 90mg		4%		
Calcium 8% • Iron 21%			Vitamin A 12% • Vitamin C	3%

* Percent Daily Values are based on 2000 calorie diet. Your Daily Values may be higher or lower depending on your calorie needs.

Directions:
1. Preheat the oven to 300 F.
2. Place the baking chocolate in a heatproof bowl and melt over a double boiler. Add the butter and mix with the chocolate as it melts.
3. Set aside the melted chocolate and allow to cool.
4. In a separate bowl, beat the eggs together with the Stevia using a handheld mixer.
5. To the egg mixture, add the salt, vanilla, and protein powder. Continue beating until all well-mixed.
6. While beating at slow speed, slowly add the melted chocolate to the egg mixture.

7. Prepare a 9-inch springform pan by lining the bottom with parchment paper.
8. Pour the cake batter into the springform pan and bake in the oven for 45 to 55 minutes, or until a toothpick inserted into the center comes out moist but not sticky.
9. Remove the cake from the oven and allow to cool before releasing from the springform panL

Low-Carb Oopsie Rolls

INGREDIENTS	Fats	Proteins	Carbs
4 eggs	16.74 g	22.11 g	1.27 g
1 1/2 cups cream cheese	102.96 g	25.56 g	12.6 g
1/4 tsp salt	0 g	0 g	0 g
1/16 tsp Stevia (powder)	0 g	0 g	2 g
1/8 tsp cream of tartar	0 g	0 g	0.25 g

Total calories: 1312 kcal
Servings: 16

Nutrition Facts	Amount	% Daily Value*	Amount	% Daily Value*
	Total Fat 7.5g	11%	Total Carbohydrates 1g	0%
	Saturated 4.4g	22%	Dietary Fiber 0g	0%
Amount per 34 g	Trans Fat 0g		Sugars 1g	
1 serving (1.2 oz)	Cholesterol 61mg	20%	Protein 3g	6%
	Sodium 150mg	6%		
Calories 82	Calcium 2% • Iron 3%		Vitamin A 6% • Vitamin C	0%
From fat 67	* Percent Daily Values are based on 2000 calorie diet. Your Daily Values may be higher or lower depending on your calorie needs.			

Directions:

1. Preheat the oven to 300 F.

2. Separate the egg yolks from the egg whites and place them in separate bowls.

3. Beat the egg whites using a handheld mixer until stiff peaks the volume has doubled.

4. Add cream of tartar to the egg whites and continue beating until stiff peaks form.

5. Add the cream cheese and salt to the bowl with the egg yolks.

6. Beat the egg yolks and cream cheese until the mixture has doubled in volume.

7. Gently fold the egg whites into the cream cheese mixture.

8. Prepare a cookie sheet by lining it with parchment paper. Place dollops of the dough into the cookie sheet.

9. Bake the oopsie rolls for 25 to 30 minutes, or until they have turned golden and firm.

10. Transfer the oopsie rolls to a wire rack and let them cool before serving.

High-Protein Coconut Macaroons

INGREDIENTS	Fats	Proteins	Carbs
1 cup desiccated coconut	69.08 g	5.3 g	21.52 g
1 cup almond flour	47.43 g	20.09 g	20.47 g
2 eggs	8.37 g	11.05 g	0.63 g
1/4 tsp Stevia (powder)	0 g	0 g	4 g
1/4 tsp vanilla extract	0 g	0 g	0.14 g
1/4 tsp salt	0 g	0 g	0 g
3 tbsp coconut oil	40.8 g	0 g	0 g
3 scoops protein powder	9 g	37.5 g	16.5 g

Total calories: 2016 kcal
Servings: 24

Nutrition Facts	Amount	% Daily Value*	Amount	% Daily Value*
	Total Fat 7.3g	11%	Total Carbohydrates 3g	1%
	Saturated 4.3g	22%	Dietary Fiber 1g	2%
Amount per 17 g	Trans Fat 0g		Sugars 0g	
1 serving (0.6 oz)	Cholesterol 14mg	5%	Protein 3g	6%
	Sodium 39mg	2%		
Calories 84				
From fat 62	Calcium 5% • Iron 4%		Vitamin A 3% • Vitamin C 2%	

* Percent Daily Values are based on 2000 calorie diet. Your Daily Values may be higher or lower depending on your calorie needs.

Directions:

1. Preheat the oven to 350 F.

2. Prepare a baking sheet by lining it with parchment paper.

3. In a food processor, combine the desiccated coconut, almond flour, eggs, coconut oil, and protein powder. Pulse until all elements are well-incorporated and a smooth batter is formed.

4. Add the Stevia, vanilla extract, and coconut oil. Pulse again.

5. If the batter is too lumpy, you may add up to 1/2 cup of water.

6. Form the dough into balls and place on the baking sheet. Press down on each ball of dough to form a cookie shape.

7. Bake the cookies in the oven for 8 minutes. At this point, you need to rotate the baking tray and continue baking for another 4 minutes.

8. Remove the cookies from the oven and cool on a wire rack. The cookies can be served warm or chilled.

LACTO

Keto Avocado Popsicles

INGREDIENTS	Fats	Proteins	Carbs
1/2 avocado	14.73 g	2.01 g	8.57 g
2 tbsp lime juice	0.02 g	0.13 g	2.55 g
1/4 tsp Stevia (powder)	0 g	0 g	4 g
1/2 cup coconut milk	24.1 g	2.28 g	3.18 g
1 tbsp coconut oil	13.6 g	0 g	0 g
1/2 tbsp dark chocolate chips	3.41 g	0.62 g	3.67 g
2.5 scoops protein powder	7.5 g	31.25 g	13.75 g

Total calories: 920 kcal
Servings: 8

Nutrition Facts

Amount per 43 g
0.25 servings (1.5 oz)

Calories 115
From fat 82

Amount	% Daily Value*	Amount	% Daily Value*
Total Fat 9.6g	15%	Total Carbohydrates 4g	1%
Saturated 6.2g	31%	Dietary Fiber 1g	4%
Trans Fat 0g		Sugars 1g	
Cholesterol 1mg	0%	Protein 5g	9%
Sodium 23mg	1%		
Calcium 10% • Iron 9%		Vitamin A 6% • Vitamin C 10%	

* Percent Daily Values are based on 2000 calorie diet. Your Daily Values may be higher or lower depending on your calorie needs.

Instructions:
1. In a food process, combine the avocados, lime juice, Stevia, protein powder, and coconut milk. Blend until smooth.

2. Transfer the mixture into popsicle molds and freeze until solid. This will take at least 6 hours, but it is best done overnight.
3. In a small bowl, combine the dark chocolate chips and coconut oil. Microwave for around 20 seconds or until melted. Let cool for around 10 minutes.
4. Dunk the frozen popsicles into the melted chocolate and allow the coating to solidify. Serve

High Protein Mousse

INGREDIENTS	Fats	Proteins	Carbs
1 tbsp gelatin	0 g	0.21 g	2.4 g
1/2 cup water	0 g	0 g	0 g
1/2 cup plain yogurt	3.98 g	4.25 g	5.71 g
1 scoop protein powder	3 g	12.5 g	5.5 g
1/4 cup whole fat milk	1.99 g	1.92 g	2.92 g
2 tbsp coconut oil	27.2 g	0 g	0 g

Total calories: 456 kcal
Servings: 4

Nutrition Facts	Amount	% Daily Value*	Amount	% Daily Value*
	Total Fat 9.1g	14%	Total Carbohydrates 4g	1%
Amount per 93 g	Saturated 6.9g	34%	Dietary Fiber 0g	0%
1 serving (3.3 oz)	Trans Fat 0g		Sugars 3g	
	Cholesterol 6mg	2%	Protein 5g	9%
Calories 114	Sodium 40mg	2%		
From fat 79	Calcium 13% • Iron	4%	Vitamin A 5% • Vitamin C	5%
	* Percent Daily Values are based on 2000 calorie diet. Your Daily Values may be higher or lower depending on your calorie needs			

Instructions
1. Bring the water to a simmer over medium heat.
2. In a small bowl, combine the gelatin and hot water. Set aside for around 5 minutes.
3. To the same bowl, combine the yogurt, milk, protein powder, and coconut oil.

4. Pour the mixture onto individual containers and refrigerate for at least 2 hours. When fully set, serve and enjoy.

Avocado Lime Pudding

INGREDIENTS	Fats	Proteins	Carbs
1/2 avocado	14.73 g	2.01 g	8.57 g
1 tbsp lime juice	0.01 g	0.06 g	1.27 g
2 tbsp coconut oil	27.2 g	0 g	0 g
2 tsp vanilla extract	0.01 g	0.01 g	1.06 g
1/4 tsp Stevia (powder)	0 g	0 g	4 g
1/2 cup cream cheese	34.32 g	8.52 g	4.2 g

Total calories: 780 kcal
Servings: 6

Nutrition Facts

Amount per 45 g
1 serving (1.6 oz)

Calories 130
From fat 111

	Amount	% Daily Value*	Amount	% Daily Value*
Total Fat 12.7g		20%	Total Carbohydrates 3g	1%
Saturated 7.9g		39%	Dietary Fiber 1g	4%
Trans Fat 0g			Sugars 1g	
Cholesterol 18mg		6%	Protein 2g	4%
Sodium 89mg		4%		
Calcium 2% • Iron 2%			Vitamin A 5% • Vitamin C	4%

* Percent Daily Values are based on 2000 calorie diet. Your Daily Values may be higher or lower depending on your calorie needs.

Instructions

1. To make the simple syrup, combine the Stevia and vanilla extract in a small pot. Add 1/2 cup of water.
2. Turn on the heat to low. Stir the pot occasionally until the mixture comes to a boil.
3. Turn off the heat and set aside.
4. Cut the avocado into cubes and place into a food processor.

5. To the same food processor, combine the coconut oil, lime juice, cream cheese, and simple syrup solution.
6. Run the food processor for 2 to 3 minutes or until the mixture has reached a pudding consistency.
7. Transfer the pudding into individual bowls and chill in the refrigerator for at least an hour.

High Protein Coconut Strawberry Mousse

INGREDIENTS	Fats	Proteins	Carbs
1.5 cup coconut milk	72.31 g	6.85 g	9.53 g
1/4 cup strawberries, sliced	0.12 g	0.28 g	3.19 g
1 tsp vanilla extract	0 g	0 g	0.53 g
3 tbsp protein powder	5.66 g	15.08 g	6.11 g

Total calories: 828 kcal
Servings: 6

Nutrition Facts

Amount per 70 g
1 serving (2.5 oz)

Calories 138
From fat 110

Amount	% Daily Value*	Amount	% Daily Value*
Total Fat 13g	20%	Total Carbohydrates 3g	1%
Saturated 10.8g	54%	Dietary Fiber 1g	2%
Trans Fat		Sugars 1g	
Cholesterol 1mg	0%	Protein 4g	7%
Sodium 26mg	1%		
Calcium 4% • Iron 13%		Vitamin A 3% • Vitamin C 11%	

* Percent Daily Values are based on 2000 calorie diet. Your Daily Values may be higher or lower depending on your calorie needs.

Instructions
1. Chill the coconut milk for at least an hour before use.
2. In a blender, combine the coconut milk, vanilla extract, and protein powder.
3. Pulse the mixture until smooth.

4. Serve in individual glasses. Top with sliced strawberries

Chocolate and Coconut

Protein Bars

INGREDIENTS	Fats	Proteins	Carbs
1/4 cup desiccated coconut	17.27 g	1.33 g	5.38 g
1/4 tsp Stevia (powder)	0 g	0 g	4 g
1 tsp vanilla extract	0 g	0 g	0.53 g
1/4 cup coconut cream	20.81 g	2.18 g	3.99 g
2 tbsp coconut oil	29.2 g	0 g	0 g
2 tbsp cocoa powder, unsweetened	1.41 g	1.95 g	6.3 g
1/2 cup butter	23.04 g	0.24 g	0.02 g
1.5 scoops protein powder	4.5 g	18.75 g	8.25 g

Total calories: 1596 kcal
Servings: 12

Nutrition Facts	Amount	% Daily Value*	Amount	% Daily Value*
Amount per 24 g	Total Fat 13.6g	21%	Total Carbohydrates 2g	1%
0.5 servings (0.8 oz)	Saturated 9.7g	49%	Dietary Fiber 0g	2%
	Trans Fat 0.3g		Sugars 0g	
Calories 133	Cholesterol 21mg	7%	Protein 2g	4%
From fat 118	Sodium 70mg	3%		
	Calcium 4% • Iron 4%		Vitamin A 7% • Vitamin C 3%	

* Percent Daily Values are based on 2000 calorie diet. Your Daily Values may be higher or lower depending on your calorie needs.

Instructions:

1. In a medium-sized bowl, mix the coconut cream, desiccated coconut, vanilla extract, Stevia, and protein powder.

2. Prepare a small cookie sheet lined with parchment paper.

3. Spread the shredded coconut mixture into the cookie sheet and shape into a 1/2-inch thick flat rectangle.

4. Place the cookie sheet in the freezer for 2 hours.

5. While the coconut bars are freezing, prepare the chocolate coating.

6. In a small sauce pan, melt the coconut oil and butter together.

7. Add cocoa powder to the oil mixture.

8. Mix on low heat for about 2 minutes.

9. Let the chocolate mixture cool to room temperature.

10. Remove the coconut bars from the freezer and cut into four equal-sized bars.

11. Dip the bars into the chocolate mixture, making sure to cover all sides and to coat evenly.

12. Place the bars back into the cookie sheet and refrigerate before serving

Healthy Keto Choco-hazelnut spread

INGREDIENTS	Fats	Proteins	Carbs
1 1/2 cups hazelnuts, whole	123.02 g	30.27 g	33.82 g
1 tbsp vanilla extract	0.01 g	0.01 g	1.64 g
1/8 cup cocoa powder	1.41 g	1.95 g	6.53 g
1/4 tsp Stevia (powder)	0 g	0 g	4 g
1/4 tsp salt	0 g	0 g	0 g
2 tsp olive oil	9 g	0 g	0 g
1/2 cup coconut milk	24.1 g	2.28 g	3.18 g
2 scoops protein powder	6 g	25 g	11 g

Total calories: 1840 kcal
Servings: 16

Nutrition Facts

Amount per 25 g
1 serving (0.9 oz)

Calories 115
From fat 86

Amount	% Daily Value*	Amount	% Daily Value*
Total Fat 10.2g	16%	Total Carbohydrates 4g	1%
Saturated 2.1g	10%	Dietary Fiber 2g	6%
Trans Fat 0g		Sugars 1g	
Cholesterol 0mg	0%	Protein 4g	7%
Sodium 45mg	2%		
Calcium 5% • Iron 7%		Vitamin A 2% • Vitamin C 4%	

* Percent Daily Values are based on 2000 calorie diet. Your Daily Values may be higher or lower depending on your calorie needs.

Instructions

1. Preheat the oven at 400 F.
2. Spread the hazelnuts overs a small baking tray and roast in the oven for about 8 minutes
3. Remove from the oven and allow to cool for 10 to 15 minutes.
4. Rub the hazelnuts together in a paper towel to remove their skins.
5. In a food processor, blend the hazelnuts while adding all the other ingredients one at a time.
6. Continue blending until you get a consistency that is close to actual Nutella.
7. Store the hazelnut spread in an airtight bottle and keep refrigerated.

Peanut Butter Fat Bombs

INGREDIENTS	Fats	Proteins	Carbs
4 tbsp unsweetened peanut butter	32.94 g	16.68 g	11.32 g
1/4 cup heavy whipping cream	11.1 g	0.62 g	0.84 g
1 cup cream cheese	79.44 g	13.76 g	9.44 g
1/4 tsp Stevia (powder)	0 g	0 g	4 g
1/2 tsp vanilla extract	0 g	0 g	0.27 g

Total calories: 1200 kcal
Servings: 8

Nutrition Facts

Amount per 42 g
1 serving (1.5 oz)

Calories 160
From fat 134

	Amount	% Daily Value*	Amount	% Daily Value*
	Total Fat 15.4g	24%	Total Carbohydrates 3g	1%
	Saturated 7.1g	35%	Dietary Fiber 1g	2%
	Trans Fat 0g		Sugars 2g	
	Cholesterol 37mg	12%	Protein 4g	8%
	Sodium 137mg	6%		
	Calcium 3% • Iron 8%		Vitamin A 15% • Vitamin C 0%	

* Percent Daily Values are based on 2000 calorie diet. Your Daily Values may be higher or lower depending on your calorie needs

Directions:

1. In a medium-sized bowl, whisk the heavy whipping cream until the volume has doubled.

2. In a separate bowl, combine the cream cheese, peanut butter, Stevia, and vanilla extract. Beat with a handheld mixer until the mixture is smooth,

3. Combine the whipped cream and the peanut butter mixture. Mix on low until well-combined.

4. Place in an airtight container and chill overnight. The fat bombs are best served the next day.

High-Protein Peanut Shortbread Cookies

INGREDIENTS	Fats	Proteins	Carbs
2.5 cups peanut flour	0.83 g	78.3 g	52.05 g
1/4 tsp salt	0 g	0 g	0 g
1/4 tsp baking soda	0 g	0 g	0 g
1 cup pecans, chopped	78.45 g	10 g	15.11 g
1/4 tsp Stevia (powder)	0 g	0 g	4 g
1 cup butter	184.12 g	1.93 g	0. 14 g

1/2 tbsp vanilla extract	0 g	0 g	0.82 g
1 scoop protein powder	3 g	12.5 g	5.5 g

Total calories: 2700 kcal
Servings: 20

Nutrition Facts	Amount	% Daily Value*	Amount	% Daily Value*
Amount per 44 g	**Total Fat** 13.3g	20%	**Total Carbohydrates** 2g	1%
1 serving (1.6 oz)	Saturated 8.9g	45%	Dietary Fiber 0g	1%
	Trans Fat 0.3g		Sugars 1g	
Calories 135	**Cholesterol** 21mg	7%	**Protein** 3g	6%
From fat 114	**Sodium** 60mg	3%		
	Calcium 3% • **Iron** 3%		**Vitamin A** 5% • **Vitamin C** 0%	

* Percent Daily Values are based on 2000 calorie diet. Your Daily Values may be higher or lower depending on your calorie needs.

Directions:
1. In a large bowl, combine the peanut flour, salt, baking soda, and pecans. Mix the dry ingredients until well-combined.
2. In a separate bowl, combine butter and vanilla extract.
3. Add the wet ingredients into the dry ingredients. Mix until well-combined.
4. Lay down a piece of parchment paper and transfer the dough on top of it.
5. Shape the dough into the shape of a log with roughly 2.5 inches in diameter
6. Wrap the log in the parchment paper or plastic wrap. Place the log in the freezer and allow to harden for at least an hour.
7. Preheat the oven at 350 F.
8. Once the log is firm, cut the log into 20 equal pieces.
9. Place the slices of dough into a baking tray which has been lined with parchment paper.
10. Bake the cookies in the oven for 7 to 10 minutes or until they have turned golden.

11. Remove the cookies and place on a cooling rack.

12. Cool the cookies for around an hour before serving.

Coconut and Walnut Macaroons

INGREDIENTS	Fats	Proteins	Carbs
0.5 cup desiccated coconut	17.27 g	1.33 g	5.38 g
3/4 cup coconut milk	36.15 g	3.42 g	4.76 g
1/4 tsp Stevia (powder)	0 g	0 g	4 g
4 tbsp peanut flour	0.08 g	7.83 g	5.21 g
1 tsp vanilla extract	0 g	0 g	0.53 g
1/4 tsp salt	0 g	0 g	0 g
1/4 cup walnuts, ground	13.04 g	3.05 g	2.74 g
3/4 cup Greek yogurt, plain	0.7 g	18.34 g	6.48 g
1/2 cup butter	92.06 g	0.96 g	0.07 g

Total calories: 1620 kcal
Servings: 12

Nutrition Facts

Amount per 44 g
1 serving (1.6 oz)

Calories 135
From fat 114

Amount	% Daily Value*	Amount	% Daily Value*
Total Fat 13.3g	20%	Total Carbohydrates 2g	1%
Saturated 8.9g	45%	Dietary Fiber 0g	1%
Trans Fat 0.3g		Sugars 1g	
Cholesterol 21mg	7%	Protein 3g	6%
Sodium 60mg	3%		
Calcium 3% · Iron 3%		Vitamin A 5% · Vitamin C 0%	

* Percent Daily Values are based on 2000 calorie diet. Your Daily Values may be higher or lower depending on your calorie needs.

Directions:
1. Preheat the oven to 350 F.
2. In a large saucepan over medium heat, combine the coconut milk, Stevia, and salt. Whisk together until well combined.
3. Add peanut flour gradually while stirring.
4. Heat the mixture to a boil and allow to simmer until it has thickened.
5. Remove the saucepan from heat. Add the vanilla extract, ground walnuts, and desiccated coconut.
6. Allow to cool for 30 minutes and add the Greek yogurt. Mix thoroughly.
7. Prepare a cookie sheet by lining it with parchment paper.

8. Divide the batter into 12 equal portions and drop into heaps on the cookie sheet.
9. Bake in the oven for about 15 minutes or until they have turned golden brown.
10. Remove from the oven and transfer to a cooling rack. Cool for 15 minutes before serving.

Chocolate Chip Cookie Dough Protein Bars

INGREDIENTS	Fats	Proteins	Carbs
1 1/2 tbsp desiccated coconut	20.65 g	2.2 g	7.75 g
4 scoops protein powder	12 g	50 g	22 g
1/4 tbsp salt	0 g	0 g	0 g
2 tbsp coconut oil	27.2 g	0 g	0 g
9 tbsp coconut milk	28.8 g	2.73 g	3.79 g
1 1/2 tsp vanilla extract	0 g	0 g	0.82 g
1/4 tsp Stevia (powder)	0 g	0 g	4 g
2 tbsp dark chocolate chips	13.64 g	2.49 g	14. 69 g
1/2 cup butter	92.06 g	0.96 g	0.07 g

Total calories: 2176 kcal
Servings: 16

Nutrition Facts	Amount	% Daily Value*	Amount	% Daily Value*
	Total Fat 12.4g	19%	**Total Carbohydrates** 3g	1%
	Saturated 8.7g	43%	Dietary Fiber 0g	1%
Amount per 29 g	Trans Fat 0.2g		Sugars 1g	
1 serving (1 oz)	**Cholesterol** 16mg	5%	**Protein** 4g	7%
	Sodium 128mg	5%		
Calories 136	**Calcium** 8% · **Iron** 8%		**Vitamin A** 8% · **Vitamin C** 5%	
From fat 108	* Percent Daily Values are based on 2000 calorie diet. Your Daily Values may be higher or lower depending on your calorie needs.			

Directions:
1. In a small bowl, combine the desiccated coconut, protein powder, and salt. Whisk together until well-combined.

2. In a separate bowl, combine coconut oil, coconut milk, butter, and vanilla extract. Stir in Stevia until well-incorporated. Gradually add the flour mixture while continuously stirring. Gently fold in the chocolate chips into the dough mixture.
3. Prepare a loaf plan by lining the bottom and the sides with parchment paper.
4. Pour the dough mixture into the loaf plan, making sure to press firmly into the surface of the pan. Chill in the refrigerator for at least 2 hours.
5. Remove the dough from the pan and cut into 16 equally sized bars. Serve while cold.

Oatmeal Coconut Cookies

INGREDIENTS	Fats	Proteins	Carbs
1 cup oat bran, cooked	1.88 g	7.03 g	25.05 g
4 scoops protein powder	12 g	50 g	22 g
1/2 tsp baking powder	0.01 g	0 g	1.17 g
1/4 tsp salt	0 g	0 g	0 g
1/4 tsp Stevia (powder)	0 g	0 g	4 g
2 tbsp desiccated coconut	22.11 g	1.7 g	6.89 g
3/4 cup coconut oil	163.5 g	0 g	0 g
1/4 cup coconut milk	12.05 g	1.14 g	1.59 g

Total calories: 2230 kcal
Servings: 10

Nutrition Facts

Amount per 58 g
1 serving (2 oz)

Calories 223
From fat 182

Amount	% Daily Value*	Amount	% Daily Value*
Total Fat 21.2g	33%	Total Carbohydrates 6g	2%
Saturated 17.3g	87%	Dietary Fiber 1g	3%
Trans Fat 0g		Sugars 0g	
Cholesterol 1mg	0%	Protein 6g	12%
Sodium 85mg	4%		
Calcium 14% • Iron 10%		Vitamin A 7% • Vitamin C 7%	

* Percent Daily Values are based on 2000 calorie diet. Your Daily Values may be higher or lower depending on your calorie needs

Directions:

1. Preheat the oven at 375 F.

2. In a blender, combine the oats, protein powder, salt, Stevia, and baking powder. Pulse for just 3 to 5 seconds.

3. Add in the coconut milk and coconut oil. Pulse again until the mixture is uniformly moistened.

4. Fold in the desiccated coconut into the dough.

5. Prepare a baking sheet by lining it with parchment paper.

6. Divide the dough into 10 equal portions and arrange on the baking sheet.

7. Bake in the oven for 6 minutes.

8. Remove from the oven and cool for at least 10 minutes before serving

Creamy Peanut Butter Popsicles

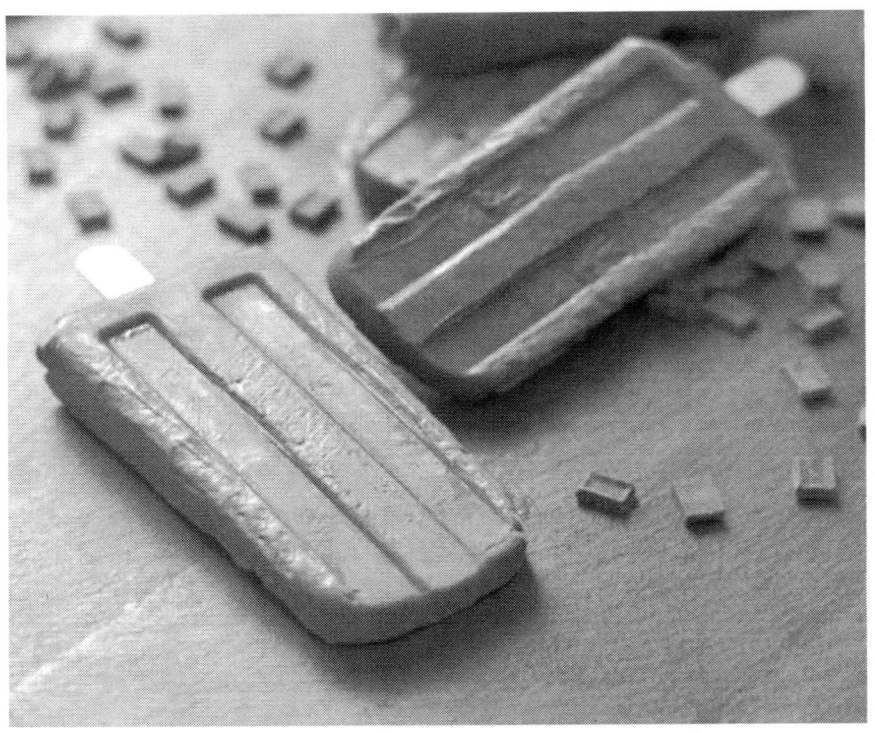

INGREDIENTS	Fats	Proteins	Carbs
2 cups cream cheese	158.87 g	27.52 g	18..88 g
1 cup unsweetened peanut butter	132.79 g	67.23 g	45.64 g
1/4 tsp Stevia (powder)	0 g	0 g	4 g

1/2 tsp vanilla extract	0 g	0 g	0.27 g
3/4 cup heavy cream	33.3 g	1.85 g	2.51 g

Total calories: 3432 kcal

Servings: 12

Nutrition Facts

Amount per 68 g
1 serving (2.4 oz)

Calories 286
From fat 233

Amount	% Daily Value*	Amount	% Daily Value*
Total Fat 27.1g	42%	Total Carbohydrates 6g	2%
Saturated 10.9g	55%	Dietary Fiber 1g	5%
Trans Fat 0g		Sugars 4g	
Cholesterol 53mg	18%	Protein 8g	16%
Sodium 223mg	9%		
Calcium 5% • Iron 22%		Vitamin A 29% • Vitamin C 0%	

* Percent Daily Values are based on 2000 calorie diet. Your Daily Values may be higher or lower depending on your calorie needs.

Directions:

1. In a large bowl, combine the cream cheese, peanut butter, vanilla extract, Stevia, and heavy cream. Mix together using a handheld mixer until smooth.
2. Spoon the mixture into popsicle molds, taking care to tap on the molds to release air bubbles. Place popsicle sticks into the center of each mold.
3. Freeze for at least 4 hours, preferably overnight.
4. Remove the popsicles from the molds by running under hot water. Serve immediately.

Peanut Butter Cheesecake Bites

INGREDIENTS	Fats	Proteins	Carbs
1 3/4 cup cream cheese	139.01 g	24.08 g	16.52 g
1 tsp vanilla extract	0 g	0 g	0.53 g
1/4 cup heavy cream	11.1 g	0.62 g	0.84 g
1/4 cup unsweetened peanut butter	33.2 g	16.81 g	11.41 g
3 tbsp coconut oil	40.8 g	0 g	0 g
1/4 tsp Stevia (powder)	0 g	0 g	4 g

2 tbsp coconut oil	27.2 g	0 g	0 g
2 tbsp 85% dark chocolate chips	6.82 g	1.25 g	7.34 g

Total calories: 2570 kcal
Servings: 10

Nutrition Facts	Amount	% Daily Value*	Amount	% Daily Value*
	Total Fat 25.8g	40%	**Total Carbohydrates** 4g	1%
Amount per 59 g	Saturated 15.3g	77%	Dietary Fiber 1g	2%
1 serving (2.1 oz)	Trans Fat 0g		Sugars 3g	
	Cholesterol 49mg	16%	**Protein** 4g	9%
Calories 257	**Sodium** 173mg	7%		
From fat 225	**Calcium** 5% • **Iron** 8%		**Vitamin A** 17% • **Vitamin C** 0%	

* Percent Daily Values are based on 2000 calorie diet. Your Daily Values may be higher or lower depending on your calorie needs.

Directions:

1. In a large bowl, combine the cream cheese, peanut butter, heavy cream, Stevia, vanilla extract, and 3 tbsp coconut oil. Whisk together using a handheld mixer until smooth.
2. In a heatproof bowl, combine the chocolate chips and 2 tbsp coconut oil. Melt the chocolate over a double boiler or in the microwave.
3. Using the melted chocolate, brush the bottoms and sides of your muffin molds. Place the molds in the freezer for 5 minutes.
4. Retrieve the muffin molds and brush another layer on top of the frozen chocolate. Return to the freezer and cool for another 10 minutes.
5. Retrieve the muffin molds. Place a few spoons of the cheesecake mixture into the muffin mold, taking care to flatten the tops.
6. Freeze the cheesecake mixture for 15 to 20 minutes.
7. To finish off, top each cheesecake cup with the remaining chocolate. Return to the freezer and cool for another 20 to 30 minutes.
8. Serve cheesecakes bites while cold.

No-Bake Pecan and

Coconut Bar

INGREDIENTS	Fats	Proteins	Carbs
1 cup almond flour	47.43 g	20.09 g	20.47 g
1/4 cup butter	46.07 g	0.48 g	0.03 g
1/4 tsp salt	0 g	0 g	0 g
1/2 cup pecans, halved	35.63 g	4.54 g	6.86 g
1/2 tbsp desiccated coconut	8.98 g	0.69 g	2.8 g
3 tbsp unsweetened peanut butter	24.71 g	12.51 g	8.49 g

Total calories: 1680 kcal
Servings: 12

Nutrition Facts	Amount	% Daily Value*	Amount	% Daily Value*
Amount per 22 g 1 serving (0.8 oz)	Total Fat 13.6g	21%	Total Carbohydrates 3g	1%
	Saturated 4g	20%	Dietary Fiber 2g	6%
	Trans Fat 0.2g		Sugars 1g	
Calories 140	Cholesterol 10mg	3%	Protein 3g	6%
From fat 115	Sodium 94mg	4%		
	Calcium 3% • Iron 6%		Vitamin A 6% • Vitamin C 0%	

*Percent Daily Values are based on 2000 calorie diet. Your Daily Values may be higher or lower depending on your calorie needs

Directions:
1. In a large bowl, combine the butter, almond flour, salt, Stevia, desiccated coconut, peanut butter, and pecans.
2. Mix the dough thoroughly.
3. Prepare a baking dish by lining it with parchment paper. Spread the dough on the baking dish, taking care to keep it a single even layer.
4. Place the baking dish in the refrigerator and chill for at least 2 hours.
5. Slice into 12 equal-sized bars and serve.

High-Protein Chocolate Mousse

INGREDIENTS	Fats	Proteins	Carbs
1/2 cup cream cheese	39.72 g	6.88 g	4.72 g
1/4 cup heavy cream	11.1 g	0.62 g	0.84 g
1/4 cup butter	46.07 g	0.48 g	0.03 g
1/4 cup dark chocolate	10.66 g	1.95 g	11.48 g
1/4 tsp Stevia (powder)	0 g	0 g	4 g
2 scoops protein powder	6 g	25 g	11 g
2 tbsp walnuts, chopped	20.87 g	4.87 g	4.39 g

Total calories: 1464 kcal
Servings: 3

Nutrition Facts

Amount per 105 g
1 serving (3.7 oz)

Calories 488
From fat 392

Amount	% Daily Value*	Amount	% Daily Value*
Total Fat 44.8g	69%	Total Carbohydrates 12g	4%
Saturated 22.4g	112%	Dietary Fiber 2g	8%
Trans Fat 0.6g		Sugars 4g	
Cholesterol 99mg	33%	Protein 13g	27%
Sodium 191mg	8%		
Calcium 27% • Iron 19%		Vitamin A 35% • Vitamin C 12%	

* Percent Daily Values are based on 2000 calorie diet. Your Daily Values may be higher or lower depending on your calorie needs.

Directions:

1. In a medium-sized bowl, combine the butter, cream cheese, and Stevia. Blend using a handheld mixer until smooth.
2. Place the dark chocolate in a heatproof bowl and melt over a double boiler or in the microwave.
3. Pour the melted chocolate into the cream cheese mixture. Blend until well-combined.
4. In a separate bowl, whip the heavy cream until its volume has doubled.
5. Fold the whipped cream carefully into the cream cheese mixture, making sure to preserve its volume.
6. Spoon the mixture into small glasses and top with chopped walnuts. Refrigerate the mousse in for at least 30 minutes before serving.

Walnut and Coconut

Yogurt Bombs

INGREDIENTS	Fats	Proteins	Carbs
3/4 cup walnuts, chopped	57.25 g	13.37 g	12.04 g
1/4 cup desiccated coconut	17.27 g	1.33 g	5.38 g
1/2 cup butter	92.06 g	0.96 g	0.07 g
1/4 tsp Stevia (powder)	0 g	0 g	4 g
1/4 tsp salt	0 g	0 g	0 g
1 cup yogurt	0.39 g	10.19 g	3.6 g

Total calories: 1620 kcal
Servings: 12

Nutrition Facts	Amount	% Daily Value*	Amount	% Daily Value*
Amount per 28 g	**Total Fat** 13.9g	21%	**Total Carbohydrates** 2g	1%
1 serving (1 oz)	Saturated 6.6g	33%	Dietary Fiber 1g	2%
	Trans Fat 0.3g		Sugars 0g	
Calories 135	**Cholesterol** 21mg	7%	**Protein** 2g	4%
From fat 120	**Sodium** 113mg	5%		
	Calcium 2% • Iron 2%		Vitamin A 5% • Vitamin C 0%	

* Percent Daily Values are based on 2000 calorie diet. Your Daily Values may be higher or lower depending on your calorie needs

Directions:

1. Preheat the oven at 350 F.
2. Spread the chopped walnuts and desiccated coconut on a foil-lined baking sheet and place inside the oven.
3. Toast for 5 to 6 minutes.
4. Remove the baking tray from the oven and set aside to cool.
5. Place the butter in a glass or ceramic bowl and melt using the microwave.
6. In a large bowl, combine the yogurt, melted butter, salt, and Stevia. Mix thoroughly.
7. Add the toasted walnuts and coconut to the yogurt mixture. Mix thoroughly until the dry ingredients are uniformly distributed.
8. Prepare a baking sheet by lining it with parchment paper.
9. Pour the yogurt mixture into the baking sheet, taking care to keep an even layer.
10. Place the baking sheet into the refrigerator and chill for at least an hour.
11. Once it has set, slice the yogurt bombs into 12 equal portions. Serve while cold.

Blueberry Cheesecake Fat Bombs

INGREDIENTS	Fats	Proteins	Carbs
1 1/2 cups cream cheese	119.16 g	20.64 g	14.16 g
1/2 cup butter	92.06 g	0.96 g	0.07 g
1/4 tsp Stevia (powder)	0 g	0 g	4 g
1 tsp vanilla extract	0 g	0 g	0.53 g
1/4 cup coconut oil	54.5 g	0 g	0 g
1 tbsp blueberries, frozen	0.16 g	0.11 g	3.04 g
1/2 cup coconut oil	109 g	0 g	0 g
1/4 tbsp Stevia (powder)	0 g	0 g	4 g

Total calories: 3444 kcal

Servings: 14

Directions:
1. In a medium-sized bowl, combine the butter and cream cheese. Using a handheld mixer, blend the two together until they are well-combined.
2. To the same bowl, add the Stevia, vanilla extract, and coconut oil. Mix again until well-combined.
3. In a mini cupcake tray, spoon a portion of the cream cheese mixture into each mold. Fill up each mold to about the 3/4 level and level the top using the back of a spoon.

4. Place the cupcake tray into the freezer for at least 20 minutes.

5. In a blender or food processor, combine the frozen blueberries, Stevia, and coconut oil. Blend until the mixture is smooth and the blueberries have been reduced into very small bits.

6. Pour the blueberry mixture over the top of each cupcake mold.

7. Return the cupcake tray to the freezer. Freeze for at least 4 hours before serving

No-Bake Keto Cheesecake

INGREDIENTS	Fats	Proteins	Carbs
1/2 cup almond flour	23.72 g	10.05 g	10.24 g
1/2 cup walnuts, ground	26.08 g	6.09 g	5.48 g
1/4 tsp Stevia (powder)	0 g	0 g	4 g
1 tsp cinnamon	0.03 g	0.1 g	2.1 g

1/4 tsp salt	0 g	0 g	0 g
1/4 cup butter	46.07 g	0.48 g	0.03 g
2 cups cream cheese	158.87 g	27.52 g	18.88 g
3/4 cup sour cream	18.29 g	6.04 g	12.25 g
1 cup butter	184.12 g	1.93 g	0.14 g
1 tsp vanilla extract	0 g	0 g	0.53 g
1/2 tsp lemon juice	0.01 g	0.01 g	0.17 g
1/4 tsp Stevia (powder)	0 g	0 g	4 g

Total calories: 4028 kcal
Servings: 11

Nutrition Facts

Amount per 86 g
1 serving (3 oz)

Calories 368
From fat 334

	Amount	% Daily Value*	Amount	% Daily Value*
	Total Fat 38.1g	59%	Total Carbohydrates 5g	2%
	Saturated 20.9g	105%	Dietary Fiber 1g	3%
	Trans Fat 0.8g		Sugars 2g	
	Cholesterol 98mg	33%	Protein 4g	9%
	Sodium 234mg	10%		
	Calcium 8% • Iron 2%		Vitamin A 23% • Vitamin C 1%	

* Percent Daily Values are based on 2000 calorie diet. Your Daily Values may be higher or lower depending on your calorie needs.

Directions:

1. Prepare the crust first. In a skillet, lightly toast the almond flour and the ground walnuts for about 2 to 4 minutes.
2. In a small bowl, mix the toasted nuts and mix 1/4 tsp Stevia, cinnamon, salt, and butter. Mix until all components have been well-combined.
3. Take a pie pan or deep dish firmly press the crust mixture into the bottom. Refrigerate the pie crust for the meantime.
4. To make the cheesecake filling, take a large bowl and combine the sour cream and cream cheese.
5. Using a handheld mixer, blend the two together until the mixture is smooth. Add vanilla extract, lemon juice, the remaining Stevia, and butter. Beat the mixture again until all components have been well-incorporated.
6. Pour the cheesecake mixture into the prepared pie crust. Level the top surface of the cheesecake using a spatula or the back of a spoon.

7. Refrigerate the cheesecake for several hours, preferably overnight. Serve while cold.

Coffee Cheesecake Bites

INGREDIENTS	Fats	Proteins	Carbs
2 cups almond flour	94.87 g	40.19 g	40.95 g
1 cup butter	184.12 g	1.93 g	0.14 g
2 cups cream cheese	158.87 g	27.52 g	18.88 g
1 cup heavy cream	44.4 g	2.46 g	3.35 g
1/4 tsp Stevia (powder)	0 g	0 g	4 g
1/4 cup sour cream	6.1 g	2.01 g	4.08
2 tbsp powdered coffee	0.03 g	0.73 g	4.52 g

Total calories: 4832 kcal
Servings: 16

Nutrition Facts

Amount per 67 g
1 serving (2.4 oz)

Calories 302
From fat 266

Amount	% Daily Value*	Amount	% Daily Value*
Total Fat 30.5g	47%	Total Carbohydrates 5g	2%
Saturated 15.3g	77%	Dietary Fiber 2g	6%
Trans Fat 0.5g		Sugars 2g	
Cholesterol 74mg	25%	Protein 5g	9%
Sodium 114mg	5%		
Calcium 7% • Iron 3%		Vitamin A 17% • Vitamin C 0%	

* Percent Daily Values are based on 2000 calorie diet. Your Daily Values may be higher or lower depending on your calorie needs.

Directions:
1. In a medium-sized mixing bowl, combine the almond flour and 1 cup butter. Mix until both ingredients are well-combined.

2. Pour the crust mixture into a pie pan. Press the mixture firmly to the bottom of the pan, making sure that it is evenly spread.

3. Cover the pan with plastic wrap and place in the refrigerator while you prepare the filling.

4. In a large bowl, combine the cream cheese, heavy cream, sour cream, and Stevia. Using a handheld mixer, whisk all ingredients together until the mixture is smooth and stiff.

5. Pour the cheesecake mixture into the pie pan. Spread the top layer evenly using a spatula or the back of a spoon.

6. Sprinkle the coffee powder over the top of the cheesecake.

7. Place the cheesecake in the refrigerator and chill for at least 4 hours.

8. Cut into individual portions and serve.

Easy No-Bake Chocolate Cookies

INGREDIENTS	Fats	Proteins	Carbs
2 tbsp butter	23.04 g	0.24 g	0.02 g
1/4 cup desiccated coconut	17.27 g	1.33 g	5.38 g
3/4 cup unsweetened peanut butter	99.59 g	50.43 g	34.23 g
1/4 tsp Stevia (powder)	0 g	0 g	4 g
1/4 tsp salt	0 g	0 g	0.14 g
1/2 tbsp dark chocolate chips	4.26 g	0.78 g	4.59 g

Total calories: 2370 kcal
Servings: 30

Nutrition Facts

Amount per 13 g
1 serving (0.5 oz)

Calories 79
From fat 61

Amount	% Daily Value*	Amount	% Daily Value*
Total Fat 7.2g	11%	Total Carbohydrates 2g	1%
Saturated 2.4g	12%	Dietary Fiber 1g	2%
Trans Fat 0g		Sugars 1g	
Cholesterol 3mg	1%	Protein 3g	5%
Sodium 36mg	2%		
Calcium 1% • Iron 10%		Vitamin A 8% • Vitamin C 0%	

* Percent Daily Values are based on 2000 calorie diet. Your Daily Values may be higher or lower depending on your calorie needs.

Directions:

1. In a medium-sized bowl, combine the butter and the peanut butter. Mix well until well-combined.
2. To the same bowl, add the Stevia, salt, and the desiccated coconut. Mix well.
3. Gently fold in the dark chocolate chips into the dough mixture.
4. Scoop portion-sized spoonful into a baking pan.
5. Place the baking pan in the refrigerator and chill for at least 30 minutes
6. Serve the cookies cold. They can be stored in the refrigerator for a week.

High-Protein Vanilla Chia Pudding

INGREDIENTS	Fats	Proteins	Carbs
1 3/4 cup coconut milk	84.36 g	7.99 g	11.11 g
1 tsp vanilla extract	0 g	0 g	0.53 g
1 tbsp chia seeds	7.69 g	4.14 g	10.53 g
2 scoops protein powder	6 g	25 g	11 g

Total calories: 1110 kcal
Servings: 6

Nutrition Facts	Amount	% Daily Value*	Amount	% Daily Value*
Nutrition Facts Amount per 79 g 1 serving (2.8 oz) Calories 185 From fat 137	**Total Fat** 16.3g	25%	**Total Carbohydrates** 6g	2%
	Saturated 12.7g	63%	Dietary Fiber 2g	6%
	Trans Fat 0g		Sugars 0g	
	Cholesterol 1mg	0%	**Protein** 6g	12%
	Sodium 30mg	1%		
	Calcium 14% • **Iron** 19%		**Vitamin A** 6% • **Vitamin C** 7%	

*Percent Daily Values are based on 2000 calorie diet. Your Daily Values may be higher or lower depending on your calorie needs.

Directions:
1. In a large bowl, combine all the ingredients and mix thoroughly.
2. Portion the pudding into individual jars or glasses. Place in the refrigerator for at least 4 hours, or preferably overnight.
3. Serve the pudding while cold.

Salted Peanut and Coconut Fat Bombs

INGREDIENTS	Fats	Proteins	Carbs
3/4 cup peanuts, ground	50. 13 g	24.5 g	20.22 g
1/4 cup desiccated coconut	17.27 g	1.33 g	5.38 g
1/8 tsp Stevia (powder)	0 g	0 g	2 g
1/4 tsp salt	0 g	0 g	0 g
1/2 cup coconut oil	109 g	0 g	0 g

Total Calories: 2300 kcal
Servings: 20

Nutrition Facts	Amount	% Daily Value*	Amount	% Daily Value*
	Total Fat 11.8g	18%	**Total Carbohydrates** 2g	1%
Amount per 21 g	Saturated 7.5g	38%	Dietary Fiber 0g	2%
1 serving (0.7 oz)	Trans Fat 0g		Sugars 0g	
	Cholesterol 10mg	3%	**Protein** 2g	4%
Calories 115	**Sodium** 91mg	4%		
From fat 103	**Calcium** 1% • **Iron** 1%		**Vitamin A** 2% • **Vitamin C** 0%	

*Percent Daily Values are based on 2000 calorie diet. Your Daily Values may be higher or lower depending on your calorie needs

Directions:

1. Preheat the oven to 350 F.
2. In a foil-lined baking sheet, spread the desiccated coconut. Place this in the preheated oven and toast for 5 minutes.
3. Set aside the desiccated coconut to cool.
4. In a medium-sized bowl, combine the cream cheese, coconut oil, Stevia, and desiccated coconut. Blend all the ingredients together using a handheld mixer until smooth.
5. In a shallow dish, mix the ground peanuts and salt. Stir until you have a uniform composition.
6. Form the cream cheese mixture into balls. Roll each ball on the ground peanut mixture, making sure all parts are well-covered.
7. Place the fat bombs in a baking tray lined with parchment paper.
8. Chill the fat bombs in the refrigerator for at least 2 hours. Serve while cold

Quick Keto Hot Chocolate

INGREDIENTS	Fats	Proteins	Carbs
1 cup whole milk	7.98 g	7.69 g	11.66 g
1/4 cup heavy cream	11.1 g	0.62 g	0.84 g
3 tbsp cocoa powder	1.62 g	1.61 g	5.94 g
1/16 tsp Stevia (powder)	0 g	0 g	2 g
1/4 tsp cinnamon	0.01 g	0.03 g	0.56 g
1/8 tsp salt	0 g	0 g	0 g
2 scoops protein powder	6 g	25 g	11 g
2 tbsp coconut oil	27.2 g	0 g	0 g

Total calories: 728 kcal
Servings: 4

Nutrition Facts		Amount	% Daily Value*	Amount	% Daily Value*
		Total Fat 13.5g	21%	Total Carbohydrates 8g	3%
Amount per 101 g		Saturated 9.1g	46%	Dietary Fiber 0g	2%
0.5 servings (3.6 oz)		Trans Fat 0g		Sugars 4g	
		Cholesterol 19mg	6%	Protein 9g	17%
Calories 182		Sodium 145mg	6%		
From fat 118		Calcium 24% • Iron	9%	Vitamin A 13% • Vitamin C	9%

* Percent Daily Values are based on 2000 calorie diet. Your Daily Values may be higher or lower depending on your calorie needs.

Directions:
1. In a saucepan, warm the whole milk over low heat.
2. In a blender, combine the heavy cream, protein powder, cocoa powder, cinnamon, Stevia, salt, and coconut oil. Mix until smooth.
3. When the milk has started to boil, take it off the heat. Add the milk to the blender.
4. Blend until you get a smooth and frothy texture.
5. Serve in individual mugs.

Low-Carb Chocolate Mousse

INGREDIENTS	Fats	Proteins	Carbs
1/4 cup butter	46.07 g	0.48 g	0.03 g
1 cup cream cheese	79.44 g	13.76 g	9.44 g

1 tbsp cocoa powder	0.74 g	1.06 g	3.13 g
1/2 cup heavy cream	22.2 g	1.23 g	1.67 g
1/16 tsp Stevia (powder)	0 g	0 g	2 g

Total calories: 1422 kcal
Servings: 6

Nutrition Facts

Amount per 59 g
1 serving (2.1 oz)

Calories 237
From fat 218

Amount	% Daily Value*	Amount	% Daily Value*
Total Fat 24.8g	38%	Total Carbohydrates 3g	1%
Saturated 14.7g	74%	Dietary Fiber 0g	1%
Trans Fat 0.3g		Sugars 2g	
Cholesterol 77mg	26%	Protein 3g	6%
Sodium 146mg	6%		
Calcium 5% • Iron 2%		Vitamin A 18% • Vitamin C 0%	

* Percent Daily Values are based on 2000 calorie diet. Your Daily Values may be higher or lower depending on your calorie needs.

Directions:

1. In a medium-sized bowl, combine the butter and the Stevia. Blend using a handheld mixer until completely incorporated.

2. Add the cream cheese and blend again until smooth.

3. Add the cocoa powder and blend again.

4. In a separate bowl, whip the heavy cream until it has doubled in volume

5. Gently fold the whipped cream into the cream cheese mixture, taking care not to overmix.

6. Transfer the mousse into individual cups or glasses and chill in the refrigerator for at least 30 minutes before serving.

Vegan Lime Cheesecake

INGREDIENTS	Fats	Proteins	Carbs
1/2 cup almond flour	23.72 g	10.05 g	10.24 g
2 tbsp coconut oil	27.2 g	0 g	0 g
1/4 tsp salt	0 g	0 g	0 g
2 cups cream cheese	158.87 g	27.52 g	18.88 g
1 tsp vanilla extract	0 g	0 g	0.53 g
1/2 cup coconut milk	24.1 g	2.28 g	3.18 g
3 tbsp lime juice	0.11 g	0.16 g	3.16 g
1/2 tbsp lime zest	0.01 g	0.05 g	0.48 g
1/4 cup coconut oil	54.5 g	0 g	0 g
1/4 tsp Stevia (powder)	0 g	0 g	4 g

Total calories: 2816 kcal
Servings: 16

Nutrition Facts			
Amount per 48 g			
1 serving (1.7 oz)			
Calories 176			
From fat 156			

Amount	% Daily Value*	Amount	% Daily Value*
Total Fat 18g	28%	**Total Carbohydrates** 2g	1%
Saturated 11.5g	57%	Dietary Fiber 0g	2%
Trans Fat 0g		Sugars 1g	
Cholesterol 32mg	11%	**Protein** 3g	5%
Sodium 143mg	6%		
Calcium 4% • **Iron** 3%		**Vitamin A** 8% • **Vitamin C** 2%	

* Percent Daily Values are based on 2000 calorie diet. Your Daily Values may be higher or lower depending on your calorie needs.

Directions:

1. In a medium-sized bowl, combine the almond flour, 2 tbsp coconut oil, and 1/4 tsp salt. Mix well.
2. Transfer the flour mixture into a pie pan and press firmly on the bottom using the back of a spoon.
3. Refrigerate the pie pan with the crust and allow to chill while you prepare the filling.
4. In a large bowl, combine the cream cheese, vanilla extract, and coconut milk. Whisk using a handheld mixer until it has increased in volume.
5. Add the lime juice and lime zest and whisk again.
6. Add the coconut oil and fold gently.
7. Pour the cheesecake mixture into the pie pan with the crust.
8. Refrigerate the cheesecake for at least 6 hours. For best results, allow to set overnight.
9. Serve while cold.

Healthy Peanut Butter

Frozen Yogurt

INGREDIENTS	Fats	Proteins	Carbs
2 cups Greek yogurt	0.78 g	20.38 g	7.2 g

1 cup unsweetened peanut butter	132.79 g	67.23 g	45.64 g
1 1/2 tsp vanilla extract	0 g	0 g	0.8 g
1/4 cup cocoa powder	2.82 g	3.89 g	12.53 g
1/8 tsp Stevia (powder)	0 g	0 g	4 g
1 cup coconut milk	48.21 g	4.57 g	6.35 g

Total calories: 2160 kcal
Servings: 10

Nutrition Facts

Amount per 72 g
.8 servings (2.5 oz)

Calories 216
From fat 155

Amount	% Daily Value*	Amount	% Daily Value*
Total Fat 18.5g	28%	Total Carbohydrates 8g	3%
Saturated 6.5g	33%	Dietary Fiber 2g	8%
Trans Fat 0g		Sugars 4g	
Cholesterol 1mg	0%	Protein 10g	19%
Sodium 105mg	4%		
Calcium 4% • Iron 31%		Vitamin A 20% • Vitamin C 0%	

* Percent Daily Values are based on 2000 calorie diet. Your Daily Values may be higher or lower depending on your calorie needs.

Directions:

1. Combine all ingredients in a blender. Blend until very smooth.

2. Transfer the mixture to an airtight container and place in the freezer. Freeze for 3 to 4 hours before serving.

3. Stir the mixture every hour while it is freezing.

Edible Cookie Dough

INGREDIENTS	Fats	Proteins	Carbs
1/2 cup almond flour	23.72 g	10.05 g	10.24 g
1 tbsp desiccated coconut	11.05 g	0.85 g	3.44 g

1/4 tsp Stevia (powder)	0 g	0 g	4 g
1/4 tsp salt	0 g	0 g	0 g
4 tbsp butter	46.07 g	0.48 g	0.03 g
1 tbsp vanilla extract	0.01 g	0.01 g	1.64 g
1/4 cup heavy cream	11.1 g	0.62 g	0.84 g
3 tbsp coconut milk	9.6 g	0.91 g	1.26 g
1 tbsp dark chocolate chips	6.82 g	1.25 g	7.34 g
2 scoops protein powder	6 g	25 g	11 g

Total calories: 1476 kcal
Servings: 12

Nutrition Facts

Amount per 26 g
1.5 serving (0.9 oz)

Calories 123
From fat 93

Amount	% Daily Value*	Amount	% Daily Value*
Total Fat 10.7g	16%	Total Carbohydrates 4g	1%
Saturated 5.7g	28%	Dietary Fiber 1g	3%
Trans Fat 0.2g		Sugars 1g	
Cholesterol 16mg	5%	Protein 4g	7%
Sodium 69mg	3%		
Calcium 7% • Iron 6%		Vitamin A 7% • Vitamin C 3%	

* Percent Daily Values are based on 2000 calorie diet. Your Daily Values may be higher or lower depending on your calorie needs.

Directions:

1. In a large bowl, combine the almond flour, protein powder, desiccated coconut, Stevia, and salt. Mix well.

2. Add the butter, heavy cream, and vanilla extract. Mix well until you get a uniform composition and a creamy texture.

3. Add the dark chocolate chips and gently fold them in.

4. Using your hands, roll the cookie dough into balls and set on baking tray.

5. Refrigerate the cookie dough balls and chill for at least an hour before serving.

OVO

Macaroon Fat Bombs

INGREDIENTS	Fats	Proteins	Carbs
1/4 cup almond flour	11.88 g	5.03 g	5.13 g
1/4 cup desiccated coconut	17.27 g	1.33 g	5.38 g
3 egg whites	0.17 g	10.79 g	0.72 g
1/4 tbsp Stevia (powder)	0 g	0 g	4 g
1 tbsp coconut oil	13.6 g	0 g	0 g
1/4 tbsp vanilla extract	0 g	0 g	0.42 g

Total calories: 486 kcal
Servings: 6

Nutrition Facts	Amount	% Daily Value*	Amount	% Daily Value*
	Total Fat 7.2g	11%	Total Carbohydrates 3g	1%
	Saturated 4.7g	23%	Dietary Fiber 1g	2%
Amount per 28 g	Trans Fat 0g		Sugars 0g	
1 serving (1 oz)	Cholesterol 0mg	0%	Protein 3g	6%
	Sodium 29mg	1%		
Calories 81				
From fat 60	Calcium 1% • Iron 2%		Vitamin A 0% • Vitamin C 0%	

* Percent Daily Values are based on 2000 calorie diet. Your Daily Values may be higher or lower depending on your calorie needs.

Instructions:

1. Pre-heat the oven at 400 F.

2. In a medium-sized bowl, mix the almond flour, desiccated coconut, and Stevia.

3. Melt the coconut oil in a small saucepan over low heat and add the vanilla extract.

4. Add the melted coconut oil to the flour mix and blend until well-incorporated.

5. In a separate bowl, whisk the egg whites until you get stiff peaks.

6. Gently fold the egg whites into the flour mix. Be careful not to overmix so you do not lose the volume from the egg whites.

7. Divide the mixture into 8 portions and spoon each portion into a muffin cup.

8. Bake in the oven for 8 minutes or until the macaroons have started to turn golden brown.

9. Remove from the oven and let cool for 15 to 20 minutes before serving.

Keto Fudge Brownies

INGREDIENTS	Fats	Proteins	Carbs
1/2 cup almond flour	23.72 g	10.05 g	10.24 g
1/2 cup unsalted butter	92.06 g	0.96 g	0.07 g
1/4 cup 85% dark chocolate	10.66 g	1.95 g	11.48 g
1/4 tsp Stevia (powder)	0 g	0 g	4 g
4 eggs	16.74 g	22.11 g	1.27 g
1/2 tsp vanilla extract	0 g	0 g	0.27 g
1/2 tsp baking powder	0.01 g	0 g	1.17 g
1/2 cup walnuts, chopped	38.15 g	8.91 g	8.02 g
1/4 tsp salt	0 g	0 g	0 g

Total calories: 1888 kcal
Servings: 16

Nutrition Facts	Amount	% Daily Value*	Amount	% Daily Value*
	Total Fat 11.3g	17%	**Total Carbohydrates** 2g	1%
Amount per 27 g	Saturated 4.7g	24%	Dietary Fiber 1g	3%
1 serving (0.9 oz)	Trans Fat 0.2g		Sugars 1g	
	Cholesterol 56mg	19%	**Protein** 3g	6%
Calories 118	**Sodium** 98mg	4%		
From fat 98	**Calcium** 3% • **Iron** 3%		**Vitamin A** 5% • **Vitamin C** 0%	

* Percent Daily Values are based on 2000 calorie diet. Your Daily Values may be higher or lower depending on your calorie needs.

Directions:

1. Preheat the oven to 325 F

2. In a small bowl, mix butter and chocolate. Melt over a double boiler and mix until smooth. Set aside to cool.

3. In a medium-sized bowl, combine the eggs, vanilla extract, Stevia, and salt. Mix using a hand mixer until thoroughly combined.

4. Add the butter and chocolate mixture and mix further until all ingredients are well-incorporated.

5. In a separate bowl, combine the almond flour and baking powder.
6. Add the dry ingredients into the wet ingredients and fold together until well-combined.

7. Prepare a baking pan by lining the bottom and sides with parchment paper.
8. Pour the brownie mixture into the pan. Sprinkle the crushed walnuts over the top.
9. Bake in the oven for 25 to 28 minutes. The brownies are best when a still a little fudgy. To test, stick a toothpick into the center. Take care to bake only until the toothpick still comes out a little fudgy.
10. Remove from the oven and allow to cool for 30 to 45 minutes.
11. Remove the whole batch from the baking pan and cut into 20 individual portions.

Coconut Crepes

INGREDIENTS	Fats	Proteins	Carbs
4 eggs	16.74 g	22.11 g	1.27 g
1/2 cup coconut milk	24.1 g	2.28 g	3.18 g
1/2 tsp vanilla extract	0 g	0 g	0.27 g
1 tbsp coconut oil	13.6 g	0 g	0 g
1/2 cup desiccated coconut	34.54 g	2.65 g	10.76 g
2 tbsp almond flour	15.98 g	6.77 g	6.9 g

Total calories: 1124 kcal
Servings: 4

Nutrition Facts	Amount	% Daily Value*	Amount	% Daily Value*
	Total Fat 26.3g	40%	Total Carbohydrates 6g	2%
Amount per 97 g	Saturated 17.6g	88%	Dietary Fiber 1g	4%
1 serving (3.4 oz)	Trans Fat 0g		Sugars 1g	
	Cholesterol 164mg	55%	Protein 8g	17%
Calories 281	Sodium 71mg	3%		
From fat 223	Calcium 6% • Iron 13%		Vitamin A 5% • Vitamin C 1%	

*Percent Daily Values are based on 2000 calorie diet. Your Daily Values may be higher or lower depending on your calorie needs.

Directions:

1. In a large mixing bowl, combine the eggs, coconut oil, coconut milk, and vanilla extract. Mix thoroughly.

2. In a separate bowl, mix together the almond flour and desiccated coconut until well-combined.

3. Add the dry ingredients to the dry ingredients. Whisk together until you get a smooth batter with no lumps.

4. Set aside the batter for 10 minutes to allow it to slightly thicken.

5. Prepare a shallow frying pan by rubbing its surface with a small amount of coconut oil. Heat the pan over medium heat.

6. Pour around 1 tbsp of batter into the frying pan. Tip and rotate the pan to spread the batter as thinly as possible.

7. Cook for around 2 minutes or until the sides are crispy and the crepe can be easily slid off the pan. Flip the crepe and cook for an additional 30 seconds.

8. The crepe can be served with some unsweetened chocolate syrup or nuts.

Zucchini Bread with

Chocolate Chips

INGREDIENTS	Fats	Proteins	Carbs
3/4 cup almond flour	35. 6 g	15.08 g	15.37 g
1/4 cup dark chocolate chips	10.66 g	1.95 g	11.48 g
1 tsp baking soda	0 g	0 g	0 g
1/2 tsp salt	0 g	0 g	0 g
1/4 tsp Stevia (powder)	0 g	0 g	4 g
1 1/2 cups zucchini, grated	0.07 g	0.45 g	0.51 g
4 tbsp coconut oil	54.4 g	0 g	0 g
4 eggs	16.74 g	22.11 g	1.27 g

Total calories: 1288 kcal
Servings: 8

Nutrition Facts	Amount	% Daily Value*	Amount	% Daily Value*
	Total Fat 14.7g	23%	Total Carbohydrates 4g	1%
	Saturated 7.7g	38%	Dietary Fiber 2g	6%
Amount per 44 g	Trans Fat 0g		Sugars 1g	
1 serving (1.6 oz)	Cholesterol 82mg	27%	Protein 5g	10%
Calories 161	Sodium 335mg	14%		
From fat 127	Calcium 4% • Iron 6%		Vitamin A 3% • Vitamin C 1%	

* Percent Daily Values are based on 2000 calorie diet. Your Daily Values may be higher or lower depending on your calorie needs.

Directions:

1. Preheat the oven at 350 F.

2. In a good processor, combine the almond flour, sea salt, Stevia, and baking soda. Pulse 2 to 3 times.

3. Add in the eggs, coconut oil, and the shredded zucchini. Continue pulsing until all the ingredients are well-combined.

4. Remove the blades of the food processor and toss in the chocolate chips. Using a spatula, gently fold in the chocolate chips into the dough.

5. Prepare a loaf pan by lining the bottom and sides with parchment paper.

6. Transfer the better into the prepared loaf pan.

7. Bake in the oven for 35 to 40 minutes.

8. Remove the bread from the oven and cool for 2 hours on a wire rack before serving.

Peanut Butter Meringue Bites

INGREDIENTS	Fats	Proteins	Carbs
2 cups egg whites	0.83 g	52.97 g	3.55 g
1 cup unsweetened peanut butter	132.79 g	67.23 g	45.64 g
1/2 tsp Stevia (powder)	0 g	0 g	8 g

Total calories: 1784 kcal
Servings: 8

Nutrition Facts	Amount	% Daily Value*	Amount	% Daily Value*
	Total Fat 16.7g	26%	Total Carbohydrates 7g	2%
	Saturated 2.6g	13%	Dietary Fiber 2g	7%
Amount per 94 g	Trans Fat 0g		Sugars 4g	
1 serving (3.3 oz)	Cholesterol 0mg	0%	Protein 15g	30%
	Sodium 219mg	9%		
Calories 223				
From fat 140	Calcium 2% • Iron 32%		Vitamin A 25% • Vitamin C 0%	

* Percent Daily Values are based on 2000 calorie diet. Your Daily Values may be higher or lower depending on your calorie needs.

Directions:
1. Preheat the oven at 200 F.
2. Prepare a baking sheet by lining it with parchment paper.
3. In a large bowl, whisk the egg whites using a handheld or tabletop mixer.

4. Continue whisking the egg whites until soft peaks have begun to form. At this point, gradually add in the Stevia while continuing mixing.

5. Once the meringue has become stiff, add in the peanut butter.

6. Mix again on lower speed to blend in the peanut butter. The meringue will deflate a little, but that is fine.

7. Using a scoop, measure out individual portions of the meringue and place on the baking sheet. Repeat this until there is more space on the baking tray or until the meringue mixture has all been used up.

8. Bake at 200 F for an hour. Make sure to not open the oven door during this period.

9. After 1 hour, turn off the oven and leave the cookies inside for another hour.

10. Remove the meringue bites and allow to cool for a few minutes before serving.

Flaxseed and Peanut Muffins

INGREDIENTS	Fats	Proteins	Carbs
1 1/2 tbsp flaxseed, ground	4.43 g	1.92 g	3.03 g
1/4 tsp Stevia (powder)	0 g	0 g	4 g
1/4 tbsp baking powder	0.02 g	0 g	1.78 g
1/4 tbsp cinnamon, ground	0.02 g	0.08 g	1.61 g
1/2 tsp salt	0 g	0 g	0 g
1/2 cup coconut milk	24.1 g	2.28 g	3.18 g
2 tbsp coconut oil	27.2 g	0 g	0 g
1 egg	4.18 g	5.53 g	0.32 g
1/2 tsp vanilla extract	0 g	0 g	0.27 g
3/4 cup almond flour	35.6 g	15.08 g	15.37 g
1/2 cup peanuts, chopped	33.4 g	16.33 g	13.47 g

Total calories: 1392 kcal
Servings: 12

Nutrition Facts	Amount	% Daily Value*	Amount	% Daily Value*
	Total Fat 10.8g	17%	Total Carbohydrates 4g	1%
Amount per 29 g	Saturated 4.5g	23%	Dietary Fiber 2g	6%
1 serving (1 oz)	Trans Fat 0g		Sugars 1g	
	Cholesterol 14mg	5%	Protein 3g	7%
Calories 116	Sodium 137mg	6%		
From fat 93	Calcium 4% • Iron 5%		Vitamin A 0% • Vitamin C 0%	

* Percent Daily Values are based on 2000 calorie diet. Your Daily Values may be higher or lower depending on your calorie needs.

Directions:

1. Preheat the oven to 350 F.

2. Prepare a muffin tin by adding silicone cupcake liners to each mold.

3. In a medium-sized bowl, combine the ground flaxseed, Stevia, baking powder, cinnamon, salt, almond flour, and chopped peanuts. Mix thoroughly until well-combined.

4. In a separate bowl, combine the coconut milk, coconut oil, vanilla extract, and egg. Whisk together until you have a uniform composition.

5. Add the dry ingredients into the wet ingredients, and gently mix using a spatula. Ensure that the components are well-mixed.

6. To each muffin mold, add a heaping tablespoon of the batter. The muffins will expand as they bake, so only will each mold to the halfway point.

7. Bake in the oven for about 20 minutes, or until the tops of the muffins start to turn brown.

8. Remove from the oven and let the muffins cool for at least 15 minutes before serving.

Fluffy Microwave Mug Cake

INGREDIENTS	Fats	Proteins	Carbs
3/4 tsp coconut oil	3.4 g	0 g	0 g
2 eggs	8.37 g	11.05 g	0.63 g
3/4 cup almond flour	35.6 g	15.08 g	15.37 g
1/2 tsp baking powder	0.01 g	0 g	1.17 g
1/4 tsp salt	0 g	0 g	0 g

Total calories: 570 kcal
Servings: 6

Nutrition Facts	Amount	% Daily Value*	Amount	% Daily Value*
Amount per 28 g 1 serving (1 oz)	**Total Fat** 7.9g	12%	**Total Carbohydrates** 3g	1%
	Saturated 1.4g	7%	Dietary Fiber 2g	6%
	Trans Fat 0g		Sugars 1g	
Calories 95 From fat 67	**Cholesterol** 55mg	18%	**Protein** 4g	9%
	Sodium 118mg	5%		
	Calcium 6% • **Iron** 4%		**Vitamin A** 2% • **Vitamin C** 0%	

* Percent Daily Values are based on 2000 calorie diet. Your Daily Values may be higher or lower depending on your calorie needs.

Directions:
1. In a tall and straight ceramic mug, drizzle the coconut oil and brush it along the edges.
2. Into the mug, add the eggs, almond flour, baking powder, and salt.
3. Whisk the mixture until it is smooth and well-incorporated. Tap the mug a few times to remove any air bubbles in the batter.
4. Microwave the batter on high for 3 minutes.
5. Turn the mug over a plate and tap its sides to loosen the cake. If needed, run a knife along the inside surface of the mug.
6. Slice the roll of bread into individual portions. Serve while hot.

Peanut and Chocolate Cookies

INGREDIENTS	Fats	Proteins	Carbs
2 eggs	8.37 g	11.05 g	0.63 g
3/4 cup coconut oil	163.5 g	0 g	0 g
1/4 tsp Stevia (powder)	0 g	0 g	4 g
2 tbsp unsweetened baking chocolate	26.16 g	7.16 g	14.21 g
1/2 tsp baking powder	0.01 g	0 g	1.17 g
3/4 cup coconut oil	163.5 g	0 g	0 g
1/2 tsp salt	0 g	0 g	0 g
2 cups almond flour	94.87 g	40.19 g	40.95 g
1/2 cup peanuts, chopped	33.4 g	16.33 g	13.47 g

Total calories: 4752 kcal
Servings: 18

Nutrition Facts	Amount	% Daily Value*	Amount	% Daily Value*
	Total Fat 27.2g	42%	Total Carbohydrates 4g	1%
Amount per 41 g	Saturated 17.4g	87%	Dietary Fiber 2g	8%
1 serving (1.4 oz)	Trans Fat 0g		Sugars 1g	
	Cholesterol 18mg	6%	Protein 4g	8%
Calories 264	Sodium 95mg	4%		
From fat 235	Calcium 4% • Iron 6%		Vitamin A 1% • Vitamin C 0%	

* Percent Daily Values are based on 2000 calorie diet. Your Daily Values may be higher or lower depending on your calorie needs.

Directions:

1. Preheat the oven to 350 F.

2. Melt the baking chocolate over a double boiler or in the microwave.

3. In a medium-sized bowl, combine the coconut oil, eggs, and vanilla extract. Blend using a handheld mixer until well-combined.

4. Pour the melted chocolate into the same bowl and blend until well-incorporated.

5. To the same bowl, add the Stevia, baking soda, and salt. Mix until all the dry ingredient are well-incorporated.

6. With the handheld mixer at low setting, slowly add in the almond flour. Continue mixing until well-incorporated and the texture becomes dough-like.

7. Prepare a baking sheet by lining it with parchment paper.
8. Using your hands, form the cookie dough into balls and place on the baking sheet. Gently press down on each ball. Make sure to leave enough room between each cookie to account for expansion.
9. Sprinkle chopped peanuts over the cookies.

10. Bake in the oven for 15 to 18 minutes.
11. Remove the cookies from the oven and transfer to a wire rack. Cool for at least 20 minutes before serving.

Keto Blueberry Pancakes

INGREDIENTS	Fats	Proteins	Carbs
3 eggs	28.92 g	26.9 g	3.05 g
1/2 cup almond flour	0.3 g	0.13 g	0.13 g
2 tbsp desiccated coconut	34.54 g	2.65 g	10.76 g
1/2 tsp baking powder	0.01 g	0 g	1.17 g
1/8 tsp Stevia (powder)	0 g	0 g	4 g
1/4 cup coconut milk	12.05 g	1.14 g	1.59 g
1 tsp cinnamon	0.03 g	0.1 g	2.1 g
1/4 tsp salt	0 g	0 g	0 g
1/4 cup blueberries, frozen	0.25 g	0.16 g	4.72 g

| Total calories: | 872 kcal |
| Servings: | 8 |

Nutrition Facts

Amount per 46 g
1 serving (1.6 oz)

Calories 109
From fat 82

Amount	% Daily Value*	Amount	% Daily Value*
Total Fat 9.5g	15%	**Total Carbohydrates** 3g	1%
Saturated 6.1g	31%	Dietary Fiber 0g	1%
Trans Fat 0g		Sugars 1g	
Cholesterol 232mg	77%	**Protein** 4g	8%
Sodium 115mg	5%		
Calcium 4% • **Iron** 8%		**Vitamin A** 4% • **Vitamin C** 1%	

* Percent Daily Values are based on 2000 calorie diet. Your Daily Values may be higher or lower depending on your calorie needs.

Directions:

1. Start thawing the blueberries at least an hour before cooking.
2. In a blender, combine all the ingredients except the blueberries. Mix until you get a smooth and thick batter.
3. Transfer the batter to a large bowl and stir in the blueberries. Let the batter sit for at least 5 minutes.
4. Pre-heat a nonstick pan over medium heat. You may lightly grease the pan with coconut oil.
5. Pour individual portions of batter onto the pan. Allow each side to cook for 2 to 3 minutes.
6. Serve the pancakes immediately.

Zucchini Brownies with Chocolate Chips

INGREDIENTS	Fats	Proteins	Carbs
1 medium-sized zucchini, grated	0.04 g	0.3 g	0.34 g
3 tbsp coconut oil	40.8 g	0 g	0 g

2 eggs	8.37 g	11.05 g	0.63 g
1/8 tsp Stevia (powder)	0 g	0 g	2 g
1 cup almond flour	47.43 g	20.09 g	20.47 g
1/2 tbsp vanilla extract	0 g	0 g	0.82 g
1/4 tsp salt	0 g	0 g	0 g
1/4 cup dark chocolate chips	10.66 g	1.95 g	11.48 g
1/2 tsp baking powder	0.01 g	0 g	1.17 g

Total calories: 1200 kcal
Servings: 12

Nutrition Facts

Amount per 23 g
1 serving (0.8 oz)

Calories 100
From fat 77

Amount	% Daily Value*	Amount	% Daily Value*
Total Fat 9g	14%	Total Carbohydrates 3g	1%
Saturated 4g	20%	Dietary Fiber 1g	5%
Trans Fat 0g		Sugars 1g	
Cholesterol 27mg	9%	Protein 3g	6%
Sodium 60mg	3%		
Calcium 4% • Iron 4%		Vitamin A 1% • Vitamin C 1%	

* Percent Daily Values are based on 2000 calorie diet. Your Daily Values may be higher or lower depending on your calorie needs.

Directions:

1. Preheat the oven to 350 F.

2. In a medium-sized bowl, whisk together the grated zucchini, coconut oil, Stevia, eggs, and vanilla extract. Continue until all ingredients are well-combined.

3. Add the almond flour, baking powder, and salt. Gently fold in the dry ingredients just until they are thoroughly integrated.

4. Fold in the dark chocolate chips, taking care not to overmix.

5. Prepare a baking pan by lining it with parchment paper.

6. Pour the batter into the pan. Level the top surface using a spatula.

7. Bake in the oven for 30 minutes, or just until a toothpick stuck into the middle comes out moist but not sticky.

8. Remove the baking pan from the oven and allow to cool for at least 30 minutes. Cut into individual squares. They can be chilled for storage or served immediately.

Healthy Green Tea Cookies

INGREDIENTS	Fats	Proteins	Carbs
1/2 cup almond flour	23.72 g	10.05 g	10.24 g
1/4 cup desiccated coconut	17.27 g	1.33 g	5.38 g
3/4 cup butter	138.13 g	1.45 g	0.1 g
1/4 tsp salt	0 g	0 g	0 g
1/4 tsp Stevia (powder)	0 g	0 g	4 g

2 tbsp green tea powder	0 g	0.02 g	0.05 g
1/2 cup walnuts, chopped	38.15 g	8.91 g	8.02 g
1 egg	4.18 g	5.53 g	0.32 g

Total calories: 2112 kcal
Servings: 16

Nutrition Facts

Amount per 24 g
1 serving (0.8 oz)

Calories 132
From fat 120

Amount	% Daily Value*	Amount	% Daily Value*
Total Fat 13.9g	21%	Total Carbohydrates 2g	1%
Saturated 6.9g	34%	Dietary Fiber 1g	2%
Trans Fat 0.4g		Sugars 0g	
Cholesterol 33mg	11%	Protein 2g	3%
Sodium 42mg	2%		
Calcium 2% • Iron 2%		Vitamin A 6% • Vitamin C	0%

* Percent Daily Values are based on 2000 calorie diet. Your Daily Values may be higher or lower depending on your calorie needs.

Directions:
1. Preheat the oven to 350 F.
2. In a large bowl, combine the butter and Stevia. Blend using a handheld the mixer.
3. Add the almond flour, desiccated coconut, green tea powder, salt, and egg. Blend using the handheld mixer until smooth.
4. Gently fold in the chopped walnuts.

5. Prepare a baking sheet by lining it with parchment paper.

6. Using your hands, form the dough into balls and place them individually on the baking sheet. Slightly flatten each ball to form a cookie shape.

7. Bake the cookies for 10 to 12 minutes, or until the bottom edges start to turn light brown.

8. Transfer the cookies to a wire rack and allow to cool for at least 15 minutes before serving

VEGAN

Coconut and Lemon Crack Bars

INGREDIENTS	Fats	Proteins	Carbs
2 1/2 cups desiccated coconut	172.7 g	13.25 g	53.8 g
3 scoops vegan protein powder	9 g	37.5 g	16.5 g
2 tbsp lemon zest	0.04 g	0.18 g	1.92 g
1/2 cup coconut oil	109 g	0 g	0 g
1/4 tsp Stevia (powder)	0 g	0 g	4 g

Total calories: 2960 kcal
Servings: 20

Nutrition Facts

Amount per 23 g
1 serving (0.8 oz)

Calories 148
From fat 123

Amount	% Daily Value*	Amount	% Daily Value*
Total Fat 14.5g	22%	Total Carbohydrates 4g	1%
Saturated 12.4g	62%	Dietary Fiber 0g	0%
Trans Fat 0g		Sugars 0g	
Cholesterol 0mg	0%	Protein 3g	5%
Sodium 14mg	1%		
Calcium 5% • Iron 5%		Vitamin A 3% • Vitamin C 4%	

* Percent Daily Values are based on 2000 calorie diet. Your Daily Values may be higher or lower depending on your calorie needs.

Directions:
1. Combine all ingredients in a large mixing bowl. Mix well.
2. Prepare a baking pan by lining it with parchment paper.
3. Pour the mixture into the baking pan and press firmly on all sides and to the bottom.
4. Place the pan into the freezer and allow to cool for at least 2 hours.
5. Remove the pan from the freezer and cut into 20 equal-sized bars. Serve while cold.

Pumpkin and Pecan Bark

INGREDIENTS	Fats	Proteins	Carbs
1/2 cup unsweetened chocolate chips	21.32 g	3.9 g	22.95 g
3/4 cup pumpkin seeds	57.88 g	35.21 g	17.36 g

3 tbsp pecans, chopped	15.5 g	1.9 g	2.68 g
1 tbsp coconut oil	13.6 g	0 g	0 g

Total calories: 1240 kcal
Servings: 8

Nutrition Facts			
Nutrition Facts Amount per 25 g 1 serving (0.9 oz) Calories 155 From fat 116	**Amount** **% Daily Value***		**Amount** **% Daily Value***
	Total Fat 13.6g	21%	**Total Carbohydrates** 5g 2%
	Saturated 4.5g	22%	Dietary Fiber 2g 8%
	Trans Fat 0g		Sugars 2g
	Cholesterol 0mg	0%	**Protein** 5g 10%
	Sodium 39mg	2%	
	Calcium 1% • **Iron** 11%		**Vitamin A** 0% • **Vitamin C** 1%

*Percent Daily Values are based on 2000 calorie diet. Your Daily Values may be higher or lower depending on your calorie needs.

Instructions

1. In a microwave-safe bowl, microwave the chocolate chips on high for seconds. Stir the partially melted chocolate and microwave for another 30 seconds. If the chocolate has not been completely melted, stir again and microwave for another 15 seconds.
2. Stir in the pumpkin seeds and chopped pecans in the melted chocolate.
3. Spread the melted chocolate on a parchment-lined baking sheet.

Refrigerate for at least an hour or until the chocolate has completely hardened. Peel off the parchment paper and break apart the chocolate into 4 equal pieces.

Almond and Walnut Sorbet

INGREDIENTS	Fats	Proteins	Carbs
1/4 cup almonds, chopped	13.48 g	5.71 g	5.82 g

3/4 cup walnuts, chopped	39.13 g	9.14 g	8.23 g
1 cup coconut milk	48.21 g	4.57 g	6.35 g
1/4 tsp Stevia (powder)	0 g	0 g	4 g
1/2 tsp salt	0 g	0 g	0.42 g
1/4 tbsp vanilla extract	0 g	0 g	0 g
1 scoop vegan protein powder	3 g	12.5 g	5.5 g

Total calories: 1104 kcal
Servings: 4

Nutrition Facts

Amount per 87 g
1 serving (3.1 oz)

Calories 276
From fat 218

Amount	% Daily Value*	Amount	% Daily Value*
Total Fat 26g	40%	Total Carbohydrates 8g	3%
Saturated 11.9g	60%	Dietary Fiber 2g	8%
Trans Fat 0g		Sugars 1g	
Cholesterol 1mg	0%	Protein 8g	16%
Sodium 169mg	7%		
Calcium 12% • Iron 18%		Vitamin A 4% • Vitamin C 6%	

* Percent Daily Values are based on 2000 calorie diet. Your Daily Values may be higher or lower depending on your calorie needs

Directions:
1. Combine all the ingredients in a large bowl. Mix using a handheld mixer until thoroughly combined.

2. Place the mixture in freezer and chill for at least 5 hours.

3. To help the sorbet develop a creamy consistency, take out the mixture every 30 minutes and give it a slight stir.

4. The sorbet can be served immediately after removing from the freezer.

5.

Almond and Avocado Sorbet

INGREDIENTS	Fats	Proteins	Carbs
1/2 avocado	14.73 g	2.01 g	8.57 g
1/4 tsp Stevia (powder)	0 g	0 g	4 g
Juice of 1/2 a lime	0.02 g	0.09 g	1.85 g
3/4 cup coconut milk	36.15 g	3.42 g	4.76 g
4 tbsp walnuts, ground	18.51 g	7.51 g	2.99 g
1 scoop vegan protein powder	3 g	12.5 g	5.5 g

Total calories: 792 kcal
Servings: 6

Nutrition Facts

Amount per 59 g
1 serving (2.1 oz)

Calories 132
From fat 101

Amount	% Daily Value*	Amount	% Daily Value*
Total Fat 12.1g	19%	Total Carbohydrates 5g	2%
Saturated 5.9g	30%	Dietary Fiber 2g	6%
Trans Fat 0g		Sugars 0g	
Cholesterol 0mg	0%	Protein 4g	9%
Sodium 15mg	1%		
Calcium 6% • Iron 9%		Vitamin A 3% • Vitamin C 8%	

* Percent Daily Values are based on 2000 calorie diet. Your Daily Values may be higher or lower depending on your calorie needs.

Directions:

1. Scoop out the meat of the avocado and sprinkle with the lime juice. Place this mixture in the freezer while you prepare the rest of the ingredients.
2. In a saucepan, bring the coconut milk to a boil.
3. Reduce the heat to a simmer and continue heating the coconut milk until it has reduced to half of its original volume.
4. Remove from the heat and allow the coconut milk to cool to room temperature.
5. In a food processor, combine the coconut milk, frozen avocados, ground walnuts, and Stevia. Pulse until the mixture is smooth.
6. Place the mixture in the freezer and allow to cool for at least 3 hours.
7. Every 30 minutes remove the sorbet from the mixture and stir slightly. This will prevent the sorbet from hardening.
8. Serve immediately while cold

Blueberry Coconut Popsicles

INGREDIENTS	Fats	Proteins	Carbs
1 1/2 cups coconut milk	72.31 g	6.85 g	9.53 g
1/4 tsp Stevia (powder)	0 g	0 g	4 g
1 tsp vanilla extract	0 g	0 g	0.53 g
1/4 cup blueberries, frozen	0.25 g	0.16 g	4.72 g
2 scoops vegan protein powder	6 g	25 g	11 g
2 tbsp coconut oil	27.2 g	0 g	0 g

Total calories: 2760 kcal
Servings: 10

Nutrition Facts			
Amount per 87 g 1 serving (3.1 oz)	**Amount**	**% Daily Value***	
Calories 276 From fat 218			
	Total Fat 26g	40%	
	Saturated 11.9g	60%	
	Trans Fat 0g		
	Cholesterol 1mg	0%	
	Sodium 169mg	7%	
	Total Carbohydrates 8g	3%	
	Dietary Fiber 2g	8%	
	Sugars 1g		
	Protein 8g	16%	
	Calcium 12% • **Iron** 18%	**Vitamin A** 4% • **Vitamin C** 6%	

* Percent Daily Values are based on 2000 calorie diet. Your Daily Values may be higher or lower depending on your calorie needs.

Directions:

1. In a blender, combine the coconut milk, Stevia, coconut oil, vanilla extract, and protein powder. Blend until smooth.
2. Add the frozen blueberries and pulse 2 or 3 times. You want the blueberries to be not completely blended so they retain their texture.
3. Pour the mixture into popsicle molds. Place the molds into the freezer and freeze for at least 5 hours. Overnight is more preferable.
4. To serve, run hot water over the molds to release the popsicles.

Healthy choco-hazelnut Bark

INGREDIENTS	Fats	Proteins	Carbs

1/2 cup hazelnuts, chopped	34.93 g	8.6 g	9.6 g
1/3 cup coconut oil	71.9 g	0 g	0 g
1/4 cup dark chocolate	8.53 g	1.56 g	9.18 g
1 tsp vanilla extract	0 g	0 g	0.53 g
1/4 tsp Stevia (powder)	0 g	0 g	4 g
1/4 tsp salt	0 g	0 g	0 g
3/4 cup walnuts, chopped	39.13 g	9.14 g	8.23 g
2 scoops vegan protein powder	6 g	25 g	11 g

Total calories: 1700 kcal
Servings: 20

Nutrition Facts

Amount per 14 g
1 serving (0.5 oz)

Calories 85
From fat 69

Amount	% Daily Value*	Amount	% Daily Value*
Total Fat 8.1g	12%	Total Carbohydrates 2g	1%
Saturated 3.7g	19%	Dietary Fiber 1g	2%
Trans Fat 0g		Sugars 1g	
Cholesterol 0mg	0%	Protein 2g	4%
Sodium 36mg	2%		
Calcium 4% • Iron 4%		Vitamin A 2% • Vitamin C 2%	

* Percent Daily Values are based on 2000 calorie diet. Your Daily Values may be higher or lower depending on your calorie needs.

Directions:
1. Preheat the oven to 350 F.
2. Arrange the hazelnuts and walnuts on a baking sheet, making sure that they are evenly spread out.
3. Toast the nuts in the oven for 10 minutes, or until they are golden and fragrant.
4. In a heatproof bowl, melt the dark chocolate over a double boiler or in the microwave.
5. Add the nuts into a food processor and blend until they are smooth.
6. To the food processor, add the melted chocolate along with the rest of the ingredients. Blend again until the mixture is smooth and well-incorporated.
7. Prepare a baking sheet by lining it with parchment paper.
8. Pour the chocolate mixture into the baking pan and spread evenly using a spatula. The layer of chocolate should be less than 1/4-inch thick.
9. Freeze the bark for at least 45 minutes. Remove from the freezer and break into individual pieces

Pecan Chocolate Bark

INGREDIENTS	Fats	Proteins	Carbs
1 cup coconut oil	218 g	0 g	0 g
3/4 cup peanut butter	99.59 g	50.43 g	34.23 g
1/4 cup dark chocolate	10.66 g	1.95 g	11.48 g
1/4 tsp Stevia (powder)	0 g	0 g	4 g
1/4 tsp salt	0 g	0 g	0 g
1 tsp vanilla extract	0 g	0 g	0.53 g
3/4 cup pecans, chopped	58.87 g	7.5 g	11.34 g

Total calories: 3750 kcal
Servings: 30

Nutrition Facts

	Amount	% Daily Value*	Amount	% Daily Value*
Amount per 18 g	**Total Fat** 12.9g	20%	**Total Carbohydrates** 2g	1%
1 serving (0.6 oz)	Saturated 7.2g	36%	Dietary Fiber 1g	3%
	Trans Fat 0g		Sugars 1g	
Calories 125	**Cholesterol** 0mg	0%	**Protein** 2g	4%
From fat 110	**Sodium** 43mg	2%		
	Calcium 1% • **Iron** 7%		**Vitamin A** 5% • **Vitamin C** 0%	

* Percent Daily Values are based on 2000 calorie diet. Your Daily Values may be higher or lower depending on your calorie needs.

Directions:

1. Place the chocolate in a heatproof bowl. Melt the chocolate over a double boiler or in the microwave.
2. In a medium-sized bowl, combine the coconut oil and peanut butter. Stir together until creamy and the coconut oil has completely melted.
3. To the same bowl, add the salt, Stevia, vanilla extract, and the melted chocolate. Mix well.
4. Add in the chopped pecans and lightly fold into the mixture.
5. Pour the chocolate mixture into a baking sheet that has been lined with parchment paper. Make sure to keep the top surface level using a spatula.
6. Place the baking sheet in the refrigerator and chill for at least 1 hour.
7. When the chocolate has set, break them into equally-sized pieces. Store the bark in the freezer.

4-Ingredient Chia Cookies

INGREDIENTS	Fats	Proteins	Carbs
1 cup unsweetened peanut butter	132.79 g	67.23 g	45.64 g
1/4 tsp Stevia (powder)	0 g	0 g	4 g
2 tbsp chia seeds, dried	30.74 g	16.54 g	42.12 g

Total calories: 2016 kcal
Servings: 16

Nutrition Facts	Amount	% Daily Value*	Amount	% Daily Value*
Amount per 23 g	**Total Fat** 10.2g	16%	**Total Carbohydrates** 6g	2%
1 serving (0.8 oz)	Saturated 1.5g	7%	Dietary Fiber 3g	12%
	Trans Fat 0g		Sugars 2g	
Calories 126	**Cholesterol** 0mg	0%	**Protein** 5g	10%
From fat 85	**Sodium** 60mg	3%		
	Calcium 5% • **Iron** 18%		**Vitamin A** 13% • **Vitamin C** 0%	

* Percent Daily Values are based on 2000 calorie diet. Your Daily Values may be higher or lower depending on your calorie needs.

Directions:

1. Preheat the oven to 350 F.

2. Prepare a baking tray by lining it with parchment paper.

3. In a large bowl, combine all the ingredients. Mix until well-combined.

4. Using a scoop, form small balls on the baking tray. Press each ball into a cookie shape using your hands or the back of a spoon. Make sure to leave space between the cookies to expand.

5. Bake in the oven for 8 to 10 minutes, or just until the cookies have turned golden brown.

6. Remove the cookies from the oven and transfer to a cooling rack. Allow to cool for about 30 minutes before serving.

Keto Candied Walnuts

INGREDIENTS	Fats	Proteins	Carbs
3 cups walnuts	234.76 g	54.83 g	49.36 g
1 tsp salt	0 g	0 g	0 g
1/2 tsp vanilla extract	0 g	0 g	0.27 g
1/4 tsp Stevia (powder)	0 g	0 g	4 g
1/2 tsp cinnamon, ground	0.02 g	0.05 g	1.05 g

Total calories: 2360 kcal
Servings: 10

Nutrition Facts	Amount	% Daily Value*	Amount	% Daily Value*
Amount per 37 g	**Total Fat** 23.5g	36%	**Total Carbohydrates** 5g	2%
1 serving (1.3 oz)	Saturated 2.2g	11%	Dietary Fiber 3g	10%
	Trans Fat 0g		Sugars 1g	
Calories 236	**Cholesterol** 0mg	0%	**Protein** 5g	11%
From fat 196	**Sodium** 233mg	10%		
	Calcium 4% • **Iron** 6%		**Vitamin A** 0% • **Vitamin C** 1%	

* Percent Daily Values are based on 2000 calorie diet. Your Daily Values may be higher or lower depending on your calorie needs.

Directions:

1. In a large pot or saucepan, combine the sea salt, cinnamon, and Stevia. Add 1/4 cup of water and mix.
2. Turn on the heat to medium setting. Stir the solution occasionally while it heats up.
3. When all the ingredients have dissolved, add the nuts and mix until the nuts have been fully coated.
4. Continue stirring the pan as the mixture starts to thicken and crystallize.
5. Remove pan from the heat and set aside for 2 to 3 minutes. Transfer the walnut mixture to a plate or serving bowl and allow to cool completely.
6. Chop the candied walnuts into individual portions and serve.

No-Bake Peanut Butter Balls

INGREDIENTS	Fats	Proteins	Carbs
1 cup unsweetened peanut butter	132.79 g	67.23 g	45.64 g
1/4 tsp Stevia (powder)	0 g	0 g	4 g
1 tbsp desiccated coconut	17.27 g	1.33 g	5.38 g
1/4 cup almond flour	11.88 g	5.03 g	5.13 g
2 tbsp coconut milk	6.4 g	0.61 g	0.84 g

Total calories: 1900 kcal
Servings: 20

Nutrition Facts

Amount per 17 g
1 serving (0.6 oz)

Calories 95
From fat 70

	Amount	% Daily Value*	Amount	% Daily Value*
	Total Fat 8.4g	13%	Total Carbohydrates 3g	1%
	Saturated 2.1g	11%	Dietary Fiber 1g	4%
	Trans Fat 0g		Sugars 1g	
	Cholesterol 0mg	0%	Protein 4g	7%
	Sodium 48mg	2%		
	Calcium 1% • Iron 13%		Vitamin A 10% • Vitamin C 0%	

* Percent Daily Values are based on 2000 calorie diet. Your Daily Values may be higher or lower depending on your calorie needs.

Directions:
1. In a large mixing bowl, combine all ingredients and mix well.
2. Prepare a baking tray by lining it with parchment paper.

3. With your hands, form the batter into small balls and place on the baking tray.
4. Refrigerate the tray for at least an hour, or until the peanut butter balls have become firm.
5. Serve cold.

Quick and Easy Peanut Butter Bars

INGREDIENTS	Fats	Proteins	Carbs
2 cups peanut butter	265.59 g	134.47 g	91.28 g
3/4 cup desiccated coconut	51.81 g	3.98 g	16.14 g
1/2 cup dark chocolate chips	21.32 g	3.9 g	22.95 g
1/4 tsp Stevia (powder)	0 g	0 g	4 g
1 tbsp coconut oil	13.6 g	0 g	0 g

Total calories: 3989 kcal
Servings: 20

Nutrition Facts	Amount	% Daily Value*	Amount	% Daily Value*
Amount per 33 g	Total Fat 17.6g	27%	Total Carbohydrates 7g	2%
1 serving (1.2 oz)	Saturated 5.5g	28%	Dietary Fiber 2g	7%
	Trans Fat 0g		Sugars 3g	
Calories 199	Cholesterol 0mg	0%	Protein 7g	14%
From fat 148	Sodium 96mg	4%		
	Calcium 1% • Iron 27%		Vitamin A 20% • Vitamin C 0%	

* Percent Daily Values are based on 2000 calorie diet. Your Daily Values may be higher or lower depending on your calorie needs.

Directions:
1. In a large mixing bowl, combine the peanut butter, desiccated coconut, and Stevia. Mix well using a spatula until all components are well-distributed.

2. Pour the peanut butter mixture into a square pan and press firmly into place.

3. Place the pan in the freezer and freeze the mixture for 30 minutes to an hour.

4. Meanwhile, combine the dark chocolate chips and coconut oil in a heatproof bowl.

5. Melt the chocolate over a double boiler or in the microwave. After the chocolate has melted, stir together the chocolate and the coconut oil. Set aside.

6. Retrieve the peanut butter slab and cut into individual bars.

7. Dip each bar in the melted chocolate mixture, making sure to cover all sides.

8. Place the peanut butter bars on a shallow baking tray and chill in the refrigerator for at least 10 minutes before serving.

Peanut Butter Chia Pudding

INGREDIENTS	Fats	Proteins	Carbs
3/4 cup unsweetened peanut butter	99.59 g	50.43 g	34.23 g
1 cup coconut milk	48.21 g	4.57 g	6.35 g
1/4 cup chia seeds, dried	7.69 g	4.14 g	10.53 g
1 tsp vanilla extract	0 g	0 g	0.53 g
1/4 tsp Stevia (powder)	0 g	0 g	4 g
1/4 tsp salt	0 g	0 g	0 g
1/2 tbsp peanuts, chopped	6.53 g	3.19 g	2.63 g

Total calories: 1800 kcal
Servings: 8

Nutrition Facts

	Amount	% Daily Value*	Amount	% Daily Value*
	Total Fat 20.3g	31%	**Total Carbohydrates** 7g	2%
	Saturated 7.5g	37%	Dietary Fiber 3g	10%
	Trans Fat 0g		Sugars 3g	
	Cholesterol 0mg	0%	**Protein** 8g	16%
	Sodium 175mg	7%		
	Calcium 4% • **Iron** 30%		**Vitamin A** 19% • **Vitamin C** 1%	

Amount per 58 g
1 serving (2.1 oz)

Calories 225
From fat 170

* Percent Daily Values are based on 2000 calorie diet. Your Daily Values may be higher or lower depending on your calorie needs.

Directions:

1. In a blender, combine the peanut butter, coconut milk, chia seeds, Stevia, and salt. Blend until the pudding is smooth.
2. Transfer the pudding into individual cups or jars.
3. Place the pudding into the refrigerator and chill for at least 2 hours.
4. Before serving, sprinkle some of the chopped peanuts over the top of the pudding. Serve while cold.

Microwave Multi-Seed Bread

INGREDIENTS	Fats	Proteins	Carbs
4 tbsp flaxseed, ground	11.8 g	5.12 g	8.09 g
1/2 tbsp desiccated coconut	8.98 g	0.69 g	2.8 g
1/2 tsp cider vinegar	0 g	0 g	0.02 g
1/4 tsp baking soda	9 g	0 g	0 g
2 tbsp coconut milk	6.4 g	0.61 g	0.84 g
1/2 tsp sesame seeds	0.86 g	0.29 g	0.16 g
1/2 tsp sunflower seeds	0.77 g	0.31 g	0.3 g
1/2 tsp pumpkin seeds	0.59 g	0.36 g	0.18 g
1/2 cup almond flour	23.72 g	10.05 g	10.24 g

Total calories: 600 kcal
Servings: 6

Nutrition Facts

Nutrition Facts	Amount	% Daily Value*	Amount	% Daily Value*
Amount per 21 g 1 serving (0.7 oz)	**Total Fat** 8.9g	14%	**Total Carbohydrates** 4g	1%
	Saturated 2.8g	14%	Dietary Fiber 2g	9%
	Trans Fat 0g		Sugars 0g	
Calories 100	**Cholesterol** 0mg	0%	**Protein** 3g	6%
From fat 74	**Sodium** 58mg	2%		
	Calcium 4% • **Iron** 5%		**Vitamin A** 0% • **Vitamin C** 0%	

* Percent Daily Values are based on 2000 calorie diet. Your Daily Values may be higher or lower depending on your calorie needs.

Directions:

1. In a medium-sized bowl, combine the ground flaxseed, desiccated coconut, baking soda, cider vinegar, almond flour, and coconut milk. Mix thoroughly.
2. Using your hands, knead the dough until the dough develops a firmer and slightly sticky texture. Form the dough into a ball.
3. Combine the pumpkin, sesame, and sunflower seeds in a shallow dish.
4. Roll the ball of dough in the seeds, making sure that all the seeds stick to the dough.
5. Place the dough on a heatproof plate. Place the plate inside the microwave.
6. Microwave on high for 1 minute. Check the consistency after 1 minute has passed. If you find the bread too soft, you may microwave for an additional 30 seconds.
7. Slice the bred into individual portions. You may toast the slices of bread in a toaster if you want to eat them crispy

High-Protein Coconut Bites

INGREDIENTS	Fats	Proteins	Carbs
1/2 cup coconut milk	24.1 g	2.28 g	3.18 g
1 cup desiccated coconut	69.08 g	5.3 g	21.52 g
1/4 tsp vanilla extract	0 g	0 g	0.14 g
1/4 tsp Stevia (powder)	0 g	0 g	4 g
2 tbsp coconut oil	27.2 g	0 g	0 g
3 scoops vegan protein powder	9 g	37.5 g	16 g

| | Total calories: | 1440 kcal |
| Servings: | 20 |

Nutrition Facts	Amount	% Daily Value*	Amount	% Daily Value*
Nutrition Facts	Total Fat 6.5g	10%	Total Carbohydrates 2g	1%
	Saturated 5.3g	27%	Dietary Fiber 0g	0%
Amount per 16 g	Trans Fat 0g		Sugars 0g	
1 serving (0.6 oz)	Cholesterol 0mg	0%	Protein 2g	5%
	Sodium 12mg	1%		
Calories 72				
From fat 55	Calcium 5% • Iron 4%		Vitamin A 3% • Vitamin C 3%	
	* Percent Daily Values are based on 2000 calorie diet. Your Daily Values may be higher or lower depending on your calorie needs.			

Directions:

1. In a food processor, blend the desiccated coconut for around 1 minute, or until the texture has become very fine.
2. Add all the other ingredients into the food processor and pulse until well-mixed.
3. Prepare a baking tray by lining it with parchment paper.
4. Using your hands, form the batter into balls and place on the baking tray. Press each ball into a cookie shape.
5. Place the tray in the refrigerator and chill for about 1 hour.
6. Serve while cold
7.

Vegan Avocado Chocolate Cupcakes

INGREDIENTS	Fats	Proteins	Carbs
1/2 cup almond flour	23.72 g	10.05 g	10. 24 g
1/4 cup avocado, mashed	8.43 g	1.15 g	4.9 g
1/4 cup dark chocolate chips	3.03 g	0.55 g	3.26 g
1/4 tsp Stevia (powder)	0 g	0 g	4 g
1 tsp baking soda	0 g	0 g	0 g
1/2 tsp salt	0 g	0 g	0 g
1/2 cup coconut oil	109 g	0 g	0 g
1/2 tbsp coffee powder	0.01 g	0.18 g	1.13 g
3/4 cup walnuts, ground	39.13 g	9.14 g	8.23 g
4 tbsp sesame seeds	19.59 g	6.54 g	3.75 g

Total calories: 1944 kcal
Servings: 12

Nutrition Facts

Amount per 27 g
1 serving (1 oz)

Calories 162
From fat 144

	Amount	% Daily Value*	Amount		% Daily Value*
Total Fat 16.9g		26%	Total Carbohydrates 3g		1%
Saturated 8.8g		44%	Dietary Fiber 2g		6%
Trans Fat 0g			Sugars 0g		
Cholesterol 0mg		0%	Protein 2g		5%
Sodium 204mg		9%			
Calcium 2% • Iron 3%			Vitamin A 0% • Vitamin C		1%

* Percent Daily Values are based on 2000 calorie diet. Your Daily Values may be higher or lower depending on your calorie needs.

Directions:
1. Preheat the oven to 350 F.
2. In a medium-sized bowl, mix the mashed avocado and coconut oil using a handheld mixer.
3. While continuously mixing, gradually add in the almond flour, Stave, baking soda, salt, ground walnuts, and coffee powder.
4. Gently fold in the dark chocolate chips using a spatula.
5. Prepare your cupcake pan by lining each cupcake mold.
6. Pour the batter mixture into individual cupcake molds, filling each one only to the halfway point.
7. Sprinkle the sesame seeds over the cupcakes.
8. Bake in the oven for about 25 minutes.
9. Remove the cupcake pan from the oven and gently transfer each cupcake to a cooling rack.
10. Cool the cupcake for at least 45 minutes before serving.

Almond and Peanut

Butter Cups

INGREDIENTS	Fats	Proteins	Carbs
1/4 cup dark chocolate	10.66 g	1.95 g	11.48 g
2 tbsp coconut oil	27.2 g	0 g	0 g
2 1/2 tbsp almond butter	22.2 g	8.38 g	7.53 g
3 tbsp coconut milk	9.6 g	0.91 g	1.26 g
5 tbsp peanut butter	41.18 g	20.85 g	14.15 g

Total calories: 1188 kcal
Servings: 12

Nutrition Facts	Amount	% Daily Value*	Amount	% Daily Value*
Amount per 18 g	Total Fat 9.2g	14%	Total Carbohydrates 3g	1%
1 serving (0.6 oz)	Saturated 3.9g	19%	Dietary Fiber 1g	4%
	Trans Fat 0g		Sugars 1g	
Calories 99	Cholesterol 0mg	0%	Protein 3g	5%
From fat 78	Sodium 26mg	1%		
	Calcium 2% • Iron 9%		Vitamin A 5% • Vitamin C 0%	

* Percent Daily Values are based on 2000 calorie diet. Your Daily Values may be higher or lower depending on your calorie needs.

Directions:
1. Prepare a mini muffin pan lining each mold with paper liners.
2. Combine the dark chocolate and coconut oil in glass or ceramic bowl. Microwave on medium for about 15 seconds and stir. Repeat this process until all the chocolate has melted.
3. Pour about a teaspoon of melted chocolate into each of the muffin liners. Place the muffin pan in the refrigerator and chill for at least 15 minutes.
4. Meanwhile, combine the coconut milk, almond butter, and peanut butter in a medium-sized bowl. Stir the mixture until you get a smooth texture.
5. Get the muffin pan and scoop about 1 tablespoon of the peanut and almond butter mixture into each muffin liner.
6. Pour the rest of the melted chocolate on top of each muffin liner.
7. Refrigerate the muffin pan for at least 2 hours.
8. Once the cups have set, they are ready to serve.

Spiced Chocolate Bark

INGREDIENTS	Fats	Proteins	Carbs
3/4 cup dark chocolate	31.97 g	34.43 g	34.43 g
1/4 tsp vanilla extract	0 g	0 g	0.14 g
3/4 cup coconut oil	163.5 g	0 g	0 g
1/4 tsp Stevia (powder)	0 g	0 g	4 g
1/2 tsp chili powder	0.2 g	0.19 g	0.7 g
1/4 tsp cinnamon	0.01 g	0.03 g	0.56 g
1/8 tsp nutmeg	0.11 g	0.02 g	0.15 g
1/4 tsp salt	0 g	0 g	0 g
3 scoops vegan protein powder	9 g	37.5 g	16.5 g
1/4 cup coconut milk	12.05 g	1.14 g	1.59 g
1/4 cup peanuts, chopped	16.73 g	8.18 g	6.75 g

Total calories: 2480 kcal
Servings: 20

Nutrition Facts

Amount per 21 g
1 serving (0.7 oz)

Calories 124
From fat 102

Amount	% Daily Value*	Amount	% Daily Value*
Total Fat 11.7g	18%	Total Carbohydrates 3g	1%
Saturated 8.7g	43%	Dietary Fiber 1g	3%
Trans Fat 0g		Sugars 1g	
Cholesterol 0mg	0%	Protein 3g	5%
Sodium 51mg	2%		
Calcium 5% • Iron 6%		Vitamin A 3% • Vitamin C	3%

* Percent Daily Values are based on 2000 calorie diet. Your Daily Values may be higher or lower depending on your calorie needs.

Directions:
1. In a heat-proof bowl, combine the dark chocolate and coconut oil.
2. Place the bowl over a double boiler, stirring the chocolate and coconut oil until it has completely melted.
3. Add the coconut milk and stir until well-incorporated.
4. While stirring, add the protein powder, Stevia, salt, cinnamon, chili powder, vanilla extract and nutmeg.
5. Prepare a baking tray by lining it with parchment paper.

6. Pour the chocolate mixture into the baking tray. Use a spatula to keep the chocolate layer leveled.
7. Sprinkle ground peanuts over the top of the chocolate.
8. Place the baking tray inside the refrigerator and chill for at least 2 hours.
9. After the chocolate has set, break the bark into individual pieces.

Keto Protein Crackers

INGREDIENTS	Fats	Proteins	Carbs
4 scoops vegan protein powder	12 g	50 g	22 g
1/2 cup desiccated coconut	34.54 g	2.65 g	10.76 g
3 tbsp sesame seeds	14.69 g	4.91 g	2.82 g
1 tbsp chia seeds	4.92 g	2.65 g	6.74 g
1 tbsp coconut oil	13.6 g	0 g	0 g
1/4 tsp salt	0 g	0 g	0 g
2 tbsp sunflower seeds	9.01 g	3.64 g	3.5 g

Total Calories: 1190 kcal
Servings: 10

Nutrition Facts	Amount	% Daily Value*	Amount	% Daily Value*
	Total Fat 8.9g	14%	Total Carbohydrates 5g	2%
	Saturated 4.7g	24%	Dietary Fiber 1g	5%
Amount per 22 g	Trans Fat 0g		Sugars 0g	
1 serving (0.8 oz)	Cholesterol 1mg	0%	Protein 6g	13%
	Sodium 87mg	4%		
Calories 119				
From fat 76	Calcium 13% • Iron 10%		Vitamin A 7% • Vitamin C 7%	

* Percent Daily Values are based on 2000 calorie diet. Your Daily Values may be higher or lower depending on your calorie needs.

Directions:
1. Preheat the oven to 300 F.
2. In a medium-sized bowl, combine the protein powder, desiccated coconut, sesame seeds, chia seeds, sunflower seeds, and salt. Mix well.
3. Add the coconut oil and continue mixing until it has been well-incorporated.
4. Prepare a baking tray by lining it with parchment paper.

5. Spread out the cracker mixture on the baking tray. Try to keep the layer 1/4 to 1/8-inch thick.
6. Bake the cracker in the oven for 1 hour.
7. Remove the tray and flip the cracker on the other side. Bake for another 15 minutes.
8. Remove from the oven and cool for at least an hour before breaking the cracker into individual pieces.

Chocolate-Coated Pumpkin Seeds

INGREDIENTS	Fats	Proteins	Carbs
4 tbsp cocoa powder	2.15 g	2.15 g	7.92 g
1/16 tsp Stevia (powder)	0 g	0 g	4 g
1 3/4 cup coconut milk	84.36 g	7.99 g	11.11 g
1 cup pumpkin seeds	49.05 g	29.84 g	14.71 g

Total calories: 1410 kcal
Servings: 6

Nutrition Facts

Amount per 94 g
1 serving (3.3 oz)

Calories 235
From fat 189

	Amount	% Daily Value*	Amount	% Daily Value*
	Total Fat 22.6g	35%	Total Carbohydrates 6g	2%
	Saturated 14.1g	70%	Dietary Fiber 1g	4%
	Trans Fat 0g		Sugars 0g	
	Cholesterol 1mg	0%	Protein 7g	13%
	Sodium 58mg	2%		
	Calcium 3% • Iron 20%		Vitamin A 0% • Vitamin C 2%	

* Percent Daily Values are based on 2000 calorie diet. Your Daily Values may be higher or lower depending on your calorie needs.

Directions:
1. In a blender, combine the coconut milk, cocoa powder, and Stevia. Blend until fully incorporated.
2. Pour the mixture into a container and add the pumpkin seeds. Stir lightly and place in the refrigerator.
3. Chill the mixture for at least eight hours, giving it a light stir every two hours.
4. Stir again before serving.

Keto Pumpkin Fudge

INGREDIENTS	Fats	Proteins	Carbs
1 1/2 cup pumpkin puree	0.17 g	1.74 g	11.31 g
1 1/4 cup butter	230.19 g	2.41 g	0.17 g
2 tbsp coconut oil	27.2 g	0 g	0 g
2 tsp cinnamon	0.06 g	0.21 g	4.19 g
1/2 tsp nutmeg	0.4 g	0.06 g	0.54 g
3/4 cup pumpkin seeds	43.41 g	26.41 g	13.02 g

Total calories: 2856 kcal

Directions: 24

Nutrition Facts

Amount per   24 g
1 serving (0.9 oz)

Calories   119
From fat   110

Amount	% Daily Value*	Amount	% Daily Value*
Total Fat 12.6g	19%	Total Carbohydrates 1g	0%
Saturated 7.4g	37%	Dietary Fiber 0g	2%
Trans Fat 0.4g		Sugars 0g	
Cholesterol 25mg	8%	Protein 1g	3%
Sodium 11mg	0%		
Calcium 1% • Iron	2%	Vitamin A 18% • Vitamin C	1%

* Percent Daily Values are based on 2000 calorie diet. Your Daily Values may be higher or lower depending on your calorie needs.

Directions:

1. Prepare a baking pan by lining the bottom and sides with aluminum foil.
2. In a saucepan, melt the butter over low heat. Add the pumpkin puree, cinnamon, and nutmeg. Stir.
3. Add the coconut oil and stir thoroughly.
4. Pour the mixture into the baking pan and level the top surface using a spatula.
5. Sprinkle the pumpkin seeds evenly over the surface of the pumpkin puree mixture.

6. Tap the bottom of the baking pan a few times to remove any air bubbles.
7. Place the baking pan in the refrigerator for at least 2 hours.
8. Once the fudge has set, carefully lift it out using the foil lining. Peel off the foil.
9. Cut the fudge into equal portions.
10. Serve while cold. These can be stored in the refrigerator for 1 week.

Homemade Keto Vegan Protein Bars

INGREDIENTS	Fats	Proteins	Carbs
1 cup almond flour	47.43 g	20.09 g	20.47 g
1/2 cup desiccated coconut	9.81 g	0.75 g	3.06 g
1/16 tsp Stevia (powder)	0 g	0 g	2 g
3 tbsp pumpkin seeds	10.84 g	6.59 g	3.25 g
1/2 cup almond butter	69.38 g	26.2 g	23.53 g
1/2 cup peanuts, chopped	33.4 g	16.33 g	13.47 g

Total calories: 1932 kcal
Servings: 12

Nutrition Facts

Amount per 27 g
0.5 servings (1 oz)

Calories 161
From fat 121

Amount	% Daily Value*	Amount	% Daily Value*
Total Fat 14.3g	22%	Total Carbohydrates 5g	2%
Saturated 2g	10%	Dietary Fiber 3g	10%
Trans Fat 0g		Sugars 1g	
Cholesterol 0mg	0%	Protein 6g	12%
Sodium 35mg	1%		
Calcium 6% • Iron 5%		Vitamin A 0% • Vitamin C	0%

* Percent Daily Values are based on 2000 calorie diet. Your Daily Values may be higher or lower depending on your calorie needs.

Directions:

1. Prepare a deep baking dish or load pan by lining it with parchment paper at the bottom and on the sides.

2. In a large mixing bowl, combine all the ingredients. Mix thoroughly until you get a thick and smooth batter.

3. Pour the mixture into the baking dish. Level the top surface using a spatula.

4. Refrigerate the mixture and chill for at least 2 hours.

5. When the bars have set, cut into individual portions. Serve while cold.

Coconut Pineapple Sorbet

INGREDIENTS	Fats	Proteins	Carbs
2 cups coconut milk	96.41 g	9.13 g	12.7 g
2 tbsp coconut oil	27.2 g	0 g	0 g
1/4 tsp Stevia (powder)	0 g	0 g	4 g
1/2 cup pineapple chunks	0.1 g	0.45 g	10.82 g

3 scoops vegan protein powder	9 g	37.5 g	16.5 g

Total calories: 1464 kcal

Servings: 8

Nutrition Facts

Amount per   80 g
1 serving (2.8 oz)

Calories   183
From fat   140

Amount	% Daily Value*	Amount	% Daily Value*
Total Fat 16.6g	26%	Total Carbohydrates 6g	2%
Saturated 13.7g	69%	Dietary Fiber 0g	1%
Trans Fat 0g		Sugars 1g	
Cholesterol 1mg	0%	Protein 6g	12%
Sodium 31mg	1%		
Calcium 12% • Iron 17%		Vitamin A 7% • Vitamin C 16%	

* Percent Daily Values are based on 2000 calorie diet. Your Daily Values may be higher or lower depending on your calorie needs.

Directions:

1. In a blender or food processor, combine the coconut milk, coconut oil, Stevia and protein powder. Blend until smooth.
2. Add the pineapple chunks. Pulse for 2 to 3 times, taking care not to preserve some of the chunks.
3. Pour the mixture into an airtight container.
4. Place the container in the freezer and freeze for at least 3 hours. Stir the mixture every hour while it is freezing.
5. Serve while cold.

Toasted Sesame and

Coconut Ice Cream

INGREDIENTS	Fats	Proteins	Carbs
2 cups coconut milk	84.36 g	7.99 g	11. 11 g
1/8 tsp Stevia (powder)	0 g	0 g	2 g
1/2 cup sesame seeds	45.91 g	15.34 g	8.8 g
1 tsp vanilla extract	0 g	0 g	0.53 g
3 tbsp coconut oil	40.8 g	0 g	0 g

Total calories: 1620 kcal

Servings: 6

Directions:

1. Preheat the oven to 300 F.
2. Spread the sesame seeds evenly on a baking sheet and toast in the oven for about 10 minutes, or until they have turned light brown. Be careful not to burn them.
3. In a food processor, pulse the toasted sesame seeds until the texture is close to that of a paste.
4. Add the coconut milk, Stevia, vanilla extract, and coconut oil. Blend until smooth.
5. Transfer the mixture to an airtight container and place in the freezer for at least 4 hours.
6. Give the ice cream a stir every hour while it freezes.
7. Serve while cold. Enjoy!

Almond Butter Fudge

INGREDIENTS	Fats	Proteins	Carbs
3/4 cup almond butter	104.06 g	39.3 g	35.29 g
2 1/2 tbsp coconut oil	34 g	0 g	0 g
1/4 tsp Stevia (powder)	0 g	0 g	4 g
2 scoops vegan protein powder	6 g	25 g	11 g

Total calories: 1644 kcal
Servings: 12

Directions:

1. In a saucepan, melt the almond butter and coconut oil.
2. Add the Stevia and protein powder. Stir until well-distributed.
3. Transfer the mixture into individual mini muffin molds.
4. Place in the refrigerator and chill for at least 2 hours.
5. Slice or pop out the pieces of fudge once they have set. Serve while cold.

Gingerbread Fudge

INGREDIENTS	Fats	Proteins	Carbs
3/4 cup unsweetened peanut butter	99.59 g	50.43 g	34.23 g
3 tbsp coconut oil	40.8 g	0 g	0 g
1/4 tsp Stevia (powder)	0 g	0 g	4 g
1/4 tbsp ginger powder	0.06 g	0.12 g	0.93 g

Total calories: 1512 kcal
Servings: 12

Directions:

1. In a saucepan, melt the coconut oil over low heat.
2. Add the peanut butter and allow to soften while stirring.
3. Add the Stevia and ginger powder. Stir until well-distributed.
4. Transfer the mixture into individual mini muffin molds.
5. Place in the refrigerator and chill for at least 2 hours.
6. Slice or pop out the pieces of fudge once they have set. Serve while cold.

Nutty Coconut Magic Bars

INGREDIENTS	Fats	Proteins	Carbs
3/4 cup almond flour	35.6 g	15.08 g	15.37 g
1/4 tsp Stevia (powder)	0 g	0 g	4 g
4 tbsp walnuts, chopped	18.51 g	7.51 g	2.99 g
1 1/4 cup coconut milk	60.26 g	5.71 g	7.94 g
2 tbsp coconut oil	27.2 g	0 g	0 g
1/2 cup peanuts, chopped	33.4 g	16.33 g	13.47 g

Total calories: 1792 kcal
Servings: 16

Nutrition Facts	Amount	% Daily Value*	Amount	% Daily Value*
Amount per 30 g	Total Fat 11g	17%	Total Carbohydrates 3g	1%
1 serving (1.1 oz)	Saturated 5.4g	27%	Dietary Fiber 1g	4%
	Trans Fat 0g		Sugars 0g	
Calories 112	Cholesterol 0mg	0%	Protein 3g	6%
From fat 93	Sodium 27mg	1%		
	Calcium 2% • Iron 5%		Vitamin A 0% • Vitamin C 0%	

* Percent Daily Values are based on 2000 calorie diet. Your Daily Values may be higher or lower depending on your calorie needs.

Directions:
1. Preheat the oven to 350 F.
2. In a small bowl, combine the almond flour, coconut oil, and Stevia. Mix well.
3. Transfer the almond flour mixture to a baking dish and press down firmly to form a crust.
4. Sprinkle the chopped peanuts and walnuts to the top of the crust.
5. Pour the coconut milk over the top of the peanuts and walnuts.

6. Bake in the oven for 35 minutes.
7. Cool down to room temperature for at least 30 minutes before serving.
8. The bars will be firmer if chilled in the refrigerator overnight.

Peanut Butter almond Bars

INGREDIENTS	Fats	Proteins	Carbs
1 cup almond flour	47.43 g	20.09 g	20.47 g
1/4 tsp salt	0 g	0 g	0 g
1/4 tsp baking soda	0 g	0 g	0 g
2 tsp vanilla extract	0.01 g	0.01 g	1.06 g
1/4 tsp Stevia (powder)	0 g	0 g	4 g
3/4 cup unsweetened peanut butter	99.59 g	50.43 g	34.23 g
1/4 cup dark chocolate chips	10.66 g	1.95 g	11.48 g
2 tsp coconut oil	9 g	0 g	0 g

Total calories: 1952 kcal
Servings: 16

Nutrition Facts	Amount	% Daily Value*	Amount	% Daily Value*
	Total Fat 10.4g	16%	Total Carbohydrates 4g	1%
	Saturated 2.1g	10%	Dietary Fiber 2g	6%
Amount per 21 g 1 serving (0.7 oz)	Trans Fat 0g		Sugars 2g	
	Cholesterol 0mg	0%	Protein 5g	9%
Calories 122 From fat 88	Sodium 102mg	4%		
	Calcium 2% • Iron 14%		Vitamin A 9% • Vitamin C 0%	
	* Percent Daily Values are based on 2000 calorie diet. Your Daily Values may be higher or lower depending on your calorie needs.			

Directions:
1. Preheat the oven to 350 F.

2. In a small bowl, combine the almond flour, salt, baking soda, vanilla extract, and Stevia. Stir until well-combined.

3. Prepare a baking pan by lining it with parchment paper on the bottom and sides.

4. Transfer the almond flour mixture into the baking pan. Press firmly towards the bottom of the pan, making sure to keep it level.

5. Bake for 12 minutes. Set aside and let cool for at least 20 minutes.

6. Spread the peanut butter on top of the crust, using a spatula to keep it level.

7. In a heat-proof bowl, combine the dark chocolate chips and coconut oil. Melt over a double boiler or in the microwave. Stir until well-combined.

8. Spread the melted chocolate over the peanut butter.

9. Place the baking tray in the refrigerator and chill for at least 2 hours.

10. Upon setting, slice into individual bars. Serve while cold.

High-Protein Almond Chocolate Fudge Bites

INGREDIENTS	Fats	Proteins	Carbs
1 cup almond butter	138.75 g	52.4 g	47.05 g
2 tbsp almond flour	11.88 g	5.03 g	5.13 g
2 tbsp cocoa powder	1.48 g	2.12 g	6.25 g
1/4 tsp Stevia (powder)	0 g	0 g	4 g
1/4 tsp salt	0 g	0 g	0 g
2 tsp coconut oil	9 g	0 g	0 g
2 scoops vegan protein powder	6 g	25 g	11 g

Total calories: 1968 kcal
Servings: 12

Nutrition Facts

Amount per 29 g
1 serving (1 oz)

Calories 164
From fat 117

Amount	% Daily Value*	Amount	% Daily Value*
Total Fat 13.9g	21%	Total Carbohydrates 6g	2%
Saturated 1.7g	9%	Dietary Fiber 3g	11%
Trans Fat 0g		Sugars 1g	
Cholesterol 0mg	0%	Protein 7g	14%
Sodium 61mg	3%		
Calcium 13% • Iron 8%		Vitamin A 3% • Vitamin C 3%	

* Percent Daily Values are based on 2000 calorie diet. Your Daily Values may be higher or lower depending on your calorie needs.

Directions:
1. Combine all ingredients in a food processor. Mix until all ingredients are well-incorporated, and you get a sticky texture.
2. Place the dough mixture in an airtight container and place in the freezer for 10 minutes.
3. Retrieve the dough mixture. Using your hands, shape them into individual balls. Place the balls on a baking tray lined with parchment paper.
4. Place the baking tray inside a refrigerator and chill for at least 2 hours. Serve while cold.

Chocolate and Pumpkin Fudge

INGREDIENTS	Fats	Proteins	Carbs
1/2 cup pumpkin puree	0.06 g	0.58 g	3.77 g
1 cup almond butter	138.75 g	52. 4	47.05 g
1/4 tsp Stevia (powder)	0 g	0 g	4 g
1 tbsp desiccated coconut	11.05 g	0.85 g	3.44 g
1 tbsp dark chocolate chips	6.82 g	1.25 g	7.34 g
2 tsp coconut oil	9 g	0 g	0 g

2 tbsp pumpkin seeds	7.26 g	4.42 g	2.18 g
2 scoops protein powder	6 g	25 g	11 g

Total calories: 2120 kcal
Servings: 20

Nutrition Facts	Amount	% Daily Value*	Amount	% Daily Value*
Amount per 21 g	**Total Fat** 9g	14%	**Total Carbohydrates** 4g	1%
1 serving (0.7 oz)	Saturated 1.7g	8%	Dietary Fiber 2g	6%
	Trans Fat 0g		Sugars 1g	
Calories 106	**Cholesterol** 0mg	0%	**Protein** 4g	8%
From fat 75	**Sodium** 10mg	0%		
	Calcium 8% • **Iron** 5%		**Vitamin A** 7% • **Vitamin C** 2%	

* Percent Daily Values are based on 2000 calorie diet. Your Daily Values may be higher or lower depending on your calorie needs

Directions:
1. In a saucepan, heat the almond butter over low heat until it is soft.
2. Add pumpkin puree, Stevia, protein powder, and desiccated coconut. Stir until well-combined.

3. Prepare a baking pan by lining it with parchment paper.

4. Transfer the pumpkin puree mixture to the baking pan.

5. In a microwave-safe bowl, combine the dark chocolate chips and coconut oil. Melt in the microwave.

6. Add the pumpkin seeds to the melted chocolate and stir thoroughly.
7. Top the pumpkin fudge with the chocolate-coated pumpkin seeds. Spread evenly.

8. Place the baking pan in the refrigerator and chill for at least 3 hours.
9. Once the pumpkin fudge has set, slice up into individual bars. Serve while cold

Almond and Pumpkin

Seed Clusters

INGREDIENTS	Fats	Proteins	Carbs
1 cup pumpkin seeds	57.88 g	35.21 g	17.36 g
1 tsp vanilla extract	0 g	0 g	0.53 g
1/4 tsp Stevia (powder)	0 g	0 g	4 g
2 tsp coconut oil	9 g	0 g	0 g
1 cup whole almonds	71.4 g	30.24 g	30.82 g

Total calories: 1600 kcal
Servings: 16

Nutrition Facts

Amount per 17 g
1 serving (0.6 oz)

Calories 100
From fat 73

Amount	% Daily Value*	Amount	% Daily Value*
Total Fat 8.7g	13%	Total Carbohydrates 3g	1%
Saturated 1.5g	7%	Dietary Fiber 2g	6%
Trans Fat 0g		Sugars 1g	
Cholesterol 0mg	0%	Protein 4g	8%
Sodium 19mg	1%		
Calcium 3% • Iron 5%		Vitamin A 0% • Vitamin C 0%	

* Percent Daily Values are based on 2000 calorie diet. Your Daily Values may be higher or lower depending on your calorie needs.

Directions:

1. In a saucepan, melt the coconut oil over low heat. Add the Stevia and vanilla extract. Stir well.
2. Add the almonds and pumpkin seeds. Stir well, ensuring that all the almonds and pumpkin seeds are coated with the coconut oil mixture.
3. Transfer the mixture to a baking sheet and spread over a thin layer.
4. Refrigerate the baking sheet for at least 3 hours.
5. When firm, break into individual clusters and serve while cold.

Multi-Seed Crackers

INGREDIENTS	Fats	Proteins	Carbs

3/4 cup almond flour	35.6 g	15.08 g	15.37 g
4 tbsp sunflower seeds	18.01 g	7.27 g	7 g
8 tbsp pumpkin seeds	28.94 g	17.61 g	8.68 g
2 tbsp chia seeds	9.84 g	5.29 g	13.48 g
8 tbsp sesame seeds	39.17 g	13.09 g	7.51 g
1/4 tsp salt	0 g	0 g	0 g
4 tbsp coconut oil	54.4 g	0 g	0 g

Total calories: 1980 kcal
Servings: 20

Nutrition Facts

Amount per 16 g
1 serving (0.6 oz)

Calories   99
From fat   79

Amount	% Daily Value*	Amount	% Daily Value*
Total Fat 9.3g	14%	Total Carbohydrates 3g	1%
Saturated 3.2g	16%	Dietary Fiber 2g	7%
Trans Fat 0g		Sugars 0g	
Cholesterol 0mg	0%	Protein 3g	6%
Sodium 39mg	2%		
Calcium 3% • Iron 4%		Vitamin A 0% • Vitamin C 0%	

* Percent Daily Values are based on 2000 calorie diet. Your Daily Values may be higher or lower depending on your calorie needs.

Directions:

1. Preheat the oven to 300 F.

2. In a large bowl, mix all the seeds together. Add the almond flour and salt. Mix until you get a uniform composition.

3. To the same bowl, add the coconut oil and 1 cup of boiling water.
4. Continue mixing until the dough develops a gel-like texture.

5. Prepare a baking sheet by lining it with parchment paper.

6. Place the dough on the baking sheet and add another piece of parchment paper on top of it. Using a rolling pin, flatten the dough.

7. Remove the paper on top and bake in the oven for about 45 minutes.

8. After 45 minutes, turn off the heat. Leave the crackers in the oven to dry.

9. Once they have dried, break the crackers into pieces by hand.

10. The crackers are best served with butter.

Dairy-Free Peanut

Butter Ice Cream

INGREDIENTS	Fats	Proteins	Carbs
1/2 cup unsweetened peanut butter	66.4 g	33.62 g	22.82 g
1 cup coconut milk	48.21 g	4.57 g	6.35 g
1/4 tsp Stevia (powder)	0 g	0 g	4 g
2 tbsp unsweetened cocoa powder	1.41 g	1.95 g	6.3 g

| 1 tsp vanilla extract | 0 g | 0 g | 0.53 g |
| 1/4 tsp salt | 0 g | 0 g | 0 g |

Total calories: 1248 kcal
Servings: 6

Nutrition Facts

Amount per 63 g
1 serving (2.2 oz)

Calories 208
From fat 162

Amount	% Daily Value*	Amount	% Daily Value*
Total Fat 19.3g	30%	Total Carbohydrates 7g	2%
Saturated 9g	45%	Dietary Fiber 2g	7%
Trans Fat 0g		Sugars 2g	
Cholesterol 0mg	0%	Protein 7g	13%
Sodium 181mg	8%		
Calcium 2% • Iron 29%		Vitamin A 17% • Vitamin C	1%

* Percent Daily Values are based on 2000 calorie diet. Your Daily Values may be higher or lower depending on your calorie needs.

Directions:

1. Combine all the ingredients in a blender. Blend for at least 30 seconds, or until the mixture becomes smooth and creamy.

2. Transfer the mixture to an airtight container and keep in the freezer.

3. Stir the mixture by hand every 15 to 30 minutes until the ice cream starts to harden. This will take around 3 to 4 hours.

4. Serve while cold.

Thank you for choosing Erin Mira Keto Vegetarian Cookbook

You may claim your Free E-book version
Just scan the code or go directly to the URL

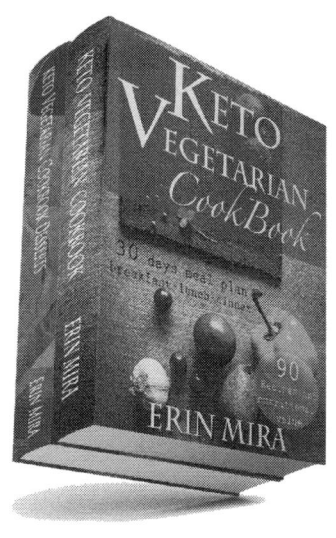

https://mailchi.mp/1299ce33357d/2-1-ketovegetarianbook

Printed in Great Britain
by Amazon